PRAGMATIC LIBERTARIANISM

ENGINEERING POPULIST CONSTITUTIONS

FOR THE 21ST CENTURY

Mark R. Blum

Dedicated to my beloved father

James Immo Blum

August 09, 1934 - June 19, 1986

Copyright © 2019 by Mark R. Blum

All rights reserved. No part of this publication may be reproduced, distributed, or transmitted in any form or by any means, including photocopying, recording, or other electronic or mechanical methods, without the prior written permission of the publisher, except in the case of brief quotations embodied in critical reviews and certain other non-commercial uses permitted by copyright law. For permission requests, write to the publisher, addressed "Attention: Permissions Coordinator," at the address below.

Harbinger Publishing; A Harbinger Publication; are Divisions of: Harbinger Consultants Incorporated

Ordering Information:
Quantity sales. Special discounts are available on quantity purchases by corporations, associations, and others.

For details contact: Kindle or **Amazon.com** and or Harbinger Publications

Publisher's Cataloging-in-Publication data
Blum, Mark.
Pragmatic Libertarianism | Engineering Populist Constitutions for the 21st Century|
Mark R. Blum.

Paperback book: ISBN: 978-1-7751695-4-3

Electronic Book: ISBN: 978-1-7751695-5-0

1. The main category of the book: 1. Politics | 2. Philosophy | 3. Libertarianism

Subject category Philosophy | Commentary on contemporary politics | Constitutional structure | Mark R. Blum.

Title. Pragmatic Libertarianism | Engineering Populist Constitutions for the 21st Century

FIRST EDITION

TABLE OF CONTENTS

1ST CHAPTER — 2
THE FUTURE IS LIBERTARIAN — 2

2ND CHAPTER — 17
THE DOCTRINE OF LIBERTARIANISM — 17

3RD CHAPTER — 86
REFORMING THE INSIDIOUS SYSTEM — 86

4TH CHAPTER — 102
FUNCTIONAL CHECKS AND BALANCES PREVENT CORRUPTION — 102

5TH CHAPTER — 152
SOCIAL MARXISM — 152

6TH CHAPTER — 166
A LIBERTARIAN ECONOMIC PLAN — 166

7TH CHAPTER — 201
THE WESTERN CULTURAL REVOLUTION — 201

8TH CHAPTER _____ 219
THE INDOCTRINATION SYSTEM_____ 219

9TH CHAPTER _____ 253
RANDOM THOUGHTS_____ 253

10TH CHAPTER _____ 282
CULTURAL CONFORMITY _____ 282

11TH CHAPTER _____ 300
THE NEW ECONOMY IS FORCING CHANGE _____ 300

12TH CHAPTER _____ 345
CONTROL THE GOVERNMENT OR THE GOVERNMENT WILL CONTROL YOU _____ 345

BIBLIOGRAPHY _____ 357

INDEX _____ 360

"Find out just what any people will quietly submit to and you have found out the exact measure of injustice and wrong which will be imposed upon them, and these will continue till they are resisted with either words or blows, or with both.

The limits of tyrants are prescribed by the endurance of those whom they oppress".

~ Frederick Douglass 1857~

1st Chapter
THE FUTURE IS LIBERTARIAN

World populations are in search of a new doctrine for society. The old right and leftist ideas have grown stale and society has moved past the industrial revolution into this new post-industrial technological era. The reality of our times is the indoctrinated and brainwashed belief that somehow the current reincarnation of communistically based socialism via "Social Marxism" is all the rage of so-called progressives. But is Social Marxism really the correct perspective for the needed social, economic and political reform? Clearly there is a social tremor rumbling in the midst of western society. The Brexit vote and Trump revolution in the United States in recent years clearly demonstrate, along with the parallel decline of the middle class, that society is in flux and that fundamental economic and social change is afoot.

Western society and its deadly lack of children is quickly headed towards extinction. Do not expect in the future to live in a western based open society without western people in charge, or at least strongly represented in the society's population. Such thinking compares to Native

North Americans thinking they would rule the United States and Canada when the first Europeans arrived. Cultural change will clearly have repercussions resulting from a lack of children in the west; and decline of family values. If this circumstance is not turned around soon at this twelfth hour this will lead to the extinction of every western nation and all western social constructs being gradually watered down into irrelevance along with western political, social and other values, including feminism will also most definitely be its victims along with minority rights. The current nihilism is nothing less than social genocide of the west perpetrated by left wingers full of ancestral and self-hatred. If social reform, true social reform, does not get in front of the current social rumblings; then, the times we are confronted with are very dangerous indeed for all concepts of liberty and individualism. The current battle against western values under the current trajectory will soon be repressive religious and other regulation, forced conversion and greater social communist repression of human rights. There is a social war going on at present and to the victors will come all the rewards of becoming the new establishment. Acts of treason and political duplicity by the current establishment in promoting the current political change, are naively based upon the assumption that these new values will lead to the accepting of the establishment. Like Neville Chamberlain, the leftists naively believe there is some benefit to the current acceptance of this change, not realizing that the acceptance of the change they advocate will be their own undoing in the end as they villainize and vandalize their own culture. There is a side to conservatives that can be leveraged to renew our perspective in that conservatism is becoming more and more a populist position, yet that perspective is very weak right now because politically it is not yet fully united as this revolution has not yet congealed. We call this perspective a free society at present; Libertarianism. In the current politically tumultuous times, there is grave danger for both the free enterprise system and individual liberty. The problem with the raising populist ideas, as they relate to liberty and libertarianism I see as follows:

A PLAN FOR CHANGE

Libertarianism at present lacks a written doctrine; unlike the volumes of text written about socialist and communist ideas. Libertarianism is floating out there like an undisciplined hippy ideology that conservatives like in principal, but that lacks definition of vision and strategic planning. Mainly due to lacking a clearly defined doctrine, which for the first time I will define in this book.

VISION FOR THE FUTURE

All great projects need a vision; a written perspective that forms a plan of what the movement seeks to achieve and where these desires seek to go in terms of objectives and perspective. Thus, I have as an educated Project Manager assembled this Project Plan to analyze the current circumstance. *If we fail to plan; - we plan to fail.*

THE POPULARITY OF LIBERTARIANISM

Libertarian ideas need to grow and mature with our times; and not advocate the stale bread ideas of maintaining the status quo. The status quo no longer exists as the economy and society has evolved and drastically changes. Libertarianism is at its core about deregulation, individual freedom with only necessary minimal regulation. Free speech, free markets and free people are libertarian values. True libertarianism is in no way fascist as some might suggest. Fascism in reality was created by the Italian and German socialists, it is a left-wing unification of the state and business with hyper nationalism added into that political ideological blend; this is a fact of history.

THE COMPETITION OF IDEAS

Conservatives who speak of free markets and family values are losing the competitive fight of ideas against the left side of the spectrum by not embracing Libertarianism. The all-important middle of society, the largest social demographic is losing its economic foothold as is human rights in the west. We feel alienated and abandoned by conventional political ideas and our Governments as a whole. The overall resulting social circumstance of economic dislocation via the technology revolution is being mitigated and delayed as it is being hijacked by the economically politicised welfare state's economic bribery. This can only be short lived, and we must prepare for the economic and social crises that will come about after the hyperinflation created by the current policies leading to full scale social and economic collapse that is on the horizon from the modern welfare states impending implosion. The left are trying to maintain a nineteen fifties economic lifestyle with Government financial handouts, while repressing majorities on behalf of minorities in a perversion of the very concepts of human rights under economic circumstance that have completely changed in reality. Add to this their social Marxism of reverse discrimination, victimhood and repression of descent. It must be realized that the future will hold tremendous opportunity for those ready with the right plan for the times that will restore a sense of economic certainty and social stability. The current circumstance can only be a paragraph in the future, as this will not stand the test of time without a Trump election style backlash, and if that fails a future of bloody civil war as a consequence.

LIBERTARIAN PROPERTY RIGHTS

Without property ownership / home ownership rights, no person can be truly free. Current land use laws are based upon feudal economic policies of Lord and Surf. The left's message has greater resonance with the middle class, that now feel they are in fact living in an economic depression, due to technological change and outsourcing manufacturing overseas causing mass underemployment and social insecurity will lead to a future of severe social unrest if not addressed with a solution.

Flexible Mortgage security will enable citizens to start businesses and entrepreneurial activities from the home.

My message here is a fundamental restructuring of the political and economic system. While some presentations may seem radical, they are not in fact, if viewed holistically as a Governmental system. Property financing is one major change here; in that during the period of highest life costs of raising children as another example; a citizen may suspend home payments without penalty upon their mortgage, and instead pay for the best schools and health care for their family; -which they themselves will determine. Then in the "empty nest, phase of life" they may double down on mortgage payments, if they choose to. These are presentations I make to illustrate that this is not a fixed system, but rather a very flexible one.

CONTROL OVER YOUR BENEFITS

Freedom of choice and control over those choices is what liberty means. Citizens will be personally responsible for controlling a variety of long-term social benefit and family plans. Each family will determine for themselves under a Libertarian state, by self-determining their voluntary "subscriptions"; or non-participation. Government will need some altruistic minded people to design and manage these non-profit Government Fiduciary Corporations', and pre-determine the benefits of different plans, and the infrastructure each of these fiduciary corporations. New laws will prevent Governments from accessing these funds and diverting them for other purposes. There will be retirement trusts and a whole host of different optional plans:

1. **Healthcare Trusts;** with different plans and associated cost. Some fiduciary healthcare plans will include their own hospitals and doctors on salary. Other plans will offer selective services all farmed out to other companies to supply services, like dental plans now function.

2. **Education Charter School Trusts;** for all manner of educations parents may want. Schools which focus on classical education, Business schools, Religious schools, Philosophical schools, Trades schools; a whole host of variety in education.

3. **A Non-profit entrepreneur funding trust;** for aspiring businesses to offer start up financing and assistance with initiating new business plans etc. and other tax-based subscriptions for citizens to voluntarily subscribe to.

4. **An Unemployment Insurance Trust;** To replace the current program. These will be via the legislature or Senate creating independent non-profit Trust Corporations by incorporating various citizen trusts, and to avail them for citizen voluntary subscription. It will be the new role of the Legislature and or Senate to debate the merits of creating new trusts, like computer applications for citizens to subscribe to if they want. The specifics of these plans and the particulars of directorships will be determined by the legislature after submission of project plans for such

services. Politicians will be kept busy managing these public non-profit fiduciary insurance plans, each with their own boards of directors providing all manner of optional social benefits.

The libertarian state does not need to be the rule of the jungle, but rather the rule of independence and voluntary subscription, or not. Government will focus upon new legislation and determining the needs of society in terms of voluntary service trusts they will create.

HOW IS IT THAT THE LEFT HAS GAINED ITS CURRENT STRENGTHENING FOOT HOLD?

Put simply, the left is better at economically / financially incentivising the working class. The liberal left is bribing the people with financial incentives of all kinds from fake, "free" health care (tax paid); to increased child tax credits; social housing, and other financial allowances. "Vote for us" they imply; and "we will give you money". Simply put, they are vote buying with tax payer's own money. In a time of decreased employment opportunities for the middle class this is a powerful incentive, that traditional fiscal and social responsibility messages of the conservative movement cannot compete with. You can be as correct or "right" as you want (pardon the pun), but that will only be proven over time as "the proof is in the pudding"; as the old expression goes.

Under current conditions, if you tout responsibility, you also come before the electorate like a naked man trying to sell clothing. The question is not purely intellectual, the question is, how do you compete with a leftist movement that is doomed to eventually fail in financial ruin, and perhaps spell the very end of western civilization from their; " bread and circuses" economic policies, that most certainly will end with all of society paying for that which can only lead to riotous social destruction, once the national accounts and assets have been given away for a party of fake fiscal prosperity, brought about by refinancing the national house. Once the nation's fake prosperity credit card based financial house has been bankrupted by their policies and ideas in the long term, like the former Soviet Union. Then people will grasp for change like a drowning man grapples to pull himself above water with anything floating.

THE OFFER:

What can the Libertarian ideology offer that can be as attractive, or preferably more attractive, than the left's bribery and remain true to their fundamental ideological principals? Libertarians must realize that when the opposing side has resorted to bribing the voting public through the draining of the public coffers, traditional conservative ideas of reducing Government expenditures, is an ideology that is not a very competitive alternative when it is the engine of the economy that is the source of the faltering of society at its root core. The conservative ideology has grown stale also. Politics is about power. So regardless of your rooted foundations, if you don't win the electorate, you will not win elections.

If you don't win elections; you're heading towards irrelevance. Under the current circumstance the stakes could not be higher for the more society becomes disenfranchised and as a result hostile, the more repressive the Government will become.

WHAT THE LEFT HAS GOING FOR IT AND LIBERTARIANS COMPARE.

Even if you disagree with it, the left has an ideology of Marxism at its core that has failed miserably economically and socially where ever it is implemented. The left has moved to a renovated version of the same ideas we now see of this discredited economic ideology with the collapse of communism in all of its former adherent nations. Now we have the so-called new communism brought to you by the same left-wing crew that has come to be known as "Social Marxism". They couldn't succeed with the economy, now they are up to implementing a renewed version of social control and citizen bribery with the public coffers. Their adherents believe that their ends are justified by their new fiscal and social totalitarian means. But it is, the same old repressive left-wing bag of tricks, put into a shiny new wrapper. Now we have new and improved communism, which having failed to run the economy, now wants to run everyone's personal lives.

Like the native residential schools' fiasco, the arrogance of the left in their desire to run all our lives never ceases to run into disastrous social experiments that destroy individual lives in the long run. The delusion of equality in a world that merely requires mutual respect, it seems is a battle that is as much intellectual, as it is pragmatic in the requirements of what must be done to combat this tyranny of controlling the individual. The core of every socialist sole is an unfathomable level of arrogance, where they think they have all the answers, and everyone else must be an idiot as they believe the rest of us are too dumb to run our own lives.

AT THE VERY CORE OF ALL CONSERVATISM IS THE FREEDOM LOVING HEART OF A LIBERTARIAN.

Freedom from excess taxation; Freedom from excess Government control, by minimizing Government; Freedom to engage in enterprise. Protection of the family, and family sovereignty protected from excessive state control and interference, and of course protection of property rights. The Libertarian ideology that is out there, it is very poorly defined. I might venture to say even being hijacked under current day political polarization. I will attempt to define a renewed doctrine in this book, which is a pragmatic and functional alternative. The Libertarian alternative is at present basically an undefined ideology. Libertarianism along with economic restructuring and reconstruction is the way forward for western nations. Under the current lethargic economic situation, we Libertarians will have to initiate a cohesive platform to move forward, and win popular elections. Polarization no longer works; ideological conversion is the only way I can see moving forward. Simply reducing the tax burden, does not any longer enthuse the working middle class thirsting for change. Without pragmatism any ideology will never gain popular traction. A society based upon voluntary subscription and payment for services, based upon user voluntary pay and subscription, based upon preferences, is Libertarian, and in fact is a true free market society.

APPEALING TO THE PEOPLE

To become competitive the Libertarian ideology must find a new way to appeal to the people. Appealing to the people will require a rethink of how Libertarian aims are to be achieved. You cannot expect to sell yesterday's obsolete technology and create enthusiasm that will or could lead to political victory. The left has extensive ideological and intellectual writings and thus subscriptions to their ideology. There must be a Libertarian middle of the road narrative, that is fresh and new, that has policies which will also provide economic incentive in the current political climate of incentivised politics. It is necessary to deregulate and restructure the economy. To build in social incentives to compete, with the political left wing under a new perspective. This is the only way Libertarians can realistically win elections and the hearts and minds of the people; to be competitive. This requires the ability to convert liberals and conservatives to be under one new "big tent"; I see as the future of Libertarianism. Without liberals and conservatives having a combined conversion, one that comes up the center, with a new and fresh perspective, gridlock is the best we can hope for.

The main doctrine of Libertarianism is free choice, not deterministic regarding what your choices and options are. If a person desires socialized medicine then, it is your right to choose this and pay for it like private insurance. This is not a right to impose such programs upon others, in this perspective I can see reconciling both the right and left wing of the political spectrum politically. The authenticity of Libertarian thinking is the right to choose to opt in or opt out. The right to pay, or not to pay, and the removal of all imposition. This can be achieved via a reformed tax system, where tax payments start at zero and are a formulation of different social program options created by Government. Like a restaurant meal, you can eat nothing and pay nothing, or choose those social benefits you desire. Government would create as fiduciary trusts various menu options, each item on the menu would have a price which determines your annual tax payment as a premium to pay. Government would incorporate various non-profit trust service businesses, creating different group service plans for citizens in; education, health care, child care as needed; gold, silver and bronze plans with varying degrees of coverage. Pensions would depend upon how many children you contributed and supported in your life; no children; no pension, as the new generation supports the old in these funds. Citizens would select, plans by category, and sign a five-year tax contract in each non-profit trust service they desire and need; depending upon their family circumstance.

1. We must be pragmatic and realize that the economic losses of industry and employment dislocation is creating massive social discontent. That the left has tapped into this discontent with free cash. That the right also must develop a system of competing politically with different incentives to capture the electorate. If several million citizens desire to create a cooperative, not for profit universal health care insurance plan, that's their right to have one, and to pay for it through their combined premiums. The key point being, it must be self-financing, and purely voluntary for the recipients. No one should be forced to partake in such plans. In fact, I would hope that there might be a dozen or so such plans all charging different premiums, so there is a variety of choice and prices.

2. There are only two political positions that matter; those who want power, and those who are in power; the rest have no say and are irrelevant. So I will move forward now with new fresh ideas, to revive Libertarianism. This new project plan is to make the Libertarian brand more competitive, and to win the current ideological war. I believe libertarianism will win in the long run, that is not just political or legislative libertarianism, but also economic. Libertarianism with a plan, to economically increase individual prosperity. To fundamentally restructure our economy, and social organization, to create prosperity and security for society. This project like

any, is a series of processes we need to reduce to work based components and strategically create a doctrine that brings together a single purpose of intentions and direction.

2nd Chapter
THE DOCTRINE OF LIBERTARIANISM

Libertarianism along with Pragmatism are the two great philosophical schools of thought that originated as uniquely North American philosophies in origin of adoption. The words of the American philosopher Ralph Waldo Emerson in his essay, "Self-Reliance" echoes repeatedly in the minds of Americans, as if a Carl Jung architype, in the psyche of every native born North American at the core of our souls. The conservative right must stop seeing the nation state as its mortal enemy. This is out of sync with the social need for national and local Government. The new libertarian thinking must initiate the perspective that the nation state and all Government, is little more than a national corporation with a social mission and citizen shareholders where:

LOCAL IS ALWAYS BETTER:

We no longer trust politicians or the political process and prefer local Government that is more manageable in smaller units, under the umbrella of a defense based, federal nation state. Local independent, smaller Government established as direct democracies like Swiss Cantons, rather than globalization. We must take back control over Government. The Swiss neutrality model that has lived in peace for over a century and has proven itself to pragmatically lead to an extremely peaceful and stable political system that justifies emulation. Local direct democracy would provide a level of ethical leadership demonstrating the ability of the nation to provide a free society that is the authentic Libertarian course going forward, that will also create political stability and economic prosperity.

WHY SWISS STYLE DEMOCRACY?

I have over the decades investigated many models of Government, being pragmatic, I searched out the best functional Government model I could find in the world. The Swiss constitutional governance model is the best I could find after many decades of research, by virtue of being a direct democracy; a peaceful nation; a stable society and life; a diverse nation; a wealthy and prosperous nation; The oldest democracy in the world, and most importantly a nation that can universally be seen as proven to be an absolute success, based upon these criteria. This is a Libertarian model of success. If you desire to see that which I espouse herein as an ideal Government in action, then a visit to Switzerland would be suggested. These are not pie in the sky ideas presented here. There is a highly successful example of what I am advocating here for Libertarian Government.

PRAGMATISM IN GOVERNMENT IS ALWAYS BETTER

Free markets and a better competitive environment necessitate innovation. This competition in all its forms is far more superior to monotone mega states like the European Union whose representatives are for the most part not even known by their constituents, and who retreat into an isolated bubble. Like pre-WWII Japanese Emperors who no longer even spoke the same dialect as that of their people due to living in isolation, over time. The issue of greatest concern is to provide a viable governable alternative to the current corrupt Governments in the west, which I will explain in greater detail in the ensuing chapters of this book.

TWELVE PRINCIPALS OF LIBERTARIANISM

1. Libertarianism is not anarchy; and thus, not anti-government as are anarchists! Libertarianism is about limiting and controlling the jurisdiction of the state and maximizing the individual's control over their own lives by respecting the individual's rights to as much free choice regarding their lives as pragmatically practical.

2. Libertarianism is about protecting individual sovereignty; protection of individual choice, by controlling the state apparatus and limiting its jurisdiction over the integrity and privacy of the individual and the family.

3. Libertarianism is about the state providing free willed options; free from state coercion such as in the standardization in education and all state organized activities providing options so as to prevent indoctrination and brain washing. Options and choices left to parents and individuals depending upon age of children, rather than having the state mandating one educational perspective that is a

Prussian system-based state indoctrination camp. Anarchy is in no way libertarianism, though they are commonly confused by society at large. Anarchist want the complete elimination of Government. Libertarians want controlled minimalist Government that is minimally authoritarian; and not controlled people.

4. Libertarianism desires-controlled state organization and regulation in their most fundamental forms and rejects the nation state becoming social engineers that manufacture constructs that basically are providing false narratives, social engineering in all its forms, and historical revisionism of history, society, and our social foundations. Thus, creating false narratives given out of perspective, from those with rudimentary knowledge and deceptive agendas.

5. The libertarian seeks to control and limit the states interference into the individual and family life; thus, seeks to regulate Government, not regulate people other than determining individual responsibilities to oneself and the cohesive family unit.

6. Libertarians reject mandatory conscription to state social engineering policies. Desire structure based upon individual responsibility and freedom. The essential perspective of libertarianism is a clear minimalist unfettered social construct.

7. Libertarians surprisingly can be left or right wing in their constructive ideas and organize national programs that are optional and never mandatory, such as national health care or education.

8. Libertarians believe in minimal taxation and voluntary self-funding state administered social benefits.

9. Libertarians believe in the elimination of all mandatory social programs. Voluntary subscription is a libertarian social policy.

10. Libertarians desire local Government, which is more manageable in smaller units like the direct democracies as practiced in Swiss Cantons at present. Libertarians like Government constitutions that control and limit Government not people's liberty.

11. Libertarians believe in free lands like all other creatures on earth. The right to one Interest free principal only mortgage from the state. That every citizen has the right to a secure home, free from all forms of seizure or judgement, collateralization, tax or other mortgage tyranny until death, and the right to relocate that residence anywhere within the nation. The right to redeem improvements upon the homestead as equity in order to relocate as a right to sell and exercise mobility.

12. Libertarians desire "opting in or out options" for Government services. Making all Government services and level of taxes payable being strictly subscriber paid based like private insurance tax payments as payroll deductions and should be based upon Government program subscriptions by citizens being strictly paid for and opted in like any private insurance without reservations. There is an efficiency of scale provided by national programs that can inure to citizens, however society should grant those who opt out of these programs to also pay less taxes commensurate with the citizen's free will. Universal Government cash incentives can be provided to all by Government but must come from consumption and other royalty-based Government income taxes, as would most Government services. Everything has a cost associated to it in reality, and thus user pay formulas must be used, and the citizen is given an opt in or out option for these group health insurance, pension plans and service programs that the Government would make available electively. Income tax would be a subscription-based tax system different for each citizen depending upon program subscriptions such as health insurance etc.

FREEDOM OF CONSCIENCE

The human world is filled with organized imposition, constantly attacking the individual. These behavioural impositions are constantly trying to subvert independent perspectives and thought, they are a blight upon liberty.

Imposers are constantly seeking conformity, for out of conformity comes control of others. Conformity of your education to create a false narrative, conformity of your ideas through media so that the official narrative is believed as a reinforcement, conformity in your family so that your children follow the narrative of the establishment. It is desired that you surrender your mind, thus it is desired that your bodies will comply. The establishment is the hierarchy of society that seeks your enslavement. If they can control your internal psychological narrative through indoctrination, your enslavement is achieved, first in your mind, then with your body and finally this could lead to the loss of your life fighting some war on their behalf. Like a captive bird you will enter the jail of your mental cage without question, in the belief that this is the only way. All governing organizations know this and thus seek to control narratives, to dumb down the population so that you will foolishly do their bidding and fight for their causes that, in reality are the shackles of upon your own life. The entire edifice of human endeavour is by intention, designed to create regimentation through indoctrination and elimination of free thought. It is difficult to combat these influences like rag tag collection of anarchists might try.

WHY ANARCHY FAILS

Anarchy can only be a solitary disruptive exercise at best, doomed to failure as it is a lone wolf solitary idea. At its very core, Anarchists discard all organization and community collaboration, this is why that ideology is weak, and always will be, mainly because it has no objective and only a desire to be disruptive. Anarchy is the undisciplined and unruly immature child of the libertarian thought in the room, lacking life experience and prudence, foolish, impudent, and even recklessly dangerous to itself and others.

THE LIBERTARIAN PERSPECTIVE

Libertarians are pragmatists that realize there must be some form of social organization, cohesion and structure. We are fundamentally constitutionalist, we seek to create organization and order to control the controllers and limit their desire, for brute force, intimidation and coercion to rule our lives. This is how the world fundamentally operates. Libertarians must realize that this is what we are up against daily, this is a constant battle to push back the "controllers". Libertarianism is about disciplined and organized freedom of the individual and the family unit within a functional social model that is based upon mutual democratic respect for the liberties and dignity of others. The world is filled with other "isms" that want to control you and your life through various kinds of economic tyranny.

TEAM WORK

Libertarianism believes in free enterprise and individualistic rights. This completely rejects communistic ideas, but not the economic reality that for certain things there can be economies of scale by pooling resources or efforts, it is not all individualism. The lone wolf is a vulnerable creature in a world full of wolf packs. Without alliances the libertarian is weak and vulnerable, this is pragmatism that the libertarian must always keep at the forefront of your efforts. Libertarians are collaborative with those who share the same values, for in unity comes strength to fend off and defeat the controllers. The group thinkers and their social tyranny are a constant threat. Through free independent thinking, the libertarian is always respectful of diversity yet vigilant to watch for controllers who seek to import control over others by giving advantage that is unearned. Unexploited teamwork and collaboration is also necessary for libertarians

ENTREPRENEURSHIP

Libertarians see the individual's free enterprise and entrepreneurship as the apex of personal development for it provides independence, as much as can be achieved as a social species to create your own economic wellbeing. Employment by others are a learning opportunity, to also obtain capital for your personal endeavours of the future. Collectivism as only of value for economies of scale, requiring equality of distribution in accordance with contribution. Libertarians see competitive entrepreneurship from innovation and creativity as natural for human beings. It is the apex of libertarianism to paddle your own canoe and being self-reliant. Yet collaborating with the greater political administration to ensure the individuals rights are always considered and respected.

THE SLIPPERY SLOPE FOR WESTERN SOCIETY

There has been an evident lessening within western society's influential managerial class to have empathy, compassion and a civic sense of responsibility for others as conservatives have had a strong sense of in past generations. The team work and team play by the owners of enterprise that existed in the past has dried up and become a kind of selfish indulgence now.

1. Social responsibility

Let us not forget that industrialists have been some of the greatest reformers of the past. From Henry Ford increasing the wages of his factory workers, to charitable endowments left by deceased business tycoons to this day. Altruism is as much a free enterprise concept as any other.

2. Ensure doctrine integrity

There has been great ruthlessness on both sides of this argument from Pinkerton guard's union busting, to Soviet era gulags. Both the right and left have on occasion lost their way. However, the acts of a few industrialists do not even begin to compare to the outright murder committed by the left in the former Soviet Union, China or even the National Socialist German Workers Party; -the fascist version of the left that pretends Nazism was a right-wing movement. Let us not forget that Stalin and Hitler were historically allies in the invasion of Poland, which started the Second World War, and both were very racist.

3. Empathy in society is critical

A callous detached and socially disconnected ruthlessness seems to have infected current day society and Government, so much so that western society and culture appears to be on the verge of collapse. Unless this trend is reversed, we, all face a very perilous future in the west. United we may stand, but if we continue as a divided people we are surely headed for a fall.

4. Remove psychopaths from positions of authority

Psychopaths that lack natural empathetic connection to others should not be in positions of authority, as they so often are right now. The inability to lead others by free will is proportional to the ability to be leaders in the provision of Justice in their dealings with others; we commonly call this lack of empathy ruthlessness or a psychopath. This is an everyday plague and tyranny upon society that we all experience from time to time as I will explain further.

5. National historical narrative is important

Both I and my family and ancestors have always lived in either Europe or America throughout recorded history, so I understand the hypocrisy compared to the cultural promise and expectations we have all grow up with. By personal experience I find we have lost our way and that this behaviour is very perplexing when you are on the receiving end of it, as I have been, and will demonstrate the barbaric current reality of western nations. The west has become psychologically chronically ill

BECOMING AN AUTHENTIC SOCIETY

We in the west have grown and been indoctrinated to expect more and a better state of affairs. It is my contention that we have lost our way in the world, and that we are no longer the beacon of light that either we ourselves expect, or those of other nations, so quick to optimistically imitate our ways, falsely hang onto as their beacon of hope for a better world. We need to strive for reform such as:

1. Eliminating pedigree politicians

Currently so many individuals I have found fancy themselves as leaders upon promotion within Government and business management. My contention is that if these individuals were authentic "leaders" and were placed upon a deserted island with a group of people, that few or none of them would be leaders of the group. Many are best described as elitist, corrupt, crony careerists and monetary motivated psychopathic social tyrants, rather than any form of real leader.

2. Eliminating divisive policies

The current crop of so called "leaders" in the west, divide and conquer the vote and society, supplying false and misleading information and diversions, this is how this system is maintained.

3. Eliminating cronyism

The truth is that in business, as in political management, there are few authentic leaders, and many unqualified cronies in positions of power, not based upon merit but rather loyalty and submission to the hierarchy. These individuals are mainly underlings, most not suited for even low-level administration jobs. Careerists, not leaders at all. Most current politicians also are not leaders necessarily for the same reasons, though the terms are often inaccurately interchanged "actor", would be a more appropriate term.

4. Eliminating social feudalism

If ever there ever was a corrupt practice to be cited in the western social political system (I refrain from calling them democracies inaccurately) it is rooted in the career politician, and a political system rooted in a feudal system of landlord post surf relationship, created by the indenture via usurious mortgages. A system that still indentures the population not as free men; -but as economic surfs.

5. Eliminating career politicians

Politics is not, and should not be a career, to serve longer than a five-year vocation in maximum duration is a hindrance upon political evolution (entrenchment is a violation of democratic ideas). The opportunity to be of public service and initiates needed change for a single 4- or 5-year term is plenty of time for a politician; otherwise politicians get an attitude of entitlement and need to be removed from office.

6. Eliminating monetary incentive attracting the corrupt

The shorter the political career, the less corruption and the better for society. If ever there is a removal of monetary rewards, irrespective of need, abandonment of these positions would occur by career politicians. Politicians are highly corruptible with influence peddling and accepting covert financial incentives and other bribes. Rare is the politician whose personal wealth does not increase exponentially while in political office, far beyond their salary. But with the levers of law enforcement within their hands nothing ever happens for their crimes, because law enforcement is not independent.

7. Eliminating political parties

Political parties have become corrupt crony clubs, they have few sincere followers, but many anticipating rewards from the public trough. Those in charge could hardly be defined as authentic or "Leaders"; instead there is a surrogate prostitution taking place, making everything only a facade of their true motives and the insincerity in their implementation of the duties and obligations of position and public office. They are only motivated by their organization's consolidation of power.

8. Removing exemption from prosecution of politicians

The root of western political administration is lacking in sincerity or authenticity and has long been rooted in a foundation of corruption in every western nation. They make laws and selectively enforce them not based upon society's needs, but rather their own political agenda giving themselves and their ilk immunity from their own laws. Clearly, the Magna Carte is no longer in force.

9. Removing pretence of integrity

Politicians don't like it when you call them out like this, because they want you to live within their phony matrix society that pretends, they have integrity. Their fear is you / the general public, seeing the elephant in the room might motivate people to do something about it. Street wise people get how the system works, but the establishment does not want you to remove the rose-colored glasses of naïve fools. Also, once the majority sees the corrupt system for what it is, the possibility of revolt in all its forms including political assassinations by the weak lone wolf citizen justice warrior who now knows the pre-determined score in these battles increases exponentially. Once you realize the system is rigged, and lacks integrity; why would you attend even any Court?

GOVERNMENT JUDICIAL AND POLITICAL ACTS

Justice occurs in the light of day, not the shadow of darkness. The secretive Courts, which hide the abuse that the system invokes upon people, who committed no crime, in the phony name of privacy in what is always a public matter —the determinations of the judiciary. This also applies in the basic human rights violation by what are called "Family Law Courts". If there were violence or any crime involved, the regular Courts could, and would deal with it. Family Courts are a parasitic crime against society, in and of themselves intended by the billion-dollar legal industry to fleece families of their wealth and transfer it to the elite class called lawyers, who later become its judges. Family Courts and their army of lawyers have committed untold damage to the family unit in western countries for generations and have played a major role in the decline of western civilization with impunity. The crime in these courts is not anything done by families, criminal courts deal with real crime. Think about it for one second.

1. Families are not criminals

A Court system that puts families on trial; no wonder the fertility rate is facing extinction in the west; - Fear of Government harassment - perhaps? Do people not see the perversion and absurdity of this? What kind of sick demented society has Courts to put "families on trial", and removes children from protesting loving parent's, stripped away from their parents loving arms and denying the families all their human rights anyways? Knowing that statistically, 90% of men who pursue equal custody as a parent (their natural right by biology), lose in these courts of tyranny.

2. Government care commonly leads to child abuse

Take the case in Canada of native children taken away from their parents to be reprogrammed and brainwashed by the Government. Here is the ultimate example of a horror story to beat even the most horrific Steven King horror story. Simply look into this case to see the reality of state parenting, Canadian Governments, who by the way also think they are great surrogate, or "co-parents" as one Ontario, Canada Government minister said in 2017, "the Government now co-parents' children". Who invited Government into everyone's family business? We are not their livestock!

> *The record of Government regarding their ability to take care of children is equal to a pedophile daycare center!*

Simply investigate Canada's disgraceful decades of Government "residential schools" as an example of Government child care. First, they were routinely run by pedophiles, who daily raped toddlers, both male and female by sodomizing them, used routine and brutal corporal punishment against the children, and outright murdered thousands of children, who lie buried in unmarked graves on the orphanage lawns across Canada. Wow, quite a record by Government child care workers! A litany of child abuse and criminal actions that went on for a hundred years right into the nineteen nineties! A sadistic tale of horrors, that the Government tried to expunge themselves of by launching a Government commission called; "The Truth and Reconciliation Commission" as a great attempt to cover up these crimes, since nothing was redressed from the crimes committed as a result of the exposure of the horrors. These children who were confiscated from their families for no justifiable reason, without any due process of law, experienced horrors throughout their youth by the reckless hand of Government that if put into a movie would leave the audience vomiting out the theatre doors and suffering from post-traumatic stress disorder just to see a fictionalized tale of what occurred. The fact is there is no

Government child care effort that has not been awash with tales of horrific child abuse. From the human vegetables of Romanian orphanages, to so called, "children's aid"; custodial arrangements where the custodial Government appointees regularly abuse the children. The fact is, take children away from their parents and their potential to be abused or even killed increases exponentially. The Dickinson tale of Oliver Twist continues to this day. Children outside of parental protection always have, and always will be in jeopardy for horrific abuse.

3. Don't allow Government to indoctrinate children

Daycares and kindergartens are the start of Government regimentation and are indoctrination factories that claim to be better than parents. They offer no proof of their Marxist implementation being of benefit for the children other than hearsay. The entire education system is designed as regimentation and social indoctrination designed to make "good citizens" in other words servants of the nation state so brainwashed that if war is declared they unthinkingly run to do the Governments bidding, as they have been so thoroughly brainwashed and regimented by the state. First created in Prussia, the system is a centralized brainwashing program of authoritarianism. Their teachers are their first military commanders of the program. The system is designed for the slaughter of innocents through indoctrination on behalf of psychopaths.

4. Government officials need to be called to account for crimes

If you want to see real Government child care simply look into native residential schools and orphanages in Canada. Not one of these child abusers, murderers or rapists has ever been criminally charged, they all are comfortably retired on Government pensions and so called, "respectable careers" behind them. That's Government care, an issue the complicit media never raises.

5. Human rights and Government complicity

Then there is the record of psychiatric institutions giving children LSD every day and performing horrific experiments (i.e.: The C. I. A. M K ULTRA brain washing project) upon innocents. There is the routine brain damage invoked by lobotomizing people, electro shocking patients in these so-called hospitals, experimenting with all manner of drugs upon patients, and performing castrations, sterilizations, and all manner of psychopathic inhumane actions and experiments. The crimes Government has committed against innocent children in a litany of horrors is a very long list indeed of Government crimes. Not to mention the rape and debauchery that went on in Government sanctioned facilities routinely. The post traumatic stress disorder, that soldiers often end up with, and too much more to list all the Governments' crimes and abuses. Virtually every western nation engaged in the same horrific human rights violations as the Nazis did in concentration camps; -after the Second World War, and since. Let us not forget all of these criminals live out peaceful comfortable retirements on

Government pensions also, probably reminiscing their psychopathic careers and relishing their mistreatment of others. This was not only in the west, in the former Soviet bloc of nations Governments were worse with gulags that imprisoned people for political crimes and once again engaged in sadistic abuse of prisoners. Left wing political types are clearly the most dangerous, they crave controlling others and have long tried to destroy people's independence. Left wing Governments have killed more people than all the wars combined.

FAMILIES ARE AN INSTITUTION NEEDING PROTECTION

Getting back to family Courts; being brought before one of these "family" Courts all a man can expect is that you will have your natural God given, biological parental rights stripped from you by these Courts of injustice without a rational reason or justification supplied.

1. Human beings are not livestock

Using the threat of violence from the state, to enforce financial extortion. Your parental rights will be stripped away without justification in most cases, but the obligation to pay the mother a monthly salary, despite your diminished sperm donor status will be ingrained in the Government to now ensure you pay their pre-determined extortion in spite of being a visitor with no authority or rights regarding the child's upbringing.

2. Government has no right to assume ownership of children

It is a proven rigged system in that less than 10% of men win even equal parental rights in "Family Courts" statistically in most western nations. These Courts of injustice are designed to justify the stripping away of parent's natural rights. Like domestic animals the Government clearly proves in these Courts that they are not Government, but rather owners of their citizens. For what gives them the right to determine human relationships, such as the human rights violation they call "custody"; - what is this but a conscious transfer of ownership of the child?

3 Child-parent biological connection must be respected

It would be more honest to simply make a law that the children are the property of the mother, then this façade would not be necessary, and families would be far better off economically. Such a law would hurt the welfare state and the Government's ability to subvert women. Since automatic custody without pretence of equality would justify the removal of the man's obligation to finance that which is in law not his. It would mean female selection of mates would require a heavy burden of personal responsibility upon women. The feminist anti male victim narrative as espoused by unscientific university humanities courses and by profiteering lawyers and capitulating vote getting politicians would have a problem, since women constituting the majority of people by gender would have to be responsible for what happens to impregnate them. Right now, in the west women have all the child ownership rights (called custody) and men only get the financial liability as granted at the mercy of the mother.

4. Courts that depend upon a person's wealth to defend yourself are tyrannical.

The reality of Family Courts is that those men that win are either very wealthy, or become very indebted, to pay for lawyers and prevent an unjustified stripping away and removal of their natural human rights from full parental rights to fractional visiting permissions.

5. Politically based family policy is tyranny

The word;" CUSTODY" is used to hide the dirty corrupt Multi-Billion Dollar business involved in this travesty of justice invoked by social communism of the feminist anti male bigoted agenda. These so-called social activists I would add by the way, are Government funded. The schools are a part of the Government's social engineering agenda, not a legitimate social movement of the people. This is done for the Government funded and subversive feminist vote. This is not a legitimate social movement; the authentic majority of women are not politicized by the Government and judicial system. The sad part is, that even a stay at home Dad who raises his children, because of his gender, will also have his parental rights stripped by the feudal western judiciary. We have a feudal Government system that operates to this day. Western society has had birthrates plummet to extinction levels because of these anti-family policies to the point of reversing population growth.

6. Judicial family interference is leading to extinction

The west is facing extinction because of greedy lawyers and corrupt politicians undermining the family with social engineering, the court industry and laws, which surely future generations will view as being a greater violation of human rights, than the human rights violations that lead to the nineteen sixties civil rights movement.

7 Social communism & engineering must be stopped

Government interference, threats, interference in private civil matters, harassment and homelessness caused by the Government has left an untold carnage of lives ruined by the Government in western nations in dealing with private and personal matters. Like all repressed by communism in all its forms, social communism's feminist agenda has literally put western civilization into its death throws. Repressive Government sponsored feminism and political correctness that represses free speech, is utilized to silence objection. By allowing Government to indoctrinate children we all become victims, as it takes decades to see reality beyond childhood school indoctrination and see the pragmatic outcome.

CURRENT IMMIGRATION TRENDS | IMMIGRATION GAMES

Current demographic reality means most western nations will end up under the yoke of Islamic fundamentalism due to their higher birth rates if current immigration trends continue for a couple generations; - Our ancestors must be crying with tears of outrage for how incompetent current generations particularly state sponsored feminists have squandered their inheritance, by allowing elites to do this to us with our own wealth, all for theft of men's wealth and political office, even social treason was not a boundary for the elites. The elite fail to comprehend that Islam is a complete system of combined religion and theocratic government the religion mandates of its adherents, which forbids the western concept of religious separation of church/mosque and Government administration.

INEQUALITY UNDER THE LAW | JAILS ARE FULL OF POOR PEOPLE DENIED A FAIR TRIAL

African American riots following police shootings or arrests demonstrate the result of generations of legal inequality, being a large population of multigenerational poor people, they are keenly aware that being unable to employ a proper court defence, that the poor receive jail sentences commonly even if innocent; that's the pragmatic reality. In western nations there is no equality before the law and minimal justice. My experiences have demonstrated for me that in real life, the tyranny of western nation's judiciary. The poor and middle class are completely unable to afford lawyers thus normally go to jail for minor acts the state calls crimes, while the wealthy commit serious crimes and get away with it, particularly white-collar crimes. It's all a great big fake façade! Until some enforcement organization other than a legislature exercising patronage appointments for law are enforcement authorities, the law will continue to only be an instrument to maintain the establishment in power, legislating for political expediency. While the crimes of politicians and the bureaucracy never get dealt with; - but rather buried out of sight.

There is no equality before the law, it is completely based upon your wealth to afford a decent lawyer who is a good debater. Under the North American system of elite crony Governments, western judiciaries consist at present mainly self-regulating, dishonourable Government patronage appointments, there is no impartiality in legal administration in America. They are members of a system that politically selects crony judges all of whom remain for decades in power and in the public trough. A French revolution style purge or mass resignations could clean up this psychopathic corruption, followed by reconstituting and reorganization of the state's operation. The problem with revolution is that without a comprehensive plan with upfront intended reforms, they risk getting hijacked by opportunists, as they often are. The causes of political corruption are resource allocation-based Government. The western nation state has become little more than a gangster club, with a police force and military to coerce social compliance in every aspect of your life including in your home and family relations. There is no benevolence in Government for the most part, only pretense indoctrinated in the schools, due to the Governments' co-opted and separate agenda. Thus because of the brainwashing and indoctrination of schools, most people do not even live in reality. It takes decades more until middle age when individuals begin to realize it has all been a lie.

PRAGMATIC EXPERIENCE PROVES IT'S ALL FIXED

The current state of western Government is that the population have become livestock; the property of the Government. These Governments regulate individuals while, they and their corporate benefactors commit crimes with impunity. Laws have become window dressing as they exist but go unenforced when they converge with politician's benefactors.

FLAWS OF HUMAN NATURE | WE HUMANS HAVE THREE BASIC FLAWS:

ONE: Impatience, which makes us easy targets to become credit slaves.

TWO: No inherited memory of past life mistakes of our ancestors so, "history repeats itself".

THREE: A late developing prefrontal cortex creating issues with our cognitive development in youth, which is exploited by the Government to turn the population against itself, create militaries and other instruments of social repression, before the young brain can process the holistic results of certain life paths and the course or product of those paths.

PSYCHOLOGICAL CONFLICT CAUSES POST-TRAUMATIC STRESS

The nation state currently causes most post-traumatic stress and human psychological damage. The result of Government education and the bait and switch of Government propaganda traumatizes the youth when they realize from childhood their whole education was a complete scam perpetrated by the Government, and the indoctrinated complicity of the nation's citizens with propaganda, in order to do the states dirty deeds, which the normal mind cannot reconcile the horror the state creates. The disgraceful, dirty deeds, the psychopathic politicians require of the youth and invoke. It's like discovering your God is the Devil. The truth is such a contradiction of the western child's childhood indoctrination that it blows the human mind to see this in reality of war, the revelation that your society is run by psychopaths. Science has uncovered that one of the last parts of the human brain to develop are logic, foresight and recognition of danger. This explains the easy manipulation and recklessness of youth. The inability to recognize the domino effect of consequences, which creates great athletes due to fearless risk taking. Good military conscripts must be young to be exploited by the Government. Men when they reach their late thirties or older, would not suit the job, because they will be more holistic in their perceptions, their prefrontal lobes are developed, and life experience creates empathy thus lessening the ability to be cruel without forethought in a normal mind.

THE ABANDONMENT OF FAMILY CARE |

WITHOUT PARENTAL GUIDANCE, THERE IS NO FOUNDATION FOR HUMANITY.

There is also a lack of parental guidance in children raised by the current crop of non-parents in the west who abandon their children that are left to fend for themselves in state and private daycares from infancy. Feminism is a state sponsored movement because the Government needs dispassionate indoctrinated people who lack individuality as much as possible. The education system is the robot factory of Government repression. Thus, getting mothers out of the way enables the states agenda to indoctrinate the children, rather than a mother's education to be an individual. The nation state hates individualism, they want socially obedient regimented robots who will serve their purposes and who believe their version of the world, even though it is a bunch of lies. Independent thinkers are of no use for psychopaths. I believe we are not Spartans and that an important part of children's developmental education parents role model as empathy, with empathy being left out of socializing children under state indoctrination, this experience is growing into a condition of social retardation. The lack of siblings as a result of their parent's economic financial enslavement causes me to wonder. How do these children learn compassion and empathy for others, by being placed in a competitive daycare environment?

Lacking the parent child empathy of parental love being demonstrated; from their first day of birth. The growth in psychopathic and narcissistic personality disorders appears to be the net effect of this socialization by parental abandonment to institutions. Institutions that will never be equipped to, impart lessons of the heart, like a mother or father can. My experience in recent decades has been that society's social skills in the west are in a steep decline in our dealings with each other. People are so miserably unhappy and dissatisfied in their lives.

Western societies have been like a sledge hammer crushing the individual along with this crushing personality. It starts with the child who scrapped his knee in daycare; - crying. Told by the teacher; "go sit over there in the corner until you feel better". Versus the soft embrace of a loving parent or mother's embrace of empathy demonstration, delivered by heart felt love for the child. This is how a psychopath is made cruel by a thousand small cuts carelessly not role modeling compassion and love, affection and the need to experience empathy that only authentic love can supply.

HISTORICAL REVISIONISM | THE FIRST THING FOREIGN OCCUPATION FORCES DO IS

KILL THE MEN OF THE VILLAGE.

Corrupted institutions of western Governments due to cronyism under the current oligarchy, subvert the political process and social institutions creating anti-democratic administration. They cannot be accused of being governed by the rule of law, as this no longer applies. The current auspices of blind belief in the concept of benevolent Government implementing Social Marxism, under the guise of political correctness, and minority rights which in reality is discriminatory affirmative action, for perceived slights that are cherry picked worldwide.

The elite have for decades been betraying and angering their founding peoples in the west. What remains of a loyal majority of their citizens, who have over the past 30 years, been grinding their teeth in silent fury at the insult and discrimination which is being directed towards their dead ancestors and used to justify targeted reverse discrimination upon their current descendants is a disgrace. Western peoples are being penalized for historical wrongs perceived in historical revisionism. This injustice is far worse than the perceived slights of social communists. Penalizing founding peoples for past Government abuses, for which even their ancestors had no say. Once again communistic ideas are tyrannizing the world. The African nations of Zimbabwe and South Africa that where once wealthy nations are now sinking into despair and extreme poverty due to social communistic ideas that are much the same as those in Western Europe being practiced at this time. Once again, a revised form of communism is a tyranny upon humanity and the destroyer of prosperity.

WESTERN MEDIA | FAKE NEWS

The education system in western societies has become "Social Communist" and originates with the intellects being complicit with the psychopathic nation state. This is making a false pretence of benevolence and innocence in their social dealings. They are in fact covering up a litany of misleading and false pretence with bandages of lies and deception. When in fact intellectual news media engineer, false and misleading narratives is what media are the architects of, thus the source, and creators of so much of western societies dysfunctions and social problems, mainly because they are operating with a hidden agenda of post-modern social engineering that is manipulative of human emotion and short comings for their own vested interest achieved by deceptive convolution.

THE INTERNET FREEDOM OF THE PRESS

The internet is now creating a change in the social conscience by providing different narratives that are changing the perspectives of average citizens, who are beginning to wake up and uncover these manipulations. The net result is the population is no longer being spoon fed the establishment's narratives, but rather alternative perspectives with argument they never heard, that was previously censored off the regular media. The world of thought has been revolutionized and now facing a challenge of authentic free thought like so many western freedoms merit is now repressed by mediocrity. The subverted media owned by the oligarchy that barks the official, manipulated, and edited story has become a dinosaur hit by the internet meteorite. Like any loser they now criticize new media and the internet in vain trying character assassination to maintain control over the people by attempting to control the narrative as they have in the past, only digging themselves deeper into a discredited sea of misinformation that society now sees through like a glass house, and has reached the tipping point or critical mass of no return. Gone are the days of imbedding reporters and intelligence service misinformation manipulation of the population, or at least it is being contested as never before. The narrative of circumstance manipulated to create false narratives by the control exercised by radio and television is over. The window into social engineering in all its forms has its drapes opened and is hopefully coming to an end due to true freedom of individuals to present all manner of narrative on all issues through free speech has arrived. The chain reaction has been the cancellation and turning off of conventional media causing the establishment to lose control of what has become a spilled can of information worms that is so disbursed as to create a new dynamic of information wars. Conventional media is quickly losing this war because at its core the old media has lost its credibility thus its ability to create narratives. Like the old media of the former Soviet Union, western state propaganda for the oligarchy's agenda, more often than not was in collusion manufacturing a narrative. To the population, the lack of free media has become apparent, the indoctrinated are becoming un-indoctrinated. These shrills of the establishment are now intellectually bankrupt of ways to deal with this revolutionary occurrence which they failed to anticipate. The brainwashing single narrative in the media is being challenged, as never before in mass media. From camera phones to the internet, the truth has conducted a prison escape.

The establishments' manipulations and secrets are being exposed, and history in the minds of the people is being rewritten. The knowledge that used to be the dominion of the intelligentsia is now no longer reclusive or secret but is becoming known by the general population. The elites arrogance is their Achilles tendon, they are so accustomed to having their way, they think it is accepted by the general population rather than manipulated as a mass indoctrination program spanning generations of brainwashed slaves who are now waking up to realize they were manipulated all along for decades to be indentured by the elite and their financial structures. The elites have been parasitically feeding upon the people's productivity for generations. I find that like the Court of France under king Louise the XVI, which could not comprehend why their heads were going to the guillotine, the current establishment is similarly socially isolated and disconnected from reality on the streets.

SOCIAL MARXISM | GOVERNMENT NEEDS TO STOP ENGINEERING AND FUNDING

PROTEST MOVEMENTS

Social economic conspiracy is the hidden bastard child of the west, born in corruption, and Governmental authority obfuscation. This is a social earthquake, that inevitably is leading to a seriously dangerous disconnect and collision between the people and the elite establishment. A circumstance of class warfare between working class and the left of center political parties. The revolution has become palpable and is approaching the tipping point of turbulent anger and generating a very unpredictable, boiling, angry mood, upon the somber and depressed populace. This is more than resentment for the collapse of Detroit and the rust belt, it's a convergence of anger against the establishment for the destruction of a comfortable lifestyle that enabled families to thrive, but no longer exists due to corporate industrial pillaging of industry. Converging with a technical revolution taking place.

The leaders of the left have departed their base, by also representing the elites that hijacked the agenda, and journeyed so far away as to no longer represent their political base. They no longer represent their traditional foundation; -the working class and unions. Instead they now represent the elites and minorities who are a new bourgeoisie. The working-class base is drifting to the libertarian spectrum. The politically correct social Marxist agenda is drifting into irrelevance, being seen for what it is as a power game of tyranny upon free speech. In fact, the traditional left is drifting so far out of sync with reality that repulsion of their fraudulent populism I predict, that within a generation, the left is heading towards extinction and total discredit. The fact is the left has implemented a tyrannical communist agenda, complete with a repressive state that believes it has the right to control society's social discourse and relationships. Like in the past, socialism always fails in their reform, because it is parasitic upon the productive. Social Marxism the final vestiges of communism, needs to be put to bed once and for all. The repressive left, with all of the baggage of their politically derived reverse discrimination, fascism and communism, including state sponsored corrected speech and fear-based governance of the population, has become a repressive political conversation where in dictionary words used can put a citizen in jail. Free speech repression has been following the usual communistic pattern of legitimized, state sponsored, top down social engineering, followed by social collapse. The enlightened lefty has become the repressive left and lost any sense of its founding principles. They no longer wish to debate with descent, now they want to imprison it. The left now resembles the far right far more than being a free speech advocate. Once again, a "left wing gulag society" is their vision for how to deal with dissent. Society has been moving towards a more libertarian model in the past thirty years. In this transformation they are taking over the lefts decades old human rights advocating. In fact, the left and the working class as a result are now divorced, due to this argument. Left wing political activism has become minority privilege over the majority or merit; the repressor of all biological human rights; repressor of family values and rights, globalist destroyer of the nation state and repressor of individual liberty and speech; Tyrannical actions speak louder than words.

Western Governmental social engineering, which is in large part a left-wing agenda, by legislating politically correct, backwards looking ethics and morality by force of Government regulation, has created deep resentments due to their unfair and brutal repression. A resentment born out of economic depression of the type that that lead to the Nineteen Thirties era German racism and blatant discrimination has taken place. The people's push back against the lefts Government by minorities has created a popular revolution. It is the new populists that will now control the agenda and is the death of the left that is coming. Like the old expression; "The road to hell is paved with good intentions". This is not the old right that is taking control but rather a new revolutionary libertarian populist movement wanting to dislodge the establishment in all its forms, both right and left in a surprise twist of outcomes. Because its foundation is the new Libertarian historical narrative the internet has created. What has happened is that elites, who I might add are normally disconnected from the population, have strayed so far into left field, that they no longer represent anyone other than fake liberalism. In fact, they have become left wing fascist in the popular conscience. The left has become so radicalized with the prioritization of minority rights and radical anti-male sentiment that expresses itself as blatant anti-male bigotry. This extends from social policy to judicial tyranny of the average man in a new form of social engineering where the nation state has become the defender of feminism and repressor of the masculine gender. The left had its start from union support, and concern over the average citizen, but those days are long gone. Now they only represent minorities, which they are also doing a poor job at, because they are creating resentment against minorities to the point that there is real threat that human rights may be redefined away from minority rights by constitutional amendment to a new form of inclusive human rights encompassing:

1. Family rights,
2. Home ownership/property rights.
3. Monetary banking reformation.
4. Restrictions upon corporate shares requiring estate co-ownership with employees.

5. Removing legislative and judicial interference by reforming the political process with a new independent law enforcement arm of Government.
6. A full constitutional revision by a complete separation of the archaic and corrupt legislature and judiciary process.
7. Children's rights to have their family relationships protected from state interference.
8. Respect for individual rights over group identity politics.
9. The rights for merit and diversity to succeed equality.

SOCIAL DYSFUNCTIONS

Separation of legislature and politics from all matters of law enforcement is necessary. People have become aware that the judicial system itself is only a system to repress them and has been used as a system of repression that in the past also included the repression of women and currently family sovereign rights, far more than any individual person could ever invoke. The judiciary has become the source of so much corruption of intents and processes. Judicial administration and law enforcement must be fully separated from the legislature to eliminate its complicity with political legislature corruption. Western marriages have now become intentionally polygamist, and every woman now has an economic guarantor for prosperity in the new surrogate husband of all women that is; the nation state vs the nation's foundation of the family; -the family has been betrayed and is under siege. Government social welfare for women has now made the state the servant of women's economic electoral demands. Further, they supplement Government welfare in all western nations that now tyrannically extorts men's wages to supplement the state's welfare policies generated due to the "women's vote". The financial benefits of marriage have become guaranteed by a family interloper being the Government acting as some sort of perverted adulterous boyfriend of women, in order to enrich the elites in the judicial establishment, that has invoked it's interference for their own profit at the expense of the institution of family via a Napoleonic divide and conquer strategy against the family and the good of society, by incentivising marital breakup for their own profit and removing the consequences of women's bad decisions. Their actions and intentional incitement have committed irreversible harm to countless relationships as to be irreparable, not to mention the damage the judiciary has done to the family that is an essential building block of society. Their greed has been permitted to take precedence over society and family's best interests. The archaic judiciary in religious terms in light of these activities can only be described as pure unmitigated social agents of evil incarnate.

No longer does Government extradite themselves from the private affairs or the personal lives of citizens, but rather the state now by self-appointment committing psychological adultery with women by directly interfering into families in every way to the point that it has become tyrannical, strictly gender based and discriminatory against men. The state has also become the new religious pontiff of society as well as the husband and head of every family in a system akin to animal husbandry by the nation state. Men and women's personal lives are now controlled by the nation state like livestock. The feminist agenda has had Government interfere in people's personal affairs so deeply as to put their honour, personal dignity, personal affairs, conversations, children's rights, personal property equity, sexuality and all the most personal aspects of one's life put on trial in a secretive human rights violation called "Family Courts". Family Courts put families on trial for their personal values and ethics, their most private affairs involving little material evidence like the Spanish inquisition, and no illegal actions are ever cited. Matters that deface the sanctity of marriage and breach the private privileged confidences of marital life are often put on trial by these interlopers. The western nation state no longer respects tradition or custom of common law and has been replaced with a communistic social engineering project called multiculturalism, designed to intentionally divide society up into small isolated groups. The Judicial establishment sees opportunity to enrich themselves in even to most private aspects of marriage for their own perverted pornography and titillation by the practitioners of the judicial process, they fail to see their own perversity and abuse of process. The states unlimited jurisdiction beyond civil society legislation has become a wide spread human rights violation used to instigate legislated social engineering. This system at its core is based upon this new corrupt vote getting mechanism, which has led to the end of human rights and democracy itself as a system that was too easily subverted to become the servant of repression. By entering the homes of the nation without citizen's commission of any crimes or other valid justification. The result of Government enforcing these social engineering programs is that western society is increasingly becoming a tyrannical police state in order to enforce the Government's new status as man / father / parent/ financial sponsor of every house in the nation and made him a eunuch.

The price of entrenched minority rights has been the tyrannical elimination and subordination of the majority's human rights, particularly for men. This is creating a coalition of those pushed aside and also anyone else with traditional family values, be they religion based or not. The state now treats minorities as the majority and has put them through affirmative action into positions of power where now minority biases are being imposed upon the majority perverting social reality, leading to perverse initiation of programs that the majority have become infuriated with. It was not enough for minorities and feminist to be given equality in protection in Government and social opportunity. It has now become Government policy that minorities like a new administration are the most favoured and preferred by the Government amongst the people. Discrimination like affirmative action in treating new generations to "need not apply" because your disqualified, being more blatantly bigoted than any previous social condition. Teaching children about a type of sexuality that promotes minority homosexuality and transgender sex changes, and hostility towards heterosexual male elders who as parents are also socially demoted as parents as disposable fodder for the new social engineering agenda of the state. The Government now has entered our private sexual lives and seeks to engineer our children's sexuality. This is the abdication of the biological jurisdiction of parents, and a very grave imposition by the Government into the most private domain and right to privacy of the children as well. But as I have demonstrated, the Government now has no boundaries regarding your privacy or your children's privacy and has even gone beyond the normal boundaries of parenthood. The agenda of homosexuality and all manner of deviation has become the Governments agenda to promote with even innocent elementary school children. This is what happens when minorities take over Government.

Callously using all of the violence that the state can muster for repression, fathers and all men under state sanction have been villainized by minority interest groups funded by the Government who make pretence of independence. These are not popular movements, these are state financed family interest repression organizations. They are Government funded to create harm and division in the family. A convenient group of minorities that Government can use as a pretence of popular support for their social engineering program. Is it any wonder that the west can no longer reach levels of reproduction that even come close to replacement levels? Government policy like a toxic soup has poisoned the majority to the point that they no longer desire to reproduce offspring. If there ever was evidence of a sick society, non-reproduction is a demonstration of a repressed disturbed society. Nothing expresses a positive outlook more than reproduction. Non-reproduction is clear evidence and symptomatic of social/cultural illness.

While historically women's unequal treatment was a social evolution without intended malice that was in fact originating with Government regulation and action. Political correctness has been a anti male form of fascist attack without any balance over the past 30 years. Men who have been exposed to the systems discrimination now see the Government as having launched an all-out war against 50% of the population that is male, from childhood to death. This combined with the working classes economic woes has been a discontent that has been highly flammable for many years. All that has been missing is a match being thrown, and the resulting fire would result in an explosion. An explosion of flames just starting to take shape created by corrupt politicians buying votes with social policy favouring minorities, as a political vote getting scheme. The impregnation of a women even with no oath of marriage, even a prostitute's pregnancy can result in a man becoming liable to financially support the woman for decades, because a man's right to freely accept or enter into a relationship contract does not any longer exist in the new fascist state designed to extricate money from men. Instead of relationships being entered into freely, the state has imposed the concept of "common law marriage" as a pseudo marriage to ensure their business of judicial interference would be unhindered by this popular trend, after they poisoned the well of marriage. The previously non-existent "common law marriage" was implemented by the judicial industry to circumvent couples opting out of marriage unions. Caused due to tyrannical state interference in their private lives, couples began having roommate situations that lawyers turned into common law marriages. True common law of the people (which this concept is not) has for millennium been the social policy of "no marriage, no right to claim support". The judiciary has in point of fact, created a fraudulent common law principal called; "common law marriage", which has no common law bases in fact. The tyranny of the judiciary is so callous as to pursue new forms of forced contract of marriage, even where no contract exists, so that this avoidance of the judicial systems profiteering does not cost the judicial industry a loss of what they perceive as their right to bilk the public by hooking them legally. They claim family wealth against the parties will. This new idea is a judicially created contract where there was no free will marriage contract between the parties. Common law marriage is a fake judicial industry created concept to pad their wallets. The new family imposed by the unelected judicial industry is to create a dysfunctional society where in a man is treated as a concubine and given into marriage against his better interest by the nation state by virtue of having shared his home with a woman. Men now worry that they may become the free life time meal ticket of a whore. The legal tradition of free will has been circumvented in favour of cash for life to women for male entrapment by pregnancy, which is legally the exclusive determination of the woman. This perversity of Government power out of its traditional role has made western nations no longer be places of freedom and human rights. Rights, which were only intended to keep the state out of the private affairs of citizens, and grant fair treatment of minorities, have transformed into a new circumstance where the nation state in western nations has no boundaries, and minorities become the alpha. In that human rights are experiencing a subversion against the family order. The defence of minorities who hide behind this new state, such as homosexuals have taken control of the state and now determine social policies for the majority in some jurisdictions.

Western nations have not only become oligarchies of the wealthy but also minoarchies (governed by minorities). Clearly minority equal rights legislation is a scam upon society, the fact is there is more diversity than similarity within each individual than within every race, religion, orientation or other difference. Also, whether a person is homosexual or not, is really a person's private business, which has no place in public discourse any more than heterosexuality has a place in public discourse. Group affiliations are being utilized to advance group agendas. This social tendency is now more political and social grandstanding than equality or human rights based upon discrimination. Social decorum, as in not respecting your personal right to privacy is being used, not to achieve the dignity of being treated with respect but are trying to achieve some sort of social dominance over the majority. This is a very dangerous posture for a minority to take, because it has the potential to create a backlash from the majority who could see their social position under threat. Human rights legislation was intended to assure equality of treatment, when it becomes perverted to seek dominance over the majority, well, being in charge puts a big bullseye upon the practitioner of dominance, when you're a fractional minority group, you don't have the backup to address a full on social assault and win, thus the repercussions of revolt can be grim indeed. Minority rights are generally accepted because they are perceived to not threaten the majority, thus they are accepted. When they try to become dominant in society, they walk over a boundary of safety into social conflict.

I foresee that there will be a serious backlash coming due to all of these developments and the outcome will be severely dangerous for minorities and minority rights. These groups have so disadvantaged the majority so as to disenfranchise them by blatant reverse discrimination, and this is a very dangerous development. Regardless of the rights legislation grants minorities, these minorities in their drunken abuse of the majority in a power grab, are in for dark times ahead. Those rights minorities now enjoy have always been at the whim of what up until now has been a silent majority. The same holds true for the minority 1% holding most of the wealth while the middle class has been destroyed for their financial advantage. For these reasons a serious social revolution is now brewing, and it is my belief that we have now only seen the tip of the iceberg with BREXIT and the election of Donald Trump in 2016. Under the current political climate even Adolph Hitler himself would stand a chance to be elected in certain western nations.

Western societies concentration of wealth into fewer and fewer hands at the expense of the middle class is the social divide and class warfare predicted by Hegelian communist theory of the 19th century. However, communistic ideas and their immature application in pre-industrial nations such as the now defunct Soviet Union and eastern bloc has largely discredited most of that ideology, but not all of it. One merely has to look at the rule of the Chinese Communist party as a possible future of Government scenario to see what the future may bring to misbehaving capitalists, while a free market exists alongside, if this continues. The vested interest of the wealthy in favouring globalism might not be in their interest, for a global capitalist system that became politicised to be like the Chinese politburo ruling class would leave nowhere to hide and could by granting their wish engineer their own demise as generational wealth systems. In this corrupt world the more mono-operational world Government becomes, the less likely the business class will control the political class.

Globalist ideology sets up monolithic Government and business for a future conflict. Given that the state always has armies and weapons, I would not bet on a globalist business community controlling a global political mechanism for too long. Nationalism is now a backlash against globalism, because the fact is people like tribal (national) identities, just as they like family sovereignty as the natural order of humanity since the beginning of time. While globalism is a worthy future goal in a few millenniums as an objective, it is currently unworkable given the planets level of human corruption from vested interest. It will most likely take the shape of global federalism and could not be a truly functional unitary state to function, unless as a tyrannical dictatorship. The larger the Government structure, the greater tendency towards dictatorship and tyranny. Smaller government structures enable greater freedom because of local affiliations and the fact everyone becomes a known entity. Large government becomes paranoid and thus tyrannical, out of fear of the unknown. Thus, by reducing the size of government we enable more honest participatory Government that enables and encourages citizen cooperation and a better sense of teamwork.

Like the industrial revolution before it, the technological revolution we are now in the middle of is bringing about radical and comprehensive change. Let us not forget that the industrial revolution caused the popularization of ideas such as communism, with its revolutions. During the Napoleonic wars in Europe mass domestic Luddite revolt was so intense that the British had to utilize in "under reported domestic unrest", more soldiers to put down domestic unrest and revolt, than they used to vanquish Napoleon Bonaparte in France. The Western nation has become so repressive that even candid talk is feared in these police states of speech repression by Government.

The modern Government unlike Egyptian pharaohs of the past have only lacked the demand that we kneel down and worship the state apparatus as a God.

Let me be upfront and candid about this provocative, which is more than I can say for the western world's current crop of politicians. A political class I might add who are currently acting like their living in the 15th century rather than the 21st. My message to my compatriots as peoples of the west is a tale written from the heart out of love (tough love). Sorry, but the truth is going to hurt your perceptions. It will hurt your pride; it will hurt your sense of self; - it will hurt your ego. Welcome to the world of pain and disappointment I too have lived in for over two decades now, as a society, we are supposed to be the world enlightened ones. However, we have screwed up. We, the peoples of critical thought, we the bosom of opportunity and liberty. We have endured so much and been villainized for it. By now, those of us who can exercise critical thinking are looking at current world affairs and wondering; what the hell is going on here? - This is a mess! Is this what the future holds?

THE POLITICALLY CORRECT, SOCIAL COMMUNIST STATE OF AFFAIRS, HAS COST US:

1. Our freedom of speech which is being repressed.
2. Our Governments have become totalitarian surveillance states of our correspondence, mail, and literature.
3. Our Governments have been subverted and spy on our speech like cold war era East Germany, so much so, we no longer recognize them.
4. Governments have prostituted themselves to become servants of anti-democratic forces and vested interest in their actions. They have become tainted and polluted by vested interest, rather than being neutral arbitrators of social peace and justice.
5. The world is in continuous war, turmoil, and greater danger from terrorism everywhere, division is everywhere.
6. Everywhere we go in Government facilities and airports, we must remove all metal objects and our shoes, and our traditional personal security has disappeared. Not due to our actions are our rights repressed, but due to foreigners and foreign wars for which no citizen desires or comprehends why we are there. Where and how has domestic peace gone?

7. The world's political diseases have now infected our entire social body like leprosy our national body is falling apart from a foreign invasion. Like cancer it is our own cells (politicians) killing our culture.

Western Governments are an ill prepared mess to deal with this state of affairs. In fact, they have contributed so much to it that has made things worse. My conclusion after study and experience is simple.

> *Let's stop looking at symptoms of this malaise;*
> *-Physician heal thyself!*

Yes, we need to look hard to cure our own problems in the west before we can go forward any further. We need to clean up our own act before we can go any further, we need therapy. The problem is internal and this my friends is an intervention! Like any therapy we need to first start with self-analysis and look at where we have been and where we are.

We need to create a vision of the future and what this social project wants to be; in open inclusive dialogue. Determine how we will go forward; for our own health and the future health of the world. Because this dysfunction is not a good or healthy state of affairs right now, and we western peoples are the world leaders. We need to clean up our act in order to exercise our leadership role in this world; because there is no one else who has the ability to step into our shoes. Because the rest of the world is an imitation of us; and our often-bad example needs reform. We must first look inside ourselves and clean up our own act first. Even, if this means we must withdraw from world involvement for a bit.

WHY NATIONS MAKE SENSE NOW AND FOREVER

1. Nations are a necessity, if only for one reason in that; Nation states constitute local, answerable Government that can, verifiably be held to account by the citizenry.

2. National leaders thus live with constituents, making the nation state the harbour of the only truly responsible form of democratic Government.

3. When the local aspect of Government disappears, tyranny is the product Government produces, as it becomes disrespectful to local interest and otherwise disengages, from the people as individuals.

4. Government in order to be humanitarian and not psychopathic or elitist, must have a two-way empathetic relationship with the people.

5. While the nation state has the authority to use force, the only way to keep the nation states in a system free of tyranny, is by a system of local checks and balances. Utilizing local administration thus preventing tyranny and its natural end product of revolutions.

6. All revolutions are the product of disengaged and aloof Governments not representing local interests.

7. A responsible national Government does not engage in foreign wars other than in self-defence. When

attacked and only in response to those who institute a violent attack utilizing military forces.

This is in keeping with the historical reality of all humanity. The anti-democratic forces of vested interest have disdain for the nation state and democracy because they desire to circumvent the influence of the people. Intending to enable the abuse of the citizenry for profit, by dilution of democratic processes through narcissistic and despotic covert autocracy. All of humanity in their private moments gripe and complain about their circumstance, but it is deserved by most, in payment for their complacency and collaboration with their tormentors out of fear.

RESTORING MERITOCRACY | ENDING CORRUPTION

Without foundations in merit, all that is left is corruption. For a society to be based upon "Justice" it can only be a meritocracy, since anything less is a circumstance of corruption. There is also within this the principal of rightful inheritance. We are by our very nature devoted to our families and whether it is in our families or businesses we have what is called inheritance and by its very nature few deny the right of the progeny of a person to inherit the property of their family as a right of succession. Yet western countries do not extend this right to matters of state. Namely matters of Government employment and preference due to family historical contribution and cultural continuity based upon being the creators of the current social order. While as a reflex this might sound to be not based upon merit, it is in fact merit based upon inheritance of the established order. This also creates social continuity, society must evolve naturally, forced social revolution spoon fed from the top down like political correctness is tyranny and also is both pejorative and condescending towards the people

The modern western nation state all too often permits foreigners to ascend to positions of Government and authority when these individuals do not fully comprehend the current culture and thus create social discord. Individuals who arrive from foreign cultures that instead of creating social cohesion create social division by their privilege of presence and demonstrate that the state is a disloyal charlatan whose validity for existence is questionable because they betray their own founding peoples. Western national Governments have consorted with foreigners in a vote buying strategy that is a betrayal the founding peoples and their culture. Founding people's culture must be protected as an inherited right. What is a nation's purpose without respecting its founding peoples? It is a truly pathetic thing which occurs when those who showed the ultimate loyalty in risking their lives in military conflict or are members of clans that have contributed to the nation for generations are unemployed and unable to obtain even menial employment, through no fault of their own are then discarded and betrayed by their own Government, living on the city's streets homeless, while foreigners are given preference for employment simply because business can exploit them for lower wages, severe work conditions, and undermine the wages and working conditions that the founding peoples who for generations paid their dues and fought so hard to achieve, in pitched street battles to stop their being exploited. This not only undermines the progress of the more senior inhabitants of industrialized nations, but also undermines the better society the foreigners sought by their immigration. In western countries it has come to be that our ideas of minority rights being protected to ensure they are treated the same as the majority has become discrimination itself of a far viler type; against the domestic population.

A system of minority rights has taken precedence over the majority culture and way of life to become a system of majority repression. This has cost western societies free speech and created a system of repression. In order for this to be accomplished, politically correct speech repression, which is just another way of saying, the majority cannot speak against their own dislocation by foreigners having precedence over the domestic population! Least you end up in court, and possibly jail, by your own Government, for speaking the truth; - Governments that now are clearly committing treasonous acts.

Ethnically subverted politicians clearly do not represent the people, but rather seek to buy votes from foreigners, while forsaking the local founding peoples. The very foundation of the nation state is a common historic identity, creating common values. This fact demonstrates that multiculturalism is an anti-national act of treason by simple logic. Multiculturalism can only be a globalist agenda because it leads to repression of the nation state. Nations that espouse multi culturalism have no legitimacy of existence, as they have no foundation in histoical ethnicity. Multiculturalism is the un-parented bastard child of nations. Clearly a communistic idea that undermines the glue of society. It is the acceptance of social divisions as normalized status and magnifies them. A citizen cannot have two masters any more than a marriage can endure ongoing infidelity by a spouse, as it is division and creates suspicion of others motives of being a fifth column that clearly does not coalesce with the domestic peoples. Multiculturalism as a policy, versus the successful melting pot policy of immigration; is a recipe for future civil war in any nation that implements it. Any time a citizen has mixed national or other foreign loyalty, the threat of terrorism is the result, thus we can see as proof the current situation, and how the elite ruling class has been able to justify the repression and abuse of domestic citizens and their fundamental human rights to our home land, because of problems from disloyalty. Multiculturalism, and its ridiculous naivety of human nature has caused a lot of problems. Yet the elites rely these acts of internal treason upon domestic ethnic populations and denied their right to defend the nation and protect themselves from the danger's politicians have created with these fantasies, which in no way demonstrate any "common sense" in their implementation. The nation state has a serious internal enemy of the people; -the globalist agenda.

Yet in those countries the foreigners come from, the same situation would be rebutted in violent revolution against the Government. Foreign immigrants know this, they often laugh at the locals behind their naïve backs or look in dismay at the discrimination against domestic citizens. The repression of local domestic citizens, who are the backbone of the nation, suffer under treason towards their upward mobility by elites, in favour of foreigners displacing the founding peoples of the nation, who see their status being diminished, their human rights being abused, their inheritance being squandered by elites, in favour of foreigners who advance often to positions of authority or Government employment, for which they should have no right to ascend to, as those positions are the birth right of domestic inheritance. Subverted by political correctness implemented by elites, in policies no citizen has ever been given a direct say concerning, because elites know the local citizenry would never agree to their own demise. Twisting of constitutional human rights legislation by courts of the elites, has created a perversity that can only be called one of the greatest treasons of history, engineered by western elites, to intentionally displace their own peoples from their rightful inheritance. Pushing the domestic population into poverty, as they undermine the middle classes existence; this is clearly some sort of covert plan or obtuse moronic level of intelligence at work. Either way, it demonstrates the elite must be removed from their entrusted positions of authority as unqualified traitors of the people.

At no time in history has such an intolerable condition been accepted by any other peoples in what is essentially the repression of the majority by the odious granting unearned privilege by any measure. Privilege to what the Government calls citizens; - naturalized as they say. That fails to grant earned privilege to the founding and indigenous people of the nation. In point of fact it is perverted domestic colonialism of the local population, for the benefit of foreigners. This is not an issue of minority rights, when it is repressive and un-acknowledging of the domestic populations often centuries of contribution, that is degrading and insulting the nation's founding people, which is given away to foreigners by Governments to buy votes for the maintenance of their privilege positions of power. Needless to say the wealthy classes are so isolated in their perspectives on society, so remote for so many generations, that they are completely ignorant and uncaring of the historical populations. They are in fact contemptuous in their actions, not to mention offensive. This is not meritocracy in action. National ethnic affinity and loyalty in governance must always take precedence. In the absence of such ethnic justification the nation state has no justification for its existence and any nation espousing these ideas in honest belief should assign its nation status to a worthier national jurisdiction. If the nation will not give preference for its own founding people first in all matters of Government, then it is not a nation and its very existence is illegitimate.

THE FOUNDATIONAL PRINCIPALS OF THE NATION STATE | THE NATIONAL FAMILY

A nation state is a common connection of human beings that consists of what is called a "culture" that is variation from other nations by connections as follows.

1. Common heritage.
2. Common food.
3. Historical connection amongst the resident people.
4. A familial feeling created by being from a common cloth.
5. Empathy thus created, giving favouritism and privilege to those who share these characteristics.
6. Being governed by those who share these characteristics noted above.
7. Domestic birth, or at least partial domestic heritage in blood, in a melting pot society that creates this national identity and affinity connections as noted in Items 1 to 7.

None of this is racially based, it is a "familial melting pot nation state". There is nothing wrong with new citizens being expected to pay admission dues for entry or protecting the integrity of the nation state and its people. Like all social common law principals of contract, those of foreign birth have the option to reject these parameters by not emigrating from a foreign land. Clearly Governments in western nations have committed grave acts of treason against the people, committed by the ruling classes. An oath of allegiance and acceptance of the national culture without reservations must be required of all foreigners seeking citizenship. The desire to remain culturally separate is justification for expulsion from citizenship.

WAGES & WORK CONDITIONS

Despite there being profuse public denial by the establishment, the reality is most employer and employee relationships are very often despotic dictatorships, which the public are aware of, but live in denial of wage slavery. This circumstance is maintained by a constant in-flux of competition to keep the labour force off balance as supplied by the Government setting minimal limits on immigration. This wage and working conditions repression is achieved in a covert fashion by a constant influx of competition - foreign workers, called immigration excluding family unification immigration which is immigration by invitation. The abuse and exploitation of foreign workers who have no knowledge of the battles lost by the workers in the service and industrial sector, are thus used as patsies by the Government in servitude to their masters in the business community to repress wage and benefit increases.

THE MIDDLE CLASS DECLINES

Youth unemployment across the western world is at record levels at present. Few companies want to employ western workers children (the owners of the nation state) because they have knowledge of the human rights their ancestors paid for with their blood on the picket line and will demand fair treatment and wages. Thus, business provides Government with false information, stating that local youth and citizens born in the nation, do not want to do certain jobs. The real fact is that these companies do not want to pay a living wage to their employees, if you compare the price of rents and the cost to raise a family, minimal wages are exploitation, compared to the wealth generated to the business owners. This is ethically comparable to a form of wage repression. In a nut shell, the very essence of the reason why real wages for the working class are below the poverty line level for 20 years with no wage increase while prices have increased by several hundred percent over the same time. These companies do not pay wages high enough that the workers can live a middle-class lifestyle. Western nations are currently experiencing a disappearing and beleaguered middle class. For more than the past two decades, western citizens have been betrayed by their own political leaders for corrupt motives of the politicians personally seeking to profit in the name of globalism.

POLITICIANS

Locally elected leaders / politicians have misled the people towards a preference for globalism and foreign trade, in the representation of the vested interest of narcissistic business interests over local interest. Corporate interests have hijacked local Governmental administration for globalism. Corporate vested commercial interest has become paramount over the people's best interest. For every activity of social significance there comes a reaction or pushback from the others affected by this circumstance. Thus, social change is never complete until the impact of change has run a full cycle and the rest of society has had sufficient time to digest the results and implications, globalism has been such a snake oil tonic sold to the public and delivered by politicians.

GLOBALISM

The Marxist based corporate agenda that has infected the west has caused a great deal of harm to the peoples of all nation states of the world by Globalism and with corrupt malfeasance of the rights of the nation state. Self-interested politicians have betrayed the best interest of the people to the point of destroying their standard of living. The west has been sold a false bill of goods through political fraud that has borne fruit which is self-evident to the working class of all nations. The digestion of this circumstance has caused considerable indigestion upon the working class & world peace, so much so that the working class now believes they have been fed food poison by the chefs of the establishment in the ultimate historical act of treason against the people of the nation state.

INVESTMENT

The intention of foreign investment is the exploitation of low wages and sending manufactured goods to high wage economies to maximize profits, all while undermining the quality of life of western nations and betraying the people in the west:

1. When foreign involvement trumps local and national interest, that elects the Government officials as is the

present case. The obvious conclusion is that, politicians are now more financially beholden to foreign and corporate interests than the nation's people.

2. Foreign companies and Governments are funding domestic political parties for favourable treatment, and political parties sell the nation like some sort of bankruptcy liquidation for their personal political gain.

3. Corporations circulate dis-information via their media, to indoctrinate the citizens with false and misleading information. This has enabled the corporate class to amass levels of wealth from wide scale corruption, never here to fore generated in the history of the world, on the backs of the workers in the corporate welfare scheme called globalization.

4. For decades now the working class have been watching their children struggle to obtain jobs now occupied by immigrants, as their own wages when they do luck into a job remain stagnant due to open borders and globalization.

5. Large domestic corporations do not generally pay taxes and create only in the neighbourhood of twenty percent of all jobs nationally. Thus, account for very minimal employment, relative to that which their companies often receive in Government handouts, in the form of loans and incentives to big corporations.

In the neighbourhood of eighty percent of jobs are on fact created by small and medium size business, who receive very little assistance from Government.

6. The real engine of the economy is small, local business which by far pays more taxes and creates more employment than the big shinny large corporate lobby groups, yet this work horse is given the least attention from any level of Government assistance.

PROPER PROJECT PLANNING AND ANALYSIS

One thing which is desperately needed in Government is the development of proper project planning and professional project management based upon research and in-depth evaluation, technology and alternative perspectives. Looking at the issues at hand via scientifically based evaluations regarding new legislation and revising existing legislation, highlighting peer reviewed university research and literature. Proper business case studies need to be reviewed for all legislative initiatives.

1. Designed to evaluate the intention of legislation, the options for creative and pragmatic solutions.

2. The long-term potential social implications. Responsible Government must consider all factors to ensure legislators take into account, the impact of legislation upon society at large.

3. Everything Government legislates does has a long-term impact upon society, that can be either positive or negative in its effects, but almost never does Government politicians give these concerns much thought, since a great deal of Government legislation is biased by nature and seat of the pants initiatives.

4. Many of the issues of legislation cited in the prior and proceeding pages illustrates the detrimental long-term effects; partisan political decision making is having upon society and has made upon society, might in the future and the impact upon society. A dictatorship legislates, a democracy must evaluate.

5. All these research papers must also be available to all legislators for each proposed law and upon request for review by citizens and journalists. Law is much too serious a matter for it to be made strictly, on a hope and a prayer.

6. In Project Management and the private sector, we call these "Business Case Studies". Before legislation is adopted; a study by academics and other professionals of the impact of all legislation should be conducted as research papers for legislators to review.

7. The creation of a legislation Project Management Department would be the agency that would

administer this process and must ensure that all reports are factual via a proper peer review process.

8. The Project Management department would require that it have a level of independence and protection from outside influence protection in law.

9. It is only with the proper information and considering different perspectives that legislators can make informed decisions prior to approving legislation in full disclosure. As it stands litigation gets better consideration than legislation. This must be changed.

Legislature debates should neither be dictated or partisan, they should be to determine the implications and discuss the potential hazards of each legislation. To refine legislation, to be of the greatest service and benefit to the nation, and its people. Business case studies could for example evaluate public healthcare in different countries and create a comparative listing of services, segregated costs, and then public opinions of favour, or disfavour of each element of variables. Recommend types of, "Non-Profit Health Care Trust Corporations" that could be created and cite the merits of different cost structures and premium rates based upon different models. Thus, Government is not only a legislator, but also implementer of options for citizen's health care as plans with different options and coverage. Remember these programs would be voluntary options. Government would create options; - not prescribe them.

The Project Management Department would conduct analysis and recommend social policies for their nation based upon this type of real business case and social research, not seat of the pants social manipulation, or an agenda as they do now. The common standard is called; "business case analysis". Governments currently initiate adhoc social projects with no analysis, and no consent from the people to implement what can only be seen as an attack upon the people's best interest. It seems that all too often, critical and important legislation within Governments is created with a hope and a prayer, on a wing it ideology, without sociological or scientific research from a neutral perspective or at least perspectives free of conflicting interests in balance.

Politicians tend to rely upon data created and supplied by biased sources and industries, subverted individuals with financial and other vested interest towards a particular outcome, information pre-prepared and suited to a particular group with a vested interest and worse of all, often opposed to the public interest, and general good of society. Government can and must rely exclusively upon their own research without outside interference. Too often at present, this information is subverted by interest groups with a vested interest in particular interest or simply a narcissistic and psychopathic profit motive. Government that does not perform its own independent analysis from the data of independent research analysis is corrupt Government.

TYRANNY OF THE SOCIAL MARXISTS | LEGISLATION FOR POLITICALLY MOTIVATED EXPEDIENCY IS TYRANNY.

Too much seat of the pants social engineering for social Marxist purposes has been initiated. It is time we should end legislation based upon the partisan, the empirical and vested interest, but rather the use of evidence and vested interest of the greatest number of citizens, which are not detrimental to society. Governments have become tyrants upon the majority of citizens in favour of minorities in a very undemocratic trend, abusing the concept of minority rights protection with minority run Government in recent decades, which seems to have no appearance of abating. If you feel your Government does not listen or give a dam about your sensible perspectives your right; it costs money to influence Government.

Representative Democracy is only a facade as every western nation that has become completely corrupted. Worst part is that this is also public knowledge in most western nations, where a placated population simply disengages from the process despite having this knowledge of this corruption. It's not mentioned in our media, but when I was in Asia a few years ago I was reading a newspaper that spoke of low to no collateral, low interest loans the Chinese give their businesses: -I never heard about this in North America, that it is going on? The Chinese economic miracle is really a state funded miracle. The real source of Chinese development clearly was and is Chinese Government grants; -generous business subsidies, is more like the real story! Seems the

Chinese economic miracle has a different bases in the provision of business capital by their Government and state-owned banks - Something western nations did in the past but don't do at present.

Overall the western economy seems to operate from self-hatred of its success and resentment of employees and founding peoples. When we change our thinking, our economy will grow again. This is as much of an attitude problem on all fronts as any other issue. Government attitudes, company attitudes and employee's attitudes from cultures of disrespect. This must change as in most such instances is a cultural issue, and a shift in attitude that crept into North America culture because we started losing respect for ourselves, our history, our abilities and our faith in our fellow man. I cannot due to reasons of brevity supply all the documents I have, which are many, to validate my claims here in. But most of them are public records, like many such records, filed with the expectation they will never be dug out of the pile. I am confident you must be aware of corruption in our countries on your own, simply by keeping your ear to the ground. I have pointed out corruption that at its root we all know, which is; generation after generation electing politicians and Governments that have sweet election time words and non-deliverance after the election. The time has come to share this knowledge and do something about this corruption. You cannot realistically expect to achieve cleanliness, if you continue to use a dirty old rag to clean up.

At first there is no human truth, only different interpretations and perspectives.

Truth can only be seen upon review of the outcome of different expectations, and how these ideas create results.

Results are the truth, therefore necessary to determine the truth. You must analyse not the intentions, but, the results of a sequence of events.

The outcome is the truth; - not the theory. The truth lies in the manifestation and the pragmatic result of idea. Justice is outcome; - not claims, desires or expectations from actions. Everything else is delusion or misapprehension.

~ M. R. Blum ~

3rd Chapter
REFORMING THE INSIDIOUS SYSTEM

I have grave apprehensions and concerns regarding the future of western civilization and heritage, what it has become, and where it is heading; clearly, towards extinction. Specifically, I am concerned regarding:

NECESSARY REFORMS

1. The corruption demonstrated by the degradation of our Governments, Judicial system, and the contamination of western values by the education system indoctrinating Social-Marxist views into the minds of the youth.
2. The influence of vested interests many of foreign origin, and its corrupting effects upon the "common good" and the nation state, which is in a shamble.
3. The often-overlooked aspect of this situation is that libertarianism is experiencing a resurgence because of social fatigue with the current circumstance of wide spread corruption.

FUNDAMENTALS OF LIBERTARIANISM

Libertarianism demands, and is equally concerned with legislature reform, as judicial reform, to get Government out of citizen's private affairs, and off the people's backs, as it is about social structure of the human matrix via constitutional design and reform of nations.

Libertarianism is concerned with the basic economic structure of society to design it in such a way that the liberty of the individual becomes entrenched into the design of the political and economic system, both creating and minimizing the creation of legislation and mandating only minimal necessary and correct legislation reflecting our beliefs. Both livelihood and employment needs and opportunities for all must be designed to attain independence and security of the person and family being addressed by a fair and equitable system of governance, providing opportunity to have personal security and respect for the freedom and integrity of the individual person.

THE BROKEN SYSTEM

Equality in the treatment of all citizens of the libertarian nation before the judicial system, and in law is a libertarian fundamental principal. Currently in western societies, there is the additional odious problem of legislators not enforcing, or selectively enforcing laws, for purely political motives and posturing. Issues like illegal immigration into the United States and other western nations go unresolved in the legislature, because laws are cherry picked for enforcement. There should be no debate where a nation has established a law; the creation of law is the time for debate. In Europe and the United States, the migrant crises has been exasperated by legislators not enforcing their own laws.

ELECTED REPRESENTATIVES

Governments have become elected dictatorships under an organized crime type system of partisan party politics, the local elected party representative has become a useless muted political eunuch, they tow the party line, essentially being useless to constituents and making party leaders dictators.

FISCAL INTEGRITY

There is the entire 2008 financial crises and further non enforcement of the law, and even indebting the nation to bail out banks, that performed illegal, even criminal actions and yet none were prosecuted for their crimes.

LEGAL INTEGRITY

This goes onto individual Court Trials and Judges who give false information during and after trials and accept political interference in the process of law enforcement, due to the non-separation of the legislature and the Judiciary in pragmatic reality.

LAWS NOT ENFORCED

There is a litany of unjust and illegal activities that go on in full public view. Despite being illegal, and Governments overlooking and never enforcing the law. The law should be carefully crafted, and amended by legislation, and never selectively enforced.

RAMPANT WHITE-COLLAR CRIME

Issues of illegal activities by Government and Corporations never see the inside of a court room in pre-Magna Carte twelfth century type judicial tyranny. The law as it is now practiced is only being used like a criminal gang to repress people's free speech rights, free expression of ideas and freedom of association with organizations; the system lacks integrity.

VESTED INTEREST

The entire Government apparatus from the legislature to the judicial system in every western nation has been both subverted, and politicised. Something needs to be done to amend the system at its core.

THE JUDICIARY | THE RULING CLASS

Elites include the entire Judiciary, the Judges and Lawyers, those that profiteer from interloping into the misfortune of others, for their own vested interest and profit in various ways.

DAMAGING THE INSTITUTION OF THE FAMILY

The cited elites that make a career out of inciting family division, and psychopathically only concern themselves with their own narcissistic financial gain, giving little thought to the damage this has done to society in destroying the family in western nations is reprehensible.

FINANCIAL EXPLOITATION

The issues cited are a form of social affliction and corruption that is perverse and insidious. To do such a thing as exploit the misfortune of families and society, in all forms of court proceedings motivated for tremendous personal financial gain only exemplifies the systems psychopathy.

ORGANIZED JUDICIAL CRIME

The same corrupted fabric creates all off-shoots of the judicial system, an industry that is incestuous, that accepts their inter-relation and abuse of privilege as some sort of entitlement tyrannically attempting to mould society without consideration of the harm-filled outcome.

THE BUSINESS THAT IS THE JUSTICE FAÇADE

In fact, it is a tyrannical dishonourable industry in its present form that is a disservice to society. Unelected appointees like divine unelected kings wield judicial power like a treacherous sward, to commit grave acts of tyranny for their own industries financial gain as they often do.

JUDICIAL REFORM | CREATING A RESPONSIBLE JUDICIARY

The current incestuous system of an unregulated judicial club called "Law Societies" demonstrate the danger of when vested interest combines with the concept of justice. These Law Societies constitute lobby groups of Lawyers and Judges that oppose all reform to their industry and counteract any progressive reform.

1. The "Judicial business", is in desperate need of being controlled to prevent abuse of the obligation people have to display respect for others, and human rights laws.

2. To ensure full enforcement of law, investigate criminal activity and regulate independently matters of law and to ensure human rights are always respected.

3. Justice is not, and should not, be treated as a business, but is a sacred trust and one of the few authentic purposes of Government, yet at this it fails also.

4. The Senate as an independent, elected judicial law enforcement regulator must be a democratically elected assembly and needs to be implemented.

5. Since Courts have since their initiation been fully corrupted and represent only vested interest and little else at present. I find this is a necessary social reform for a second independent legislate review group that I call a "Senate" (same name as present institutions of minimal useful purpose).

6. Courts have never had any truly legitimate democratic right to make laws, other than through coercion and threat of violence by authority of their paymaster; - the Government.

7. Courts can be useful social instruments to determine the validity of disagreement points of contention. Courts have a responsibility to ensure the enforcement of law, free of political agendas and other attempts at social engineering, which they are guilty of collaborating with as they have historically collaborated with every human rights violation throughout history.

8. Justice concerns itself with restitution and or removal from society at large of law breakers to prevent harm and restore victims' integrity.

9. Determining judicial outcomes and ensuring that those found guilty of intentional legal breaches pay retribution to restore of the victims' integrity. Retribution carries twice the weight of the perpetrator's rights.

10. Right now Courts are merely the enforcer of political and financial expediency of vested interest, with a financial incentive to undermine the principals of democracy and any concept of Justice.

11. There is a need for extensive reformation to prevent the current political hijacking of the state judicial apparatus for selective law enforcement which is tyranny. A nation either lives by enforcing all its laws or it has no regard for the rule of law.

12. The current system was intended to be a system of checks and balances regarding the legislature. However, under the present activist judiciary; these unelected individuals have exceeded this intention and have unto themselves determined that they can also be legislators without any constituency. They fail to see or have chosen to ignore that they have now exceeded their mandate, in that some legislators have neglected and failed their responsibility to determine and enforce the law of the land.

13. Courts have been utilized to perpetrate conspiracies of Government and injustice for a very long time.

14. Making laws is not the responsibility of Courts. Interpreting law, and enforcing laws, is their proper mandate.

15. Where Courts determine the legislature to be lacking in providing guidance in terms of laws, they shall under this new regime request that the new independent Senate with the democratically elected authority, would interpret all laws democratically, as in reality Courts should have no right, by way of not being elected and representing the people to make any law or precedent of law, which exceeds enforcement of Law or precedent.

16. Precedent is a bogus form of undemocratic law creation. Court interpretations should not have force of law.

17. Only, sovereign elected legislators should interpret laws. Currently court precedents that interpret laws have proven themselves to be nothing less than the devil's playground. Precedents are not really laws, but rather interpretations of laws created by the legislature, that inappropriately make a judge a de-facto sovereign or monarchy, thereby acquire the weight of law by a form of resurrection of the "Devine rights of Kings", within nations claiming to be democracies; this is a travesty of justice. The current judicial system in the west is a perversion of the very concept of justice. When law is not legislated specifically, and not enforce equally, when precedents are cited in Trials to have the same authority as legislated law, in English Common Law. This is thus a system that is insincere in its foundations, as it often diverges from all intentions of legislators. The result is often, making precedents in pragmatic fact; an enabler of criminality, as they become used for all manner of convoluted applications by lawyers in Trials as though law.

ELIMINATING GOVERNMENT ABUSE

Libertarians believe that due to corruption being a concern we must be vigilant concerning Government administration. This requires the Governing apparatus must be controlled and limited in its jurisdiction and activities; that out of control Government always leads to tyranny. The desire of those in power always creeps over time to encompass more than was the original intent, when it comes to Government. The Government always starts with the promise of benevolence, then gradually evolves to take over the liberties of the people. We must always be vigilant that the utopian ideas of one group do not become the next state of tyranny for those who do not desire to be controlled by your utopia or share your vision. There is a constant need to push back the controllers and their repression. Human beings always seek advantage to advance themselves, and it is this often covert, manipulative impulse, that is the essence of all human corruption. If the system has real integrity, then it will be fair and balanced. To create integrity in law enforcement which must be separate from the legislature and be independent. Combining legislature and legal enforcement into one authority is to invite corruption into government and the negative consequences of corruption which snow ball over time leading to disintegration of the social order.

THE SENATE

Libertarians via checks and balances seek to constitutionally control Government abuse caused by having too much power and authority centralized in one legislature. Also, to create a separate independent and authoritative democratically elected Senate to: Conduct judicial enquiries; Investigate any and all corruption where ever it may be found in the nation. To review and provide oversight to all law courts and agencies that administer Justice; to review all court precedents; and via vote in their assembly hall, to accept or reject each Court Precedent; in addition to conducting public hearings of enquiry into corruption and scandals as they determine by democratic vote within the Senate Assembly Hall.

FORMULATING A LIBERTARIAN FEDERAL CONSTITUTIONAL SYSTEM, MY BROAD STROKES ARE:

1. The first level of administration would be the Federal Legislature; which makes National laws; sets National Government policies; Ensures National defense and national money bills; to operate in Federal Government jurisdiction of administration and in the best interest of the Citizens and National Sovereignty.

2. The second level of administration would be the Federal; "Senate" with their constitutional jurisdiction to enforce laws and have oversight regarding the entire judicial system and to audit and review all Government expenditures.

3. The third level of Government would be the independent & sovereign "Cantons" that would be equal to; State and Municipal Government at present in terms of constitutional powers. They would be local Government via direct from citizen's rule by plebiscite and referendum rules. They would determine their own immigration policies and quantities to their Canton but could not exclude another citizen's mobility if a citizen was at birth, born in the nation anywhere. Cantons could force a national referendum to amend any act of law if a majority of Cantons sign onto a petition to have any law or constitutional provision changed. The details of these proposals would be filled by constitutional convention and ruling Governments to infill the details of these reforms. What I present here are only my broad stroke amendments and provisions. Finally, that any constitution not approved by plebiscite has no authentic legitimacy in my perspective.

THE SENATE

The intent of the Senate is to enforce equally all the laws of the Legislature continually, by holding the powers of legislated laws enforcement. Their responsibility is to streamline the judicial process so as to avail it to citizens at low cost or no cost regarding disputes. Most matters would be determined after standardized documents are completed and submitted to the courts for review of activities for illegality and Court determinations. If a court determines further police investigation of submissions is required to obtain the truth or validate presentations, all court judges would be under obligation to order any further impartial investigations the court deems necessary. In civil matters Courts under the authority of the Senate would prosecute those who breach the law, and or order restitution for damages based upon their independent investigations. Gone will be the current system where trial of rudimentary facts, drama and debate determine judicial outcomes. They will be replaced with research and fact finding. In event that an issue of contention between the Senate and Legislature takes place, a popular referendum could be called by either the Senate or Legislature to determine the solution. The Senate and Legislature can submit independent referendum questions for the plebiscite or agree to a singular question requiring resolution. This separation of powers ensures that all laws are enforced and that all of society must abide by the law, unlike at present under selective enforcement of laws.

The Government has a responsibility to enforce all laws without distinguishing people by rank or position. Laws should be very basic and respect the individual. By separating legislation from enforcement, this ensures that the legislative branch will be very cautious about creating legislation because, no person will be exempt from the law, there must be no selective enforcement of the law. Thus, laws should be as few as necessary and only when necessary, to maintain social harmony and civility of processes; to ensure peace and order with integrity. All laws made by the Government must be enforced by the Government. Governments over legislate when they are exempt from the laws they create, due to selective enforcement, as occurs now. No sane person will create fully enforced legislation that will be tyrannical, if they know it backfires in that it applies to themselves also.

The Senate would consist of at least one hundred fifty members or more (Similar numbers to the ancient Greek Jury system). Selecting amongst themselves a leader of the Senate who would be the nation's Attorney General, under oath responsible to maintain judicial integrity and prosecute illegal activities and corruption as the Senates members become aware of such practices. All Senators by oath of office and law will not be permitted to accept any gifts or moneys outside their Government salaries and will be forbidden from accepting any election campaign contributions, beyond their own moneys. Senators will serve for singular seven-year terms; with an age restriction of being no younger than 60 years of age to run for election as a Senator. Receiving a Government pension afterwards for serving honourably to ensure their financial security afterwards. Pragmatic life experience and incorruptibility should be the hallmark of a Senator. This is intended to make Senators, it is hoped: - incorruptible.

Senators must use their own personal finances to fund their election campaigns. Law enforcement must be free from all political interference making former members of the Legislature and immigrants ineligible to become Senators in their lifetimes. Senators will be given the jurisdiction to oversee all issues of law enforcement, and all law enforcement agencies, being independent separate from the legislature and all Government control. Senators would be elected by their own separate popular electoral vote. They will have authority to initiate public enquiries into issues of corruption that will be determined by Senate free votes of the Senate Assembly membership. The Senate would independently oversee all the nation's Courts, judges, commissions of enquiry and reviews of judicial processes. The Senate may levy its own budget to pay for its administration.

DEMOCRATIC PROCESSES

In a Libertarian nation, there would be a "Legislature" and an independent elected "Senate". These would also exist and be elected separately with a separate and fully detached legislature buildings, in a separate city of distance from the legislature. The two bodies of Government would be independent and not permitted to be in contact except by formal correspondence. The Legislature would conduct day to day Government business, create laws, and perform all functions of Government under independent Senate oversight for acts of illegality.

SENATE CONSTITUTIONAL AUTHORITY

The Senate would not create laws and will have authority to enforce and interpret legislation by resolution in their Assembly via request from courts dealing with specific trials or their own enquiries.

1. The Senate must preapprove, review and endorse all precedents made by Courts to take effect of law. Review all court decisions and would require Senate review of all legal interpretive presidents prior to their taking effect. Decisions that do not obtain Senate endorsements stand as having no enduring effect upon future Court hearings and may be reversed by the Senate if determined to be inappropriate by the Senate.

2. The Senates main authority will be to debate and consider all Court precedents, to enforce the law, control all law enforcement agencies, regarding legal breaches against or by any citizen or organization, regardless of rank or position. To eliminate as much bias, inequality and injustice as possible in the application of law, as a final Court of Appeal. The Senate will serve as a Supreme Court in addition to its other functions in hearing final Trials being appealed to this highest judicial Court.

3. This Senate could also launch public corruption commissions of enquiry, have authority to issue warrants, subpoena witnesses, deal with all cases of court perjury, accept evidence for purposes of prosecution, and hold trial with enquiry as a single process if the members by majority should choose to pursue such actions.

4. Senate work must be publicly broadcast and recorded except when arranging prosecutions of criminals and secret investigations. Enquiries and all court actions must be fully open to the public in person without reservation.

5. So long as these hearings are sanctioned by a vote in favour by the majority of elected Senators, the Senate shall carry out these specific duties as their responsibility and exclusive jurisdiction on behalf of the citizens of the nation in fiduciary trust for the nation's citizens.

6. Law enforcement, utilization of military and police force would be the Senates sole determination. Receipt of a request from the legislature regarding acts of war will require, a Senate determination if such actions are warranted by the legislature under particular circumstances. But not under cases of emergency defense retaliation which is the only exception.

7. Equality; every person within the nation must experience equal application and obligation to abide by the law. No longer should legislators or Government officials be exempted from law enforcement by too much concentration of power into a single legislature. A nation is not democratic that unequally applies law and enforcement of laws.

4th Chapter
FUNCTIONAL CHECKS AND BALANCES PREVENT CORRUPTION

Libertarian Governments as with all nations seeking authentic social justice need Government checks and balances of a separate legislature. Constitutionally assigned separate law enforcement powers are necessary because there is currently too much corrupt selective enforcement of the law, due to too great a level of concentrated Government authority in the hands of the legislature and or head of state, representing vested interests that allows the breach of Constitutions and the selective enforcement of laws. Thus, this non-separation at present is the essence of the current wide scale abuse of the powers of Government. Experience has demonstrated that even elected officials become corrupted by too much authority and many judges are appointed by politicians, thus a separate law enforcement legislature (Senate) is needed to remove judicial interference as is the current case. Honourable politicians otherwise are hard to find, and too often capitulate to impositions, even breaches of constitutions which should never be tolerated unilaterally from any Government officials. Primarily the Judicial Industry has become a seditious lobby group with its own very dishonourable vested financial interest in matters of law which the judicial industry pretentiously assert does not exist, even though this is pragmatic reality.

GOVERNMENT ETHICS

There is a seeming degradation of our overall humanity, in terms of empathy for our fellow citizens. It's not really a surprise because of the insidious effects of social communism and multi-culturalism. The divide and conquer judiciary which destroys families, relationship unity and trust, that is a malaise that disconnects western people in these nations from feeling any common cultural, and familial connection. Western society is in reproductive decline and headed towards extinction due to these judicial exploiters.

MULTICULTURALISM VS. MELTING POT

Multiculturalism and its social-communist fantasy of a connected global society undermines the nation state and democracy to its very core. Multiculturalism creates a callous, ruthlessness, an uncaring society, without affinity. A no-man's land, of ruthless pursuit of political advantage and money, outside the foundations of familial culture. Multiculturalism is in fact a form of long-term national sedition; no sane nation would vote for its implementation and none have that I am aware of. It has always been implemented without consent by elite politicians. By creating social and political wedges that politicians exploit for electoral advantage and purposes, multiculturalism is intended to pit one ethnic group against the other, like a Napoleonic electoral war game by design. The ideology of Multiculturalism has many flaws and contradictions as a Government policy. In the long run multiculturalism by its essential advocating undermines and harms the nation state, by segregating people based upon gender and race. Causes the raise of deep division of the state into the future and sets the stage for future civil wars. The advocating of multiculturalism is treason against the nation states cultural unity. Multiculturalism sets the stage for civil war in the future, it is the complete opposite in terms of shared multiethnic social values as its core premise multiculturalism is the promotion of social long-term division, which human history has proven to be the root core of every war in human history. The typical person of this day and age who reads the words above, is so indoctrinated by the state education system. Especially the young will most likely accuse this of being racist, which is what they have been indoctrinated by the western social marxists of the education system to believe, but that is totally false. No multicultural nation in history has ever not existed without deep internal division and or eventual (often very bloody) civil war. Multiculturalism flies in the face of reality as being as realistic as communist economic policies as; simply a fantasy!

NATIONALISM

Nationalism is not racism, it is social cohesion and partnership based upon cultural cohesion by affiliation that develops over time. Nationalism is sovereignty and commonality of peoples created by a desire to enable and achieve governance by shared social values because of ethnic, cultural or philosophical, familial affiliation, which is cultural cohesion of common values and historical narrative.

Multiculturalism is racist

The apartheid created by multiculturalism is a racist seed for social discord and is fundamentally racist in creating divisions. Solitudes of people only creates division, and ultimately the desire for separation. Any nation with a separatist organization is one of a history with a solitude of peoples. There is no difference between multi culturalism and segregation, and also apartheid, since that is its advocacy to encourage and promote ethnic and social differences rather that uniting peoples, creates ghettos as exists and are proliferating in every multicultural nation. To believe otherwise is nothing less than a real racist and fraudulent faith, without any evidence of success throughout human history and contemporary experience.

A Cultural and racial melting pot

The acknowledged failure of political correctness and of the divisions created by a melting pot society, is the only way such a society can be made to be functional. Thus, under multiculturalism, repression of freedom of speech and conscience makes it a severely dangerous social and political ideology that leads to repression of human liberty and free speech on a very slippery slope towards fascism. Pre WWII-Weimar Germany had extensive speech regulating laws that restricted civil liberties, the result within a short time was a popular election of Adolf Hitler, and the Nazi Party, under their National Socialist banner, The Nazis were a left wing socialist political party in name, and most of their policies, along with rabid anti-Semitism. Like the former Yugoslavia, Iraqi, South Africa and all multicultural segregation states, of which I mentioned a few, historical examples. Social Harmony only existed in undemocratic dictatorships that repressed social and political descent long term under multiculturalism. Non-melting pot societies are divisive, and history proves this point in virtually every civil war and genocide.

WESTERN GOVERNMENTS HAVE LOST RESPECT FOR HUMAN RIGHTS REGARDING THEIR DOMESTIC POPULATIONS.

Human rights are repressed in Europe and Canada at this time to prevent civil unrest over their policies. Government there now practices tyranny and repression of human rights and freedoms of the domestic population; we have entered a dark age. This is the end product of multicultural policies by Government. Western liberalism is now disappearing into the darkness of a new dark ages where Government human rights abuses including; State media disinformation; Judicial repression of domestic populations throughout the west in favor of Immigrant foreigners; Special exclusionary rights for foreigners, not permitted by the domestic population; Special laws to prosecute domestic citizens who oppose in any way the states anti citizen policies; A policy of propaganda and disinformation launched against the domestic population. Media censorship and control; by

Governments. These are acts of treason against their own people for a Social Marxist political agenda. This trend towards western nations human rights violations against their domestic populations is complete with news media collaboration and repression of free speech, means freedom is being replaced by propaganda style news reporting, and the official line of Government policy; that you better not contradict (or else); - as is now daily reality of Government threats and intimidation. This is a serious issue that will lead to serious political and social turmoil in the long run in these nations. Using media as propaganda, is a form of human rights treason committed against domestic populations. There has been a gradual process of terminating news media reporters for the past two decades, replacing those in the media with a free mind to report the facts, with propagandists, often foreigners and immigrants to repress domestic population's freedom of expression.

In recent decades the powers that be, have been intentionally weeding out journalists to remove "loose cannons" through layoffs and attrition. A very noticeable dumbing down of the contents of news has gone on, along with media concentration into the hands of fewer and fewer owners. It is obvious to those of us who consume the news and are old enough to see the differences of the past vs now, to the point of all media are no longer informing the public of the realities, but rather broadcasting select stories to intimidate society regarding accepting foreign cultures is at hand. Rather than a free media, that would examine the root causes of circumstances. The media is now politically bent as a result. Soviet style media propaganda has arrived in the west. Donald Trumps "Fake news", is a reality. Western media now has a greater resemblance to Soviet or Nazi era propaganda media, than anything from its past or cultural history in the west. Current media no longer promotes correction of injustice or Government reform as in the past, now it simply barks the official Government line of the social communists. It has become a media of Government shrills, "imbedded reports" with Government setting the rules of what can and cannot be reported or photographed. Corporate media limitations of free speech imposed upon reporters are also causing the trade's practitioners to live in fear of their limited job security, simply "toe the line" of their Corporate Masters, who also own the politicians. Thus, they all play a façade of independence, which in fact is an absolute illusion. Thus, the depiction of reality no longer exists in western media. In the former Soviet Union, it was said; "the Government pretends to pay us, thus we pretend to work". Any society that exists with a pretentious media, becomes blind to its errors and timely reform, thus cannot correct its course that is headed towards getting entangled and entrapped by a proverbial coral reef, of lies and deception in the echo chamber of the elite.

Lack of criticism disables a socially isolated elite living in an echo chamber. Having gone too far off course with the desires and liberties of the people. Thus, due to censorship, we can expect Government tyranny to become more common and magnified over time under social communism's political correctness, to the point that western ship is sinking due to the resulting cited social rot, damaging freedoms and liberty. They live in a" Louise the XVI Versailles fool's paradise, for trust fund elitist fools are not aware of reality. Serious social rebellion is brewing because this circumstance, and most western Governments have become discredited in the perspective of the working class. Only the most indoctrinated believe them any longer. Violent Government repression will be the cause of an eventual violent retaliatory response by the middle class upon the elite, for the elite's reactionary repression of them. I don't believe such repressive regime policies will have a good outcome when the pressure relief valve of free speech has been repressed by the state. The elite overlook the value of a free media in providing a "coal mine canary" for problems. Under politically correct repression of free speech, the pressure builds and builds until there is an eventual social explosion, then it's too late. The game has changed completely. Professor Gene Sharp's book, "From Dictatorship to Democracy" is recommended reading to help Libertarians organize our movement. The Brexit vote and subsequent election of Donald Trump is the first sign that the pressure was building. In fact, Trump has been a pressure relief valve that has been good for America and the world in that the people have finally been heard. What Trump does will determine if this is the right relief valve to calm social discord in the USA in particular? With job creation being close to equal to immigration levels, this means that immigration is taking jobs from the struggling domestic population. In the new de-industrialized America. Most likely too little, too late to stop the civil war that is being repressed under cover of foreign terrorist claims.

THE CULTURAL & RACIAL MELTING POT

Immigration needs to be diminished to match the lack of jobs. There is a population decline at the same time as a job decline in all western nations. There is a certain equilibrium that has been upset by too much immigration during economically difficult times for the working class; this is not going to have a positive outcome. There needs to be an adjustment period; an immigration holiday yet Governments in the West are doing the opposite. During such an immigration holiday, of a decade or two, we in America need to adjust our social and political system away from multiculturalism and its ghettoized minorities, in reality multiculturalism is a racist's segregation system.

1. What I am advocating is the century's old system of success in immigration called the melting pot. The melting pot formula has been largely a success, in countries built upon centuries of immigration in particular in North and South America, and around the world. This is a time proven anti-discrimination recipe for immigration success. Governments need to realize their obligations to the existing population first, otherwise the resentment they create is the creator of racist attitudes that arise due to domestic citizens struggling, and thus resenting new comers and their disrupting social harmony.

2. Not bringing in too many people of any one ethnic nationality, mixing up immigration ought to be encouraged as Government policy. Keep newcomers feeling on the outside temporarily and wanting to be on the inside. Appeasing domestic population by recognition that foreigners must earn their place, and pay their entrance dues, to become functioning members over time, and eventually becoming one people. This is how peaceful, united nations are created.

3. Foreigners should not be eligible for Government assistance or programs such as mortgages, the nation is a home; not a hotel.

HISTORY MARCHES TO THE TOON OF ITS OWN DRUMMER

My parents are of mixed European American background with Native American blood, also my wife is Asian. So, accusations of racist ideas against me are bogus, as the facts demonstrate an expressed openness to and mixture with other cultures. Advocating a melting pot of race mixing is as anti-racist as it gets; it is only creating social cohesion! Quite frankly; I am more suspicious of those that want people segregated as multi-culturalism creates by default. Ghettoization, segregation in all their forms, can only be seen as covert racism. For some odd reason, in order to encourage those who are covert racists that do not want a melting pot society, they accuse anyone who has a divergent view of racism. Clearly this is merely a trick to end debate rather than encourage open democratic discourse. Name calling behaviour by the Social Communists is in duplication from their National

Socialist past and a repeat of Nazi brown shirt policies, which engaged in the same behaviours. This is always the first sign of a weak argument, which is exactly what the politically correct and bigoted movements of history have always done. Anything politically correct ideas claim to achieve, is accomplished through simply teaching good manners and respect for other differences, something the current "daycare generation"; was not taught by Social Communist indoctrination by the school system.

LOCAL DEMOCRATIC GOVERNMENT

Libertarianism believes in grass roots local Government, local control of Government, as the foundation of good Government; because such Government is always accountable to their people. The same idea extends to immigration, in the belief that it is good for social harmony for there to be racial integration and intermixing to create one identity in the nation. Immigration must be gradual and of mixed nationalities, ensuring that no one group has excessively large numbers to create an enclave that last longer than a single generation. International sources of immigration should be determined by ability to swiftly integrate into society, and the track record of ethnic groups historically. With preference for those populations that integrate more easily determining the quantity of inflows from particular ethnic groups. The nation state has the right to determine such policies which benefit it most. Illegal immigration is to be deemed military invasion and repulsed by the nation's defence organizations utilizing all necessary force.

1. The melting pot has a very long and successful track record spanning centuries, even millenniums of success through integration, worldwide not only in the west, but on all continents. Those societies that do not have a melting pot eventually end up with a state of civil war and national division eventually when Government repression is not implemented.

2. A few geographically isolated cases of endemic social division and overt racism exist, they have always been multicultural. Group isolationism is a direct path to social division, if not alleviated by integration and inter breeding. Racism is not a universally endemic human condition, other than in places like the southern United States, where Government laws in the past forced separation of the races. People do otherwise interbreed for generations where the Government does not interfere in the process. Segregationist policies and laws of Governments create the circumstances of racism. When Government stays out of citizens' private lives, society self-heals all wounds, in one pot it develops its own recipe.

3. In fact even in the United States of America has been found that the majority of African Americans are one quarter or more of European extraction. Though much of this racial mixing was covert and due to the historical wide spread rape of female slaves, by white people involved in the slave trade, unfortunately and sadly. The skin color of your typical African American of domestic origin is many shades lighter than most Africans arriving from Africa, due

to interracial relationships. Under segregation, and other Governmental race laws, created by Governments the population is prevented from full integration of the races by Government; how does this differ from multiculturalism in promoting segregation and division of peoples?

4. Mixed race societies are not a western creation, they exist worldwide in virtually every nation. Ideas of racism exist in virtually all societies worldwide. In nations such as Brazil, where slavery existed in the past, race mixing was not illegal at about the same time. We now see one people, of one culture, living in mutual respect that now exists, and that developed post slavery, because the Government stayed out of people's personal relationship choices, which is a private matter; up until recently.

5. Left unhindered by Government interference people do integrate and melt into one people in one nation. If foreigners are introduced, so as not to threaten the predominance of the majority of people, this integration is normally accepted and peaceful. Mixed heritage children are the antidote to racism. Without segregation in the USA, the outcome most likely would have been the same as a civil rights movement over time. When racial issues become protest movements or have Nazi perspectives of force, there is a problem with Government interference. When Government becomes involved coercion is the result. Forcing or foisting change upon people usually has the opposite effect of creating opposition and descent, it is simply unhealthy to force compliance rather than winning over their acceptance voluntarily. Force never works as it corrodes good will and creates resentments.

6. Government interference in the process of racial integration has been the refusal to recognize the need to treat all people with respect, as being an obligation, we all carry on our shoulders. Integration is a personal matter that simply based upon "natural selection" referring to Charles Darwin's book, is positive genetically, due to the immunities passed down to the next generation. The concept carries its own weight based upon its own merits. But once Government starts to utilize policy in any manner upon racial and cultural integration, the outcome is to exacerbate resistance to it.

7. In the southern United States racist laws and policies, thus slowed down integration. Nazi Germany is another case of Government law interfering in the development of a racial melting pot. Many mixed-race Germans; what was called "Mischling" Germans existed. Many Germans loved American jazz music and this cultural exchange lead to many mixed-race children that were accepted in Weimer Republic, prior to the Nazi movement. Once again, we must recognize as almost always, it is Government laws and brutish use of authority, which is the biggest racist. Government interference and racially or gender based bigoted laws, which interfere in individual liberty is that which must be controlled; not the people, as is the case currently in western nations. The choice occurs when people individually intermingled and natural urges take place over time, from there to create pair bonding, which is in reality a highly personal choice, which Government has no business in involving itself in. It doesn't matter which side the Government takes, their interference always creates a negative social impact and aggravates bigotry, delays integration, and promotes racism. The road to hell, really is filled with good intentions.

BORDERS

Borders must be respected and maintained to regulate immigration, and both the degree and mixture of new population flow, to prevent separate groups from coalescing that will, compete and culturally conflict with the domestic population. The melting pot is created by having a majority population, and a mix of minorities, they melt into the population to become one in short order. Open the faucet of immigration too much and social conflict is inevitable eventually. The more divergent the minorities introduced, the fewer of their numbers it would be safe to introduce, without creating conflict. Threaten the domestic population with a deluge of too many foreign nationals as immigrants of one group, at one time; is a recipe for future civil war and social unrest. Along with all of the ugliness including genocidal tendencies within a society as in the former Yugoslavia. Diversity is good, but division is very risky if one group becomes more successful economically or receives financial handouts from Government, not available to the local domestic population. These resentments can turn into anti-immigrant racist attitudes. Economic migration is a problem not just for the host nation, but also for the brain drain foisted upon their former nation. This type of immigration provides a pressure relief valve for dictators sometimes by draining the country of its reformers, intellectuals and most educated. How can a nation advance or have a necessary revolution, if it's most talented keep migrating to first world countries to become doctors for instance that drive taxis?

WESTERN EUROPE

Many people believe that Western Europe was one race; this is absolutely false. From Genghis Khan's Asian immigrants in Hungary and elsewhere, to Africans in Portugal, Italy and Spain, over the centuries, Europeans have melted away racial differences to become fairly homogenous and mixed culturally. Even in Germany with French Huguenots and many other tribal groups settling Berlin. The Saxons, Anglos, Vikings and Britons in England etc. The list is too long to write here.

DNA tests in recent years performed upon archeologically discovered Neanderthal bones have exposed an odd new genetic fact that Neanderthal DNA exists in Europeans and Asians, and apparently this is a unique trait. There is suggestion that Europeans and Asians acquired larger brains from Neanderthals that it is suggested lead to them having higher IQs. Race mixing is not negative as it passes on immunities that would otherwise never occur, and such genetic traits that can be positively transformative, in genetics variation is strength. If a plague arises and your ancestors were never exposed to it; most likely you and your lineage will die. But if you have an ancestor say from Africa, where the disease originated, unknown to you, there is a good chance you and your family might be immune to the disease from past exposure. Genetically closed groups as is frequently the case of aristocrats with hemophilia or former Roman emperors, malformed Egyptian Pharos who inbred are a good example, as is the case with certain German religious groups in America, who have been inbreeding for generations, and have many genetic problems. Inbreeding humans is a taboo across all human cultures because past generations experienced the negative and harmful results.

EXTINCTION OF CULTURE

One of the most racially pure people of all times were and are the American Natives, due to what is estimated as almost ten thousand years of geographic isolation. Many still to this day in South America have this disease immunity problem. You could wipe out an entire tribe by going there with chicken pox for example. Native Americans were conquered easily, not by conventional weapons but rather by European diseases like the common cold, scarlet fever, small pox and other diseases as is the record of history. The Europeans inadvertently infected the natives with diseases that would make most Europeans sick, but not kill them since they had ancestral immunity. However, these common diseases from Europe would kill natives by the tens of thousands very quickly, as they had no historical immunity, thus died very quickly.

When French explorer Jacques Cartier first traveled down the St. Laurence River in Canada in 1535, he reported the entire area as fully occupied with a dense population of natives and their villages in present day Montreal along the Saint Lawrence river. A century later in the 16th century when Samuel du Champlain traveled in the same area, he reported the land was virtually vacant. When British explorer Captain James Cook visited the West Coast of North America in the late seventeen century in the area of present day city of Vancouver, he found a post apocalypse native society where the bleached bones of the dead were left un-buried and scattered all over the place, along with vacant villages abandoned. Cook commented that the land was ripe for settlement, not realizing that the land was used productively by the prior inhabitants who had since passed away several years prior.

Native American tribes in this part of the world still tell tales of how ninety percent of their population died from European diseases introduced mainly out of ignorance. These diseases followed the natives on their trade routes transported by the natives themselves who became infected and unknowingly brought the diseases from the east. In fact, had this massive plague not occurred, it is very possible that the Europeans would have been repulsed from any British or American territorial take over, due to there being millions more North American Natives. Nobody truly knows the numbers other than the fact that there were numerous abandoned villages due to the plague of disease that was running rampant across

North America and inadvertently introduced by Europeans, who themselves had no idea initially this was happening. In fact even the French Canadians, some of the earliest Europeans to arrive in North America, with 16th century technology, came perilously close to extermination at the native's hands many times during my ancestors past settlement, especially in the sixteenth century, given a larger population of natives. Europeans would not have had the manpower to conquer so many native North Americans, even though the natives only had bows and arrows with other hand weapons, a force of millions or hundreds of thousands of natives would have been formidable.

Be they North American Natives, Amish or Hutterites, European aristocracies with haemophilia, Roman elite' and Egyptian Pharaohs with genetic defects or others. Genetic Death of a people and nations has occurred many times in the past to the present from "racial purity" as it is called. Much like animal breeding, there are few inbred animals that do not have genetic defects of some type or other. Ethnic diversity adds genetic immunities that pass down blood lines and creates superior offspring as every geneticist knows. There is not a pure breed animal, like dogs for example, which do not have some sort of genetic defect from inbreeding; - some being fatal. Many ethnic groups carry diseases or genetic defects from generation to generation, that are known within their society. Diversity in cultures, while it can genetically import benefits. Living together can be very problematic, cultures can diverge in values either subtly or greatly, and it can be filled with cultural misunderstanding resulting in disputes. None quite as great as the divergent beliefs of native North Americans and Europeans, when they first encountered each other. Particularly in the example of land disputes as in America. While natives occupied the land, they thought European ideas of land ownership were absurd. While the French were more interested in the very lucrative fur trade with the natives for several centuries, and had both good relations, limited settlements and limited population growth; often having families of mixed race (Métis) with the natives. It was the settlements in the southern thirteen colonies that wanted land for agriculture and farm settlements that created the greatest conflict over time that become outright war. The French Indian wars are a case in point of cultural diversity. Natives in America had such good relations with the French, as to be allied in a war against the thirteen British Colonies to the south. Another is after the American Revolution, in the war of 1812 when the eastern North American natives again sacrificed many lives. The natives allied themselves with the Canadians, to repulse an attempted takeover of the remaining British-French colonies to the North, by the United States. Once again natives sided with the Canadians in what would have been a successful military conquest by the newly founded United States without the natives assisting the Canadians; for certain. If cultural mixing reaches an understanding, and if done right with mutual respect, it can create deep friendships and alliances over time, as these ethnic Canadians, had hundreds of years to facilitate in the fur trade with Native North Americans. Without delving needlessly deeper; my point is that, the melting pot is the most peaceful way to integrate cultures and people for national unity and add new blood to make the nation genetically stronger. Racial inbreeding as in marrying your siblings, as every tribe on earth teaches their young, is unacceptably harmful and risky. Virtually every population on earth has taboos against inbreeding for this reason.

The history of the world contains many success stories, not just in America with divergent immigrant groups' pair bonding; but also, around the world as in Europe and Asia. When you see racial segregation, you see a circumstance that goes on for hundreds of years and becomes inflamed by becoming a powder keg of racial discontent due to inequality of opportunity that becomes institutional. Don't get this wrong though, I do believe immigrants must pay their dues to any country they relocate to. To gain social acceptance, move up the social strata too quick cause's original inhabitants to often become resentful, as occurred with the Jews in Europe. Becoming first culturally integrated takes at least one generation. Broadening one's cultural perspective requires a social and historical understanding of a culture that takes decades to understand if one is not born into it. Sociology still comes to play in these matters.

There is a great deal of pretense regarding these matters. Political correctness only stifles candid conversation thus ignores pragmatic reality. Just because we do not like what is being said, does not alter the facts of human nature in all cultures. Cultural integration takes time, of at least one generation, and sometimes several depending upon the deviation of cultures. Marxism can take on two forms one is cultural as in the west right now, and economic, as in the former Soviet Union this is a belief that morphs into totalitarian control of the individual. Communistic ideas have been a miserable failure in all its forms and mutations, because it is a fairy tale with no foundation in science, sociology or psychology. Thus, in pragmatic implementation social/cultural Marxism seeks to achieve its aims by the only means it has available; tyranny and repression, as it is unnatural regarding human nature. Marxism always fails and belongs in the dust bin of history as a failed experiment that's is responsible for the outright murder and genocide of people everywhere it has been attempted from The Soviet Union, to the entire former east bloc nations, to China and Cambodia. Communism has been the most vicious and murderous ideology ever in the history of humanity, made up of intolerant fanatics who are in denial of reality. The second most murderous philosophy has been Islam, which is not just a religion but also a complete social philosophy from the 15th century. Their view upon the world is a desire for conquest in the name of creating Islamic states. Western Social Communists seriously underestimate how dangerous this ideology is for all human rights as we believe in the west. It is very much like the fanaticism of fascism and is completely incompatible with western ideologies that in the end will lead to conflict or serious social tyranny; if allowed to become entrenched in the west. The greater the dissimilarities, the smaller the base population western nations should accept at any one time of any one immigrant group for quicker integration of immigrants.

Nothing is better than being raised from birth in a culture to provide deep insight. Cultural Integration takes time. After centuries of habitation, even the Jews of Germany in the nineteen thirties were integrating with Germans. The German Jews would have integrated far faster; but we can see the result of too much cultural / religious variation slowing down this progression. The image of the wealthy migrant from a foreign land moving to Germany as a Hasidic Jew with black coat, beard and top hat who stood out as a separate group in Germany society created a separate identity, which is difficult to integrate. Much like Muslim women in the west today wearing bourkas etc., under such divergent differences social integration is slow, when they come to the west in large numbers. It is much quicker to integrate secular immigrants. There was a lot of resentment because Jewish integration was very slow. I have to wonder if the Jewish population were all dressed like contemporary Europeans prior to the holocaust if the discrimination of the National Socialist German Workers Party has occurred. The danger of course for the minorities to experience discrimination is always if a greater proportion of the domestic population is homogenous, and being in a nation of historical, thus cultural and racial hegemony; as in Germany in the nineteen thirties; unlike America in such nation's immigrant integration must be even and slower.

There has to be enough time for the natural integration of peoples living together to take place completely, because demonstrative divergent religions and race slows down the social integration process, but it does occur. The greater the cultural points of difference, the slower and fewer in numbers of the migrants that must be introduced to reduce the appearance of being perceived as a threat to the dominant culture. Granted most racism is committed by Governments compared to individuals. Clearly affirmative action is a very bigoted and racist policy that creates social stress and resentment, in addition to the belief that the recipient of such favour is, an underqualified foreigner or other obtaining privilege unearned. Whether in a grocery line or a job opportunity, people resent que jumpers. Thus, such things do cause resentments and disrupt social harmony. Many Jews fought in the German army, on Germany's side in WWI, and some even during WWII, only to find out their relatives were being murdered back home; much to their chagrin and trauma. Nationalism is rooted as an extension of a cultural and historical community through heritage that hands down character, social perspective and social values. Outward differences in different nations, reflect differences and reality in cultural values.

For me, like most people with a heritage in America, Western nations have been indoctrinated with certain expectations starting in the schools. Ethics and ideas concerning our society, as all societies embrace their own culture. My society's history is my cultural heritage, identity, and my ancestor's legacy after four hundred years of the melting pot; -my inheritance is due to generational foundations from centuries of residence. This has also made my families cultural heritage to become very mixed, so mixed as to be, "of the land, and from this land". With no foreign allegiance being of; French, Native American, German and Jewish ancestry and we speak English with my children each adding in other heritages of the other parent. So, their children's heritage may be four or more heritages. To some people of other nations this may seem like a lot of blending, but in America this is not unusual amongst my peers of similar historical vintage. We are, and have been a very tolerant people, we have by our tolerance, been far too forgiving to our politicians and their treasonous vested interests. Despite racial and cultural combinations, I can connect, and have a common perspective with my fellow citizens for one reason; we are of the similar culture. In this I am referring to as western culture; the western Reformation, The Renaissance, The Trade Union Movement, Laws Preventing Child Labour, the end of Slavery, The Sexual Revolution, Women's equal rights, and general social fights for human rights, social programs, and dignity against Government repression the people on our continent have endured. When I see anything depicted from my nations past, it is my past and that of my ancestors; thus, I am connected and so are my compatriots, just as in any and all other nations this historical connection leaves my people feeling at home and connected to our culture and our land. As with all peoples; "our history is our culture" and anyone who claims we in America do not have a culture, displays an extraordinary level of historical illiteracy and ignorance to implore such audacious insult and degradation upon us. Every nation has a story which created the character of its people. Those who offensively insult North Americans by suggesting we are without culture only display offensive bigoted insult upon the nation's people and their ancestors.

 History makes the nation and the character of the people for it is our story; our values; our character with no apologies! History is evolutionary, and no child or descendant is guilty of the crimes of their ancestors; that is just ludicrous! After four centuries of building nations in America, our culture is as vibrant as that of any nation on earth. We are not in America nations of immigrants, we earned our right and identity from our historical journey that built this continent and is our culture. The people's history is culture! One unique quality is our welcoming attitude to foreigners immigrating here. We are not nations of immigrants, any more than any other people's whose ancestors migrated anywhere centuries ago are. We have a very unique culture in that our ancestors came to American in almost every case seeking one thing; Social Liberty from Government, Liberation from our past, and most importantly the opportunity to recreate ourselves and cast out our past. Any immigrant who does not comprehend or respect these values should not come to America.

THE CURRENT MIGRATION CRISIS IN THE WEST

It is the epitome of ignorance to think that mass migration of illiterate refugees from the third world, whose culture does not embrace or comprehend western cultural history, or our historical evolution are a good social fit. Under current circumstance it is risky to introduce large numbers of foreigners who are the products of a low quality and biased religious based education systems, it creates ghettoization of ethnic groups. The risk of multiculturalism is also of civil war or Balkan style racial cleansing dangers long term. Many of these foreigners where never taught our nation's history in school or have any familial connection to our nations; thus, do not understand western cultural realities. Thus, unlike previous migration between western nations post WWII these new third world economic migrants have no cultural connection to western institutions or comprehension of the freedoms and privileges in the west. Freedoms were earned via the sacrifices of a nation's ancestors, history is the legacy of cultural heritage. Peoples who do not have a western family heritage from a cultural history perspective, that did not historically fight these social battles in the west, cannot, and don't fully understand western culture, other than perceiving the west as a place that gives away free stuff and money, that we call our social programs. The very idea that some person who immigrates to the west in a decade or two suddenly shares or understands these issues is unrealistic and highly provocative towards the domestic population. It is absolutely illusionary to think foreigners share or comprehend the depth of these issues, and also realize it is these same working-class people who really pay for Government created employment scarcity brought about by unskilled and uneducated immigrants that repress domestic workers employment opportunities and wages. This is where racism festers over time; as the fault line that is rumbling.

It is bad enough that society is operated by socially remote elites. Having elites and immigrants running the country is incitement to violent and bloody civil war or revolution, and outright class warfare. The reason being that, elites are already socio-economically separate from the general population. "These bourgeoisie", if they now add to their number's bourgeoisie foreigners, the outcome of this is complete alienation of the working class as has occurred in most Western nations. The divorce will now be complete creating the foundations for bloody future civil war. I have no idea how far this will go, because the outcome I predict will depend largely upon the elite experiencing an awakening or not. The elite's prudence is about to be tested. I see that if the current immigration trend continues, both America and Europe are going to end up impoverished, and in a state of terrorism and civil warfare, brought about by western Governmental ineptitude. I foresee the founding people themselves; not foreign terrorists, as the targeted enemies of the state in a civil war now brewing. Citizens born in the west will launch covert terrorism against their own repressive Governments, brought about by technology-based employment dislocation, corrupt Government administrations and immigration intended to dilute their existence. This will ultimately bring down the current establishment I predict. There is no war more insidious than civil war.

It is really sad that the children in many western nations have been severely misguided by the education system to be are so brainwashed as to become tools of the elite, due to social communist indoctrinating education system. Today's graduates and students more than any in previously generations desire to bringing down the system of their ancestors, as they are educated to become enemies of the people, acting as a fifth column, due to false nihilistic social communist ideas acquired at school. Historically inaccurate revisionist narratives are delivered in the education system that is being abused to corrupt and indoctrinate the youth. Youth who do not realize where their vested interest lies, since they are so brainwashed in the schools that have replaced parental wisdom with social communism. Political correctness, speech repression. It is the Soviet indoctrination system introduced to the formerly free west. Meanwhile education in business and comprehension of how to succeed in our economy is not taught, because the teachers having spent their lives on the Governments payroll have not got any idea regarding how the economy and business actually operate.

Those who are entrepreneurial struggle needlessly. This is why business books often become best sellers, due to the thirst for that knowledge. Clearly there is a disconnect, between reality, pragmatism, and the education system. Like the old adage; "Those that cannot do teach". This is not healthy for our society to have an education system that is so weak in providing students with essential knowledge of; history, how the economy works, and how to start a business, this needs to change. Western social benefits are now nonchalantly distributed by Governments in the west to domestic and foreign immigrants, as if these elites were Santa Clause. These social programs were fought for, paid for, and earned by the domestic working class today and their ancestors, were hard earned privileges, fought for, costing many their lives. The annoyance this causes the working classes, who know the history, needless to say, are not at all impressed, or pleased to see elites and their elitist Courts giving away the benefits their families fought these same elites to get for themselves, and their families, in the first place being given away to foreigners who never paid even one cent into the system. The same elites whose ancestors often fought against the people getting such social security programs being implemented, now throw this money at foreigners in an underhanded vote buying scheme.

THE PRESENT ECONOMIC STRUGGLE IS TOO LATE.

Perhaps this is just a natural part of human evolution that all civilizations eventually collapse. Technological change at present means that manual labour jobs are in short supply for the domestic population and taking the few jobs of this nature away from domestic populations has created a great deal of resentment. This means for example that many migrants, educated in Arabic writing are in fact functionally illiterate and will have a very difficult time integrating into our society; most likely never. Especially with a religion that is exclusionary unto itself, self-ghettoization will be the result, with a second generation like in Europe, not feeling they belong in the society and being resentful with a chip on their shoulders that will be acted out upon. Once again, Government creates a problem for future generations to deal with.

THE IMPLOSION OF THE WEST

It is the very people who are the bedrock of the west, the working class, poor women with children, who are be harmed the most by the impoverishment of social welfare, due to funds being diverted to fund economic migrants flooding in as fake foreign refugees, who do not have the education to work in any position other than unskilled jobs. Just as western society is struggling to keep its collective head above water, and such employment which is the best they can aspire to is quickly diminishing. It has throughout history been men who have always done the fighting to destroy a corrupt social order. Men as a group have suffered the most injuries from social Marxism and they have had their fill of it. The shock from street fights at the beginning of the coming civil wars will cause the social Marxists a great deal of trepidation as their eyes will be opened to the reality of the anger of the working class as it comes out onto the streets to shut them down, along with the establishment. Suddenly the social Marxists will realize, all has been a delusion when the long-suffering silent majority finally speaks up in a spontaneous explosion of rage and anger. This will bring about the political systems demise after decades of social and economic decline. The outcome is not necessarily all bad, since in the end, the west will be a changed place and Governments will be toppled to bring about real change. The elite initiated this, by their total ignorance of the issues regarding the working class. Ultimately the current mass immigration policies of multiculturalism that has been the tipping point and will sever all loyalty to the elite. Once the die is cast and outcome has commenced, it shall be too late to reverse it without horrible consequences. The Elite will be viewed as traitors and social pariah, who by treasonous policies destroyed many western nations. As radical as it may sound, I believe there will come a period of a bloody revolution against the elites as deadly and vicious as the post French Revolution Reign of Terror. The elite and even the establishment, will face angry mob justice and regime change. The calm before this storm is the present situation. Like the aristocracy in Versailles under Louise the XVI they have no clue regarding what is brewing. Their deluded world goes on as the populous is gathering to storm the palace. The elite are going to no longer be immune from public retribution, along with the resulting violent cultural warfare. They should not have angered and betray the working-class silent majority, for they are doers, and once the movement starts its advance it will not stop like a ball rolling down a hill until the job is complete. The current social engineering will bring great social upheaval, and you can bet there will be a hunt to find and punish these left-wing politicians, legal representatives and social engineers in the schools who engineered this social discord. The next two decades will definitely not be boring. The current social engineering program is an invitation for future fascism and the resulting purge of Marxists. This is all so unnecessary and avoidable; - it is depressingly sad, that university education systems were used as a tool to create social hatred in humanities education against one's own society, rather than social cohesion. I also foresee university defunding as retribution for this situation, and higher educational institutions being shut down as too expensive a manner to deliver a curriculum by new Governments. Many of the intellectual elite will be removed from their positions by the mass closure of university departments by defunding them, which will reduce their numbers. There shall be as a result a reduction in such institutions. Afterwards there shall be a reformation to purge higher education of biased social agendas. A replacement to more online technical education, that will be state monitored for attempting any future social engineering through indoctrination via a system of curriculum review to replace political indoctrination with holistic perspectives that must provide both sides of every element of education to encourage divergent perspectives creating greater understanding that the world is not black and white, but rather fluid and full of alternatives. Education will be purged of those that have been using education for political ends. A Libertarian society must have free thinkers who understand diversity and society is subjective to perspectives in a given social matrix of time. This was and remains the proper objective of education, being to open the mind and not to close it.

THE BOURGEOISIE VS. THE WORKING CLASS

To maintain power, the bourgeoisie social communists and their "Frankfurt School" University elite sought to achieve the combined acquiescence of the working class and business class to control society by their social subversion. Otherwise by themselves, the University based bourgeoisie have neither the finances, the influence, nor the wealth to rule. Their only source of power and influence has been the sedition of the minds of the youth, particularly by political correctness and other social communist policies. The population needs to demographically ally ourselves with authentic working-class leaders not bourgeoisie "Frankfurt School" wannabes, since by ourselves, individually, we have no ability to bring about change which will protect us and our liberties. We will only have authentic Libertarian Government, when the shackles are removed from the productive. In recent decades, Government has increasingly been subverted by multicultural and minority group politics echoing the "Frankfurt School's" socially subversive philosophies based upon communism coming to fruition. These ideologies of social subversion have been increasing in their influence over time and away from democratic influence exercised by the working class. The Frankfurt Schools education indoctrination program has become many western nations political policies based upon communistic social nihilism. These ideas they espouse are socially corrosive, divisive and destructive, because they are in no way based upon merit. It can be seen as "mediocrity fights meritocracy". It is underhanded, covert and subversive social competition. The jealousy of humans against the advancement of others based upon merit is gilded in communism. In fact; communism is purely based upon envy and excuses for failure, which put down others to elevate themselves.

While in the past few decades these ideologies have operated under the radar of western society with little notice. It is time we citizens in the west must realize that our diet has been poisoned by precepts that are completely dedicated to undermining and subverting western civilization with the intent of implementing "social communism". There is no altruism in communism, it is filled with jealous bile. This is why, when in power it is the most murderous ideology ever in human history, responsible for the imprisonment and mass murder in the hundreds of millions of people; so great are communism's ideological crimes, as to make even Hitler's "final solution", look like a mere Boy Scout Troop; by comparison. However economic communism has been discredited. The original intent of this sedition foisted upon western society was created by Frankfurt School communists to undermine the west. The Frankfurt

School's program of social sedition via; multiculturalism, political correctness, and other precepts originating with them has infected western nations. Given that communism has been proven to be economically a failure, these seditious concepts are a metamorphic gift for Islamic demographic conquest of Western Europe, handed on a silver platter to Islamists because of the nihilism they infected within Western European, and America society following in tandem. However, at the eleventh hour the momentum of resistance has started to build. Two examples of this western turn around and epiphany regarding the social manipulations at work have been Brexit (thanks to Nigel Wright) in England, and the election of Donald Trump as president of the United States in America. Trump's election was as much a loss of confidence in the traditional elite bourgeoisie social managers by the working class, as an unconscious repudiation of the current Frankfurt School nihilism within society that is part of the working-class nausea at this time, with the political system.

The ruling class and their banking interest's phony social agenda of promoting their specific vested interest, has created a drift from their traditional base the working class and; without appropriating the working class they are losing all political power by this new configuration. The internet has opened up alternative perspectives and demonstrated that we are not alone, in fact; we are united in our conscious desires. When the working class is set adrift like this politically, due to all this corruption and sedition, the outcome can lead almost anywhere in the political and social spectrum. We want and need Liberty from all of the lies and manipulations. This reminds me of politics in the Nineteen-thirties in that anything is possible since the system as an egg has been cracked open! We have only a scent and small tastings right now of this opportunity, and of its potential. Most importantly how far this paradigm shift will go, and what will be its direction, the next two decades will determine. The next millennium of human life on this planet will be altered for better or worse as a result of what you and I do at this time. Will it be Liberty or more servitude; - our actions will determine the outcome. I believe we are now not approaching a new chapter in human political and social evolution. We are approaching an entirely new book. A rewrite of every political and social construct is now possible to create a system based upon honesty and finally reflect real integrity; - when the wind goes in our direction, we need to open our sails to receive it and take our Liberty! This is the time and opportunity for humanity to embrace Libertarianism, utilize the patterns set out in this document, to finally liberate mankind from our shackles created by the controllers. This repudiation of the current system is one of disdain with the current system itself. I believe that the workings of Frankfurt School in the sedition and undermining of society have been a corrupting influence upon western society. Their actions have been very harmful in creating narcissistic and detrimental social manipulations. However, the results of their philosophies seem to have woken up western society sufficiently and having an unintended consequence upon society in western nations, so as to put it to an end finally, by exposing the detrimental effects in dividing society against itself. This circumstance has in fact demonstrated the corruption of the system. Validating the Libertarian Argument, by pragmatically and clearly demonstrating, that the current model of the centralized social communist state only becomes increasingly repressive and tyrannical over time, as western nations have seen their culture hijacked as in the case of the Frankfurt School's social contamination. hat the affairs of state must be managed in close proximity to and by the people themselves under "Libertarian Direct Democratic Cantons" and "Constitutional limitation and control of the mega or Federal state apparatus"; as I present in these writings.

THE NEW SOCIAL CONFIGURATION

Due to Donald Trump, the patriotic amongst the elite of the population have created a new political reorganization with the working class to defeat the elite Frankfurt School bourgeoisie. The election was a severe repudiation and slap across the face of the elite for forgetting their base. The foundation of the social communism has always been advancement from co-opting the working classes vote under various socialist political parties, with university connections. The bourgeoisie and their mediocrity have never been wealth creators; unlike the wealthy or the working class, both of which have for the most part have a good work ethic combined with a rugged Libertarian individualism. While the social communists may poo-poo this alliance, the fact is that philosophically, it is they the university elite bourgeoisie that are the odd man out. Unexpectedly, this social division is not unlike a predicted Marxist class war, in which the elite paradoxically take from the others. The elite in this case are social communist I am referring to from universities who are so removed from the working class as to fantasize this is their constituency when in fact the working class find them and their ideas to be repugnant. However, in the, "theme park of university fantasy lands", their fantasies lack pragmatic realism, and they are so isolated and deluded within their echo chamber as to be in fact schizophrenic in their social ideas and constructs. There are in fact many parasitic social strata that enrich themselves by utilizing Government legislation to promote their ideologies. By indoctrinating the youth with Frankfurt School precepts in Universities and schools. They are in league with what we know as professional politicians, who for their own vested interest and profit abuse Government position and sell state policy for their own advancement.

THE WORKING CLASS

The Social Communism of the "Frankfurt School" "Politically correct Movement", creators of the concept of Multiculturalism based upon their ideology of Cultural Marxism, have no credibility with the working class, who are too pragmatic to buy into such social engineering ideas, which can only proliferate via indoctrination in academia; removed from pragmatic reality. There is a new and odd alliance in the political configuration of the business class and working class in favor of Donald Trump, this cross of class lines has seldom occurred in history. It reminds me of the western powers during WWII allying with Stalin's Communist Government. Essentially the thinking was that at least Donald Trump speaks his mind, and second, he is not part of the corrupt establishment.

THE CURRENT CLASS SYSTEM

Government has become imbedded with scams and scammers, it seems the public good has been discarded by a corrupt elite, seeking only their private enrichment. Groups of elites have subverted Government to the point that it no longer works for the people. Lobbyists such as the lawyer's; with their exploitive child custody laws, Government funded gender lobby groups and, speech control, political correctness, profit oriented interest group politics, have brought about the elimination of impartial Government regulatory determination of social policy, product health and safety, and have even corrupted the judiciary. Government and privately funded fake social protest organizations are the new elitist scam to manufacture their particular social narrative. Frankfort School ideas are indoctrinating students in high school by teachers in University and post-secondary education through courses based upon post modernism. They indoctrinate the rebellious youth to manufacture politically motivated perceptions of dissent. When in fact the protest groups are financed by the Government or lobbyists, none of it is organic. This decent is not in any way legitimate, but rather a form of radical movement that is the way of Government manufactured justification for state interference into private family matters. Simply research who is funding these trouble making organizations and see their real agenda; - simply follow the money.

Governments now engineering political protest, political lobby groups and coalitions. Their making private making private family issues a Government concern, as a form of social distraction by politicizing private and personal affairs.Government Ministries indoctrinate multiculturalism and other deluded ideas, because it is political policy. The people are incited to fight and squabble amongst themselves, thus they overlook the nation's inadequacies. To serve their covert corporate masters who create these issues intentionally with Government. The elite live in complete arrogance regarding the social change created by these actions, which impact the working class very negatively. Western society lost all sense of pragmatism, which used to be called "common sense". Society is now a division of social strata. The divisions are becoming deeper, under social communism, which is founded in socialism that has betrayed the foundations of western representative Government; that being the working class.

Governments in the west now pursue policies that do not represent the values of the working class and in fact harm the working class. Like a magician this sleight of hand is very effective to keep the population divided for easy conquest and control of the agenda for their exploitive sponsors. Study after study of family dynamics has proven that intact families are be best incubator for child development, even if the parents have issues. Yet Government ignore the volumes of studies proving this, because it is not in their policies of division to encourage family cohesion. The fact that most individuals in jail are the products of single parent households or broken families does not concern the Government apparently. The interesting twist on the Trump revolution is the question of: "can the class alliance between the wealthy and the working class be maintained for a prolonged time?" They do share common desires on completely different planes of social strata. Libertarian's share a desire for less Government intervention and more independence in our lives.

THIS HAS ALL BEEN ENGINEERED

There are no mistakes or accidents concerning social engineering issues and intended destruction of the family in western nations; -it is all by intention! The Politically correct movement is a Social Marxist movement to silence opposition to Government curriculum policy as devised by the Frankfurt school. These policies are intended to enable Government to indoctrinate the children, thus control society by Government narrative, it is essentially the tail wanting to wag the dog. This Government project must be stopped. Stop creating gender based divisive Government departments and agencies and using Government policy to interfere in society by funding radical feminist and minority rights groups and anti-male discrimination invoked by Government policy that takes many forms. Government and business must stop being permitted to fund artificial protest groups and lobby groups, advocating social policy by employing and paying protesters to covertly make pretence of popular movements for the corporate media to broadcast and mislead the people about society. The manipulation from news media (fake news) acting, must stop and be made illegal to broadcast fraudulent popular protest, for political manipulation of the people's opinions intentionally. Stop the judicial industries citation that men are poor parents as a complete lie; multiple psychological and sociological studies have proven this. No one questions the male widower, but in the separation of a marriage the man is always depicted by lawyers as a deadbeat parent who must compensate financially for his ignorance and inability to raise their children. The Judicial business regarding family law is an absolute travesty of Justice that goes on primarily because it is very lucrative for what I see as the "judicial mafia", which is all about extorting money from the financially more successful male gender. Even when a stay at home father raising the child requests his parenting be recognized he is not respected. Stop the courts from systematically and dogmatically deny fathers and children of their rights of paternal care, by stripping fathers' rights away without justification in any breaches of the law. It's all about falsely depicting all men as bad negligent parents, as an excuse to deny parental rights, and create excuses to maintain the judicial gravy train. By a process of outright anti-male bigotry. We can see that statistically this is going on, in that men lose their rights for equal custody over ninety percent of the time, because contrary to the cited mythology, men do want to attend to and raise their children.

Eliminate all family courts and conduct these matters under rules of evidence, not hearsay. Stop the Judicial industries extorting men for money. If equal parenting is recognized this means no money gets transferred to the mother, if the father takes care of the child equally, thus the lawyer who depends upon the father to pay his billings must currently attack the father in court by fabricating some excuse. The corrupt Judicial industry has a vested financial incentive to oppose all equal parenting legal reform and has via their Barristers lobby groups and associations done just that as a matter of public record.

Support families. The family in the west and marriage are in steep decline. The numbers of children in western countries is at extinction levels because it is too hazardous for men to marry. The blame for the extinction of family values in the west falls completely in the lap of the judicial tyranny being invoked in their venomous family destroying self-enriching industry. Here is the cancer of the west rooted in the judiciary in collaboration with the enforcers of extortion; the Government. Poking their greasy family money laden hands in private family matters; regardless of the very detrimental effect upon children in parental alienation and society in general. Stop indoctrinating children with Government promoted sexual and social justice ideas, such as historical revisionism that imagines a patriarchy. This is not without motive, as this puts the Government in place to be able to indoctrinate your children once the father has been deleted in the nation states soldier factory. This has backfired against the state by causing the extinction of western children. No family values, no children, once again Government intervention severely damages society.

We also need political reforms to:

1. Introduce laws making corporate and foreign influence and bribing electoral public officials by financial campaign contributions illegal and enforcing these laws.

2. Making political parties in the Senate and Legislature illegal, requiring all votes be free votes of local politicians to reflect the desires of local constituents.

3. Place the majority of Governing authority into the hands of local "Cantonal" type direct democracies following the Swiss model.

4. Constitutionally controlling all Government bodies so as to limit their jurisdiction, to control Government and hinder Government attempts to engineer society.

5. Altering the Judicial system so that it follows processes that the Senate will determine.

6. We need a Senate to oversee the entire system of justice as an elected nonpartisan judicial tier of Government. A Senate that is independent and elected with all law enforcement oversight powers.

EXPLAINING SOCIAL ENGINEERING

Social engineering is taking place and it is not by accident or unintentional. Let me be clear that there exists in society psychopathic vested interests, that are here to exploit society regardless of the repercussions to society at large, for their own financial advantage. They are in no way altruistic, but rather via neurodiversity psychopathic individuals and social influences perverting the social consciousness. Historically we might call them "evil people"; - they do exist. They are the same type people who commit acts of torture, rape, run concentration camps and gulags and all the evil in the world. To deny this reality is to live in a pretentious cartoon world. The type of bigoted anti-family social engineering policies implemented by Government and the judicial industry, I have described. They have created a very harmful anti-family culture and displays the danger of a political matrix running rough shod over society's best interest.

The second force is creeping social Marxist engineering derived from the "Frankfurt school" along with political correctness, that has run havoc over western nations with rudimentary social justice historical revision that has created false narratives. These narratives known as "social justice" have little bases in real human interactions and are being indoctrinated in University campuses under political correctness. They reflect the smallest of minorities, which bear no relevance upon society at large. Their motivations vary from power grabs to the most common financial gain though attempting to gain preferential treatment for employment opportunities and the ever-present claim of victimhood.

Government policies within their institutions that includes schools, have damaged the family in so many ways in recent decades. There is a Government imposed, engineered, and created sociological matrix. This matrix has gravely harmed western society to the point of extinction at present. The average person lacks the perceptive intelligence to see these psychopathic realities distorting and perverting society, as it takes many insidious forms, such as:

1. Government creation of artificial social divides that penalize current people where no crimes were committed; except in very rare cases.

2. Creation of victimhood through fictionalized historical narratives, to justify reverse discrimination, for imagined and perceived past wrongs and creating a culture of victimhood imposed upon the majority population.

3. Issues are raised regarding matters that even the current complainants cite based upon historical revisionism stories not involving their generation personally, thus having no firsthand knowledge.

4. Granting unearned job opportunities and gender-based nepotism to those lacking qualification, such as minorities and those lacking credentialed merit.

5. This is the very divisive ideology created at the Frankford School designed to divide and destroy western civilization.

6. Government sponsored institutional undermining the family, in schools and courts, by bigoted attacks against masculinity, villainizing heterosexuality and fathers, must be stopped.

7. Government sponsored post-secondary indoctrination. Socially engineering the youth by creating inaccurate historical perspectives of victimhood, must be stopped.

8. Women being indoctrinated to see themselves as victims in a state sponsored "feminine victim culture", to intentionally create a distorted and perverted perspective of history and the family is an insidious type of Frankfurt school ideology of psychological manipulation.

9. Schools radicalizing women with false and distorted historical narratives and revisionism to create extreme anti-male feminism with false narratives being taught by Universities humanities programs that have no bases in scientific foundations, must be stopped.

10. Government bigotry with exaggerated narratives of criminal spousal and child abuse villainizing all men as brutes and abusers, utilizing the worst-case scenarios of criminal cases to tar all men, as being such a way, creating a scenario that does not exist in reality, other than an extreme minority of dysfunctional and rare family scenarios to tar all men with strategic bigotry, must stop.

11. Frankfurt School ideologies like multiculturalism must be stopped as a segregationist ideology.

12. Ideologies, like globalization, that remove interactive democratic Government, must be stopped.

13. Government school systems methodology of misleading the youth with false historical narratives, intended to exploit their rebelliousness, as a social engineering tactic in order to distract from a Governmental globalist agenda to disengage society from the political processes must be stopped.

14. Clearly these political ideologies are on their last leg as the middle class has had its fill of these lies created

by the communist Frankford School. This scam is on its last leg and experiencing push back by the majority who are clearly being discriminated against and under the attack of the state. This social engineering by western nations has to be stopped.

The experience of all ages and nations, I believe, demonstrates that the work done by slaves, though it appears to cost only their maintenance is in the end the dearest of any. A person who can acquire no property can have no other interest but to eat as much and to labour as little as possible. Whatever work he does beyond what is sufficient to purchase his own maintenance, can be squeezed out of him by violence only, and not by any interest of his own.

Book III, Chapter II

The Wealth of Nations

~ Adam Smith ~

5th Chapter
SOCIAL MARXISM

The current backlash is a uniquely western revolution that is well on its way to becoming a growing political movement, that is about to radically transform western politics and society. The Trump matrix allied with the electorally, numerically, superior working class; created a new election winner by getting the "king maker", the working class vote alongside. This left the elites with divided minorities and no large base of support, only manipulative minorities. On the surface these two groups, the working class and the wealthy have little common ground: - They both want independence, and Government that stays out of their private affairs. The genius of Donald Trump is he understood the current class warfare well enough, to see how divided America has become. This was the Trump revolution, his genius to intellectually see where the division was, and wedge it open like a clam with his political knife. This has brought about the toppling of the white-collar elite bourgeoisie and their social control operations temporarily. The cause continues to spread spontaneously across Europe, with Brexit and local elections. I predict eventually not only the rest of both North Americas, but also South America and worldwide. Peoples are beginning to be mentally deprogrammed from the state's indoctrination by open worldwide communication via the internet. The extortion of people by central banks in the financial realm, as will be explored in one of the following chapters, will follow this reform in tandem I believe we cannot reform only Government to repair the system and end the parasitic exploitation.

FOLLOWERS OF THE SOCIAL COMMUNISM ARE PASSÉ

The Frankfurt school conspiracy of social engineering the west has finally been exposed as a cold war period, KGB sedition project. Vying for positions in Government, the Frankfurt School's sedition by infiltration project, would see communists put into positions of academic administration where they could by autocratic rule, implement their communistic disinformation policies from above in the educational hierarchy of the west, and could remove all opponents in academia; today they have largely succeeded. This is an excellent example of long-term Soviet-Communist espionage planning, and social infiltration. The Soviets excelled at sedition as an infiltration technique. The Social Marxist KGB engineered espionage program for destruction of western society still goes on and must come to an end. The fall of the Berlin wall was their official funeral, yet communism still haunts us via the, Frankfurt School. Social Communism, multiculturalism, political correctness, control of media, Globalism are all a part of the program as designed by the Frankfurt School social engineering program that is well documented, in plain sight to read their social manipulations planned. The program consists of:

- Politically correct speech control.

- Multiculturalism.
- Globalization.
- Destruction of the family.
- Radical feminism.

Frankfurt School Professors were all avowed communist from Germany, working on plans for the KGB in the west to subvert the west into becoming a communist dictatorship, by undermining the social structure to create social instability providing opportunity for a communist takeover from the civil war created by these divisive policies: "Divide and conquer". The Frankfurt school's indoctrination includes many professional politicians and especially academics and young academics. Political correctness is their weapon of choice to silence opposition to their agenda. Political correctness, multiculturalism, extreme feminism and social engineering teaching social communism in university humanities courses, to indoctrinate the youth, and espousing another of their communist ideas; Globalism. This is the legacy of these professors and their creations, circulated worldwide also; all recoded in publicly available documents. Add to these corrupt western politicians, who for their part, did not care if the working class was impoverished, as they sold off their positions of authority to others, even if their behaviour was a fiduciary conflict of interest. There was no obstacle to corrupt politicians or the Frankfurt school. The political classes' outright sold-out their own people, for their own narcissistic personal financial benefit; which distracted the powers that be as long as they themselves lived well, that was the political ruling classes' only concern is self-interested social deception. A sense of entitlement and greed are their motivations. Their civil service is used to being repressive towards the working class, despite in reality being white collar workers themselves, they have become very condescending towards others of the working class. Deception and greed are their ethics. Perhaps this is the result of getting away with their two-faced corrupt politics for far too long. Clearly the left-wing elite have no sympathies for the working class either. Left wing political parties have followed the Frankfurt school and become political parties of minorities. They certainly do not represent the people, after decades of betrayal by their ideology; this has become clear concerning the left.In 2016 the people took a chance and elected Donald J. Trump as President of the United States. I believe this may be the start of a preference for non-traditional candidates and a new Libertarian resurgence, as we realize how absolutely incompetent big Government has been. In essence western society is fed up with the University based Social Communist ideology and all its tenants, also the parasitic pilfering and constant lies of politicians. The ruling class in the west have characterized the working class as idiots and see themselves as their better. This condescending reality has not escaped the working classes detection. Having no political options remaining, the working class switched loyalties to the wealthy Donald Trump in the United States, and the rest of the world is waiting for the same type of revolution hoping for reformation. The fundamental roots of this radical shift in politics was economic, combined with disconnected politicians.

This is the product of the seeds planted by the Frankfurt school's sedition which has been exposed not only in its conspiracy, but also the seeds in society of social communism's destruction of social cohesion in the west as is currently under way. The Frankfurt school team worked for decades creating subversive communist ideas, literature, promotion and infiltrated of the North American (western) educational systems as administrators who brought in and promoted more like-minded individuals, by identifying ways to implement communist ideology, through sedition. The education system of the west was seen by the KGB to be a key into the homes and minds of western nations to manipulate the minds of the youth and exploit this western weakness; pure genius as a long-term espionage program and strategy! Indoctrinate your enemy as explained by Soviet dissident Yuri Bezmenov in many videos now available on YouTube, by attacking inside its borders, and infiltrate institutions to utilize the naivety of youth. None of the social communist changes such as political correctness, multiculturalism and others are organic; they are part of an old cold war, KGB infiltration program. Unfortunately, the Frankfurt school members were not exposed or deported to the former Soviet Union during the cold war. Obviously Western intelligence was far too focused upon foreign wars, and doing the bidding of their corporate oligarch masters, to see the enormity long term of the threat within the nation infiltrating and creating education-based sedition or realizing what it would become when manifested in the future (today). Then there is big Government, and their distraction by social engineering and other self-interested policies by vested interests. Tyrants always resort to violence which is an admission that his victim is superior to him. Tyranny is the exasperation of the intellectual inferior. Utopian ideas almost always fail, because they are tyrannical by nature. What do you do in Utopia with those who disagree with your ideology? Usually those that disagree are persecuted as in the former genocidal Soviet Union or forced to leave if you're a Hutterite; your utopia is my hell on earth!

THE SOVIET CONNECTION

The former Soviet Union via the KGB was very good at manifesting local sedition in other countries. They had agents all over the world facilitating those who espoused communist ideas in key positions during the cold war. During the cold war one of the groups they covertly supported was the "Frankfurt School". Russian President Vladimir Putin is well aware, I am convinced of these undercover efforts. Being a former KGB man and now leader of Russia, he has clamped down on seditious social communist movements in his country, since he knows how effective the seditious enemy within the state can be. For decades social communist activities went on in the west, right under the noses of western Governments. They swayed unsuspecting politicians towards social communist, socially divisive policies without their knowing what was afoot; multiculturalism, political correctness, globalism and other communist ideologies covertly supported by the former Soviet Union, via the spy agency the KGB. One leader was not fooled by this social deconstruction project is former KGB man Vladimir Putin, now President of Russia. Clearly, he knew where the ideology came from, and passed laws to ensure his country was not infected by the social division diseases that were devised to create social discord by the Frankfurt school under the assistance of the KGB in the old Soviet sedition plot. The creation of social communist social division was the KGB's greatest success. The Soviet era dissident Yuri Bezmenov can be found on YouTube videos explaining in great detail how this was accomplished. While US intelligence services focused on foreign wars, the Soviets focused upon internal sedition inside the borders of the United States, Canada and Western Europe, left alone by western Governments security apparatus, whom it appears did nothing to counter act this sedition.

I encountered a Russian gentleman in the Hong Kong airport in 2010 by chance. We sparked up a conversation while I was waiting for a connecting airline flight, as he was also. Was it boredom, or simply wanting to confess his sins, I have no idea, to me it was an entertaining conversation at the time. This rather elderly gentleman told me he was soon retiring, and that he had spent his career in the KGB working all over the world. He informed me of this KGB program quite by chance in our conversation that started out quite harmlessly regarding the trend of Western men marrying Asian women. He seemed very matter of fact; stoic, and very highly intelligent, he spoke with a thick Russian accent in a very slow, calm, very matter of fact way. I don't think he cared if I believe his story or not. He explained to me that; this western cultural change of political correctness etc. was a KGB creation. I had no reason to doubt he was what he claimed to be, given we were in the Hong Kong China airport. So, there was little reason for me to doubt the truth of his comments, I am just nobody I thought. He seemed to have no fear in telling me this story. On one level it was just a random airport waiting room conversation between two foreigners far from home. I thought most likely everything he was telling me was either the absolute truth or a complete fiction, but he connected all the dots to the story. Years later I must admit that the more I researched it, the more it appears the facts of what he called, "The Frankfurt School"; which he claimed the KGB planted like a seed in the United States to circulate sedition, to be the absolute truth. I felt convinced by his demeanor and depth of detail that he must be some kind of spy or Government intelligence officer, because he knew so much about cultural Marxism and its foundations in the "Frankfurt School". "This was an old KGB program"; he explained. "The intention of the program during the cold war was a strategy to promote sedition through the Universities". The intention he said, was to, "create social division, and by disinformation and spreading dead end philosophies, create social division that would be insidious, like planting a hidden virus into a computer that eventually completely corrupts the computer making it unworkable and useless". For decades during the cold war this KGB operation was circulating sedition via works coming out of the Frankfurt School and thus I have explained it herein. It was a bizarre and fascinating revelation. Boy, have we been scammed! I have no idea why he confessed all this to me, perhaps he just wanted to get if off his chest by telling this to a random Canadian guy would make no difference. He seemed to laugh it all off as somehow being comical. My impression according to him was that even the KGB underestimated, and were amazed by how well this ploy actually worked out. He did say that, they never thought that post-modernist ideas would be so broadly accepted, since its genesis is the undermining of society by depicting everyone as a victim, thus falsely blaming society for every misfortune that has befallen upon the person. Like he said, "we all have normal misfortune that's just life". But, "turning that misfortune into a fictional conspiracy of the patriarchy was pure genius". I asked him what his job was in the KGB. To which he burst out in a roaring laugh that echoed down the halls of the airport building. Then once he calmed down, with a great big grandfatherly smile, he looked me in the eye and said in a whisper, tapping my lap with his right index finger; "Trouble maker", he said. "Yea"; he said; "I spent my life all over the world making trouble that was my job". I nodded at him and muttered under my breath; - "hmmm, interesting". I turned away from him and went silent as did he and I went inward into my own mind deep in thought. I considered; what if nothing he said is a lie?

What if everything that synchronicity has just informed me of is all true? I thought, this is perhaps the greatest true conspiracy story ever in history. It takes war to an all new level. No armies, no killing with weapons, just releasing socially toxic ideas, and letting the society and their own Government destroy itself. This makes physical military conflict look like monkeys flinging stones at each other. After seven years of independent research, I verified by fact checking the old Soviet spy's story by researching the details he exposed to me during that fate filled meeting in Hong Kong airport back in 2010. Our flights arrived and boarding was announced over the airport speakers, and I told him it was a pleasure talking to him. The old gentleman tipped his head in a bow with a smile and we departed company, never exchanging names or any other information, each going our separate ways. Strange, how the greatest secrets sometimes, leak out. If he thought I was anyone of relevance I'm without doubt, he would have never said a word about it. I have thus concluded that by not recognizing the dangers of importing European Communists, like those in the Frankfurt School, that this was the American Intelligence services greatest failure in bringing into America the Frankfurt school Trojan horse. The purpose of the KGB's social communism strategy as was explained to me was to divide the western society into camps all claiming victimhood by the society's structure. The Soviets infiltrated with communists into places of higher learning through academics. To assist in the promotion of those who philosophically were communists, communist doctrine and social communist ideas were devised in this plot to bring down the west from within, with false ideologies that would undermine social cohesion and thus bring down capitalism. The free enterprise system by indoctrinating the youth who are too pragmatically ignorant to realize what was being foisted with post modernism, would take years for them to realize they were pawns in an international espionage plot. That what they learnt in University was indoctrinated by their teachers from other teachers, then to school policies. Then this spread into the minds of pupils in schools everywhere. It was implanted in millennial minds and others to justify every rebel without a cause.

The heads of the Frankfurt school were German immigrant communists and their project was a decade's long development of strategies and ideas that could be implemented in the west to subvert the youth with divisive ideas of victimhood. Tell the kids they are victims in school, which has been their center of brainwashing since elementary. Kids in university believe anything the professors teach them, including post modernism, which as explained was a Soviet intelligence program for western cultural suicide. Young girls under the feminism banner, were and are, its greatest supporters, because always being a victim means you can do anything and still be innocent; it's a victim complex created out of an inferiority complex. It's really a very irresponsible ideology designed for immature childlike minds, but it was designed as sedition, so it only has to pollute the mind for a few years. Thus, it is taught in universities worldwide as humanities, even university faculties have demonstrated they're not so intelligent either, in buying into a seditious espionage social construct. It was a long-term espionage game plan, best yet, the brainwashed would pay the university to be indoctrinated with social sedition and rebellion, which imparted no economic benefit to the student long term; - It is a total waste of education dollars and time. The Frankfurt Schools plan did start to bear fruit decades later through their persistence, just as the Soviet Union was crumbling. This successful subversion plan encountered one serious problem; that being that the Soviet political system collapsed; the economics of communism had collapsed. Not able to admit the failure of their philosophy these communists continued with the promoting their agenda, now after years on auto pilot. We see that this aftertaste of the Soviet espionage program has borne fruit, after the collapse of their failed economic system. Yet indoctrinated western children raised under the state's education system fail to realize that most of those who graduated from this top down contamination of western children's minds, "has now born fruit". Western educators and Governments now unknowingly still indoctrinated the youth in postmodern communist ideology, in a covert long-term communist / Soviet based espionage plan. A plan that is socially toxic and designed as an espionage program to undermine the very fabric of western social cohesion through creating divisions, which would destroy western capitalism; - nothing less than pure genius!

We in the west have a big job ahead of us to deprogram our indoctrinated children, created by an education system that did not properly vet leaders in academia, but rather enabled their internal promotion and positioning of those who shared their toxic communist ideology of post modernism. To this day, we have academic institutions teaching social communist doctrine to our children still. Now we can see the results politically with a naïve ruling class that also has communist ideas and yet are blind to the fact they have been indoctrinated in their education by a KGB plot to divide western nations internally so they would be ripe for takeover by communism; - thus undermining western civilization. We need to wake up from our slumber and recognize the opposing side was playing for keeps. The flip on this is, it was intended to create a flip to communism, and it looks like it handed western civilization over to Islam as an unintended consequence. The outcome has yet to play out.

I think a person who takes a job in order to live - that is to say, for the money - has turned himself into a slave. Work begins when you don't like what you're doing. There's a wise saying: make your hobby your source of income. Then there's no such thing as work, and there's no such thing as getting tired. That's been my own experience. I did just what I wanted to do. It takes a little courage at first, because who the hell wants you to do just what you want to do; they've all got lots of plans for you. But you can make it happen.

~ Joseph Campbell ~

6th Chapter
A LIBERTARIAN ECONOMIC PLAN

Some people who claim to be libertarian might be wondering if what is espoused here is libertarian in fact. Here are some key points to ponder. If you don't want any Government even one that is controlled, no social programs etc., this is where there is a divide in concepts. If you don't want any rules, regulation or structure, then it's time to realize you're not a libertarian; -you're most likely an anarchist! Libertarianism is a realistic philosophy. Libertarianism is about voluntary subscription to having Government involvement in our lives. It's about free choice, and free will, Government free from extortion of the citizen.

1. Libertarianism is mainly about voluntary subscription to Government initiatives; it's about free will and free choice to pick Government services like cherries on a tree; "Yes, I want this or No, I don't want to pay for, or have that".
2. Libertarians see Government as an organizing necessary evil they want to control Government and not have Government control them through extortionist universal taxes and programs, but rather taxation and initiatives of Government by subscription and pay as you use systems.
3. Libertarians see Government as exploitive in terms of land use. We want to constitutionally prohibit all

property taxes and fees charged for that which is a citizen's birth right to own and use property unmolested.
4. Libertarians would give all citizens the right to Government financing of home mortgages, by having the central bank finance interest free mortgages for citizens.
5. Enabling the citizen to acquire a mortgage directly, through a Government provided, zero interest fully flexible mortgage loan. Rather than the current system of, the bank lending out money they got free from the Government and adding bank interest.

PROPERTY RIGHTS

The Libertarian dream is to provide the opportunity of every citizen to purchase and own a home interest free, to have security of your home, free from any and all forms of lien and or repossession. This to libertarians is a fundamental human right to have inviolable property rights; absolute security of home.

1. Rich or poor, pay or not; pay now or pay later, we all have the right to live unmolested in a home. This would be a way the libertarian state distributes money into the supply system and is one of two Libertarian social programs. Flexible Government home mortgages would pay builders for their efforts and constructions. Mortgages charging interest would not be permitted on non-business home property purchases.

2. Liberty begins with economic freedom and independence from mortgage indenture sanctions against your home. Mortgages would be a line of credit that the home buyer can suspend payments on anytime and still maintain all ownership rights to the home for life under special provisions.

3. This system will be the removal of fear from loss of your home and provide the security we have a human right to. This would aid economic productivity and along with other reforms, would be a complete restructure of the current economic system that would sprout invigorated entrepreneurial activity by creating the right conditions.

ENABLING SELF RESPONSIBILITY

The home ownership process outlined herein, combined with the payment of dividends to citizens as explained here will completely alter the economic and social bases of western society. Libertarianism I believe, poses a serious pragmatically superior and competitive political option to the communistic welfare state. Libertarianism frees citizens, and can provide not only greater economic individual liberty, but also personal independence of the family and individual based upon personal responsibility. Given almost a century of communist tyranny and murderous regimes that murdered millions of people wherever it has been attempted, clearly the failure of communism mandates it and all its controlling social engineering desires be relegated to the dustbin of history as a concept that is a complete pragmatic failure, out of tune with the true nature of human beings, thus always results in tyranny.

Libertarian reforms would offer freedom of optional choice and eliminate the need for welfare and other such programs in a responsible way, since even in the most difficult of circumstances having flexible shelter enables the citizen to survive and endure hardship independently, thus greatly reduces the social burden of poverty in a responsible way. There would also be the Government distribution of dividends from resource royalties and other Government income to all citizens that could be paid monthly or as an annual lump sum. Dividend payments would thus provide an incentive for citizens to desire minimal Government, as Government growth would cut into their individual shareholder dividend.

LIBERTARIAN ENABLING INDEPENDENCE

The reality is that Libertarianism is about individuals taking self-responsibility and determining for yourselves that which your family needs. Libertarianism changes the family economy and promotes personal economic growth under free enterprise.

1. Citizens will freely choose to opt into their menu choices of social programs and the education of your children.

2. What the citizen receives is selected from a menu of choices in Government program options.

3. The Government will distribute dividends from its income amongst citizens, who can buy services for the family as you desire from a Government menu of choices in each category according to your family needs.

ITS ALL ABOUT FREEDOM OF CHOICE

The defining aspect of libertarianism is that all these constructs of Government, except home mortgages will be open to private sector competition and must be on a voluntary subscription basis. The Libertarian Government will incorporate non-profit health insurance foundations. There shall be a variety of Government organized voluntary health care system policy options. A variety of public education systems in a menu for parents to choose. A public highway system plan based upon pre-purchased subscriptions. Libertarianism believes that taxes you pay should be on a voluntary subscription bases, determined by those programs you desire to freely subscribe to. Like a private insurance subscription, every family will decide what services they desire to subscribe to each year from a pool of Government programs and initiatives, and your tax rate is determined by your Government services you subscribe to.

1. Not subscribing annually does not mean you cannot access the service, it merely means that like a toll

highway you must pay each time you use it as toll for the service. Under libertarianism these Government programs are user pay by subscription or pay tolls per use. There is no income tax, thus maintenance and construction must be compensated.

2. Gas taxes on fuel as a present would continue to pay for roads and road construction so there would-be toll-free use of most roads.

3. Citizens start at a basic zero income tax payable rate and may subscribe to payments of, payroll taxes, or use national dividend earnings to pay for services. Citizens can subscribe to such programs as Government pensions, health care, road use permits etc. The other option is a payment plan if used or pay as you go options.

4. There would be a variety of public health insurance and voucher-based education systems to choose from. Personal choice is always the core of Libertarian Government services and creating fiduciary non-profit insurance corporations offering different tiers of services is one of the roles of Government, also to assign Project Managers to create optional non-profit corporations, with programs according to public need, and create the conditions for non-profit private NGO service providers. Cantons may also provide these services based upon popular determination of the Canton.

HOW WE BECAME DEBT SLAVES

Back in the middle ages and beyond, feudal land tenure was based upon land stolen by military force, taken by groups of thugs later relabelled Governments. Land theft under feudal economics grants the thief of land, the head of this state / mafia / Lord / Barron / King or other sovereign ownership by virtue of ability through repressive force called an army, the right by force to steal land and turn its utilization into an enrichment scheme. To use this scheme to indenture or enslave people to a life of servitude to pay the land thief, creating citizen's life time serfdom via indenture, with laws tailored to facilitate usury that keeps people impoverished for life. Government / Royalty creates serfdom in similar feudally based economic models. If not taking a share of the crop in perpetuity from labour production on land, then in current times by extortion or the document called mortgage loans charging interest (years of free labour output being charged) out of thin air. Causing the citizen to work longer than the value of consideration given as a loan, so that via adding usurious interest, the bank by compounding interest accumulates by two to three hundred percent more than the mortgage granted to supply the purchase price. The Government (central bank) thus provides money free to all parties in the transaction except the borrower, who in reality is completely ripped off for decades of his/her life. This is not an accident. Clearly it is fully intentional for exploitation. This raises some interesting questions that obviously demonstrate collusion, for example:

1. What entitles a financer who contributed nothing to proceeds? The capital loaned by the banks for example is not their money in reality or practice, but rather is provided / created out of thin air originally by the Government. The value of the money is the theft of the labours of the borrower mortgagee. Thus, lenders collect interest for Government issued money after contributing nothing!

2. Why does this useless usurious middle man call a mortgage loan exist at all? All funds for these transactions are a Government creation loaned to the bank; - where is the banks collateral?

3. Why not lend directly to the borrower? Of course, there would be no profit from the labours of others in exchange for nothing, from stolen land/property to which the Government has no title only extortion power over.

4. Other than to orchestrate theft from the working class to keep them impoverished by interest payments. This usurious scam of mortgages and its earlier form of feudalism has impoverished more people over the centuries than any other fraud. The end of parasitic land ownership and use rules. The end of parasitic funding the elite, on the backs of workers with exorbitant interest on loans; funding the bourgeoisie lifestyle is on its last leg.

5. Government often pretends to be charitable by creating and giving citizens welfare from money made from the land they stole from the people. Their reliance upon various forms economic deception perpetrated upon the working class due to impoverishment from land theft, is a long bitter experience.

6. Fortunately for them, the establishment have not figured out how to charge wild animals rent for their homes upon the land that is their terrestrial right to inhabit. Humans have the same natural right of occupation that has been corrupted by the parasitic brutality of the state. This is a natural birth right divinely given to us as terrestrials upon this planet. The only real value in land is in compensation for labour that belongs to the worker, less depreciation from ageing of those creations or constructions. Properties construction depreciates as they age and do not appreciate in price in reality, unless the location adds value due to supply and demand resulting from higher property densities.

7. The new economic and social structure must be implemented to enable the middle class to continue to prosper, despite technology bringing an end to full time and life time employment. The feudal economy has run its course; time for a revised economic model.

8. The land rightfully belongs to the nation's citizens. Personal homes should thus be financed by the Government interest free, tax free, and with flexible repayments that permit unlimited term payment suspensions. This feudal surf economy has leached off the working class, by force of brutality to create life time indenture forced upon us and has gone on for far too long.

9. Society must supply economic breaks to those who have children and families, in order to encourage family unity by creation of incentives. Life is like an inverted pyramid in that senior childless couples often have minor or no mortgages, while those who need such a financial break will not see this until retirement. The cost burden of families and children are temporary often spanning two decades. Why not allow the financial break of these payments when it is most needed? When children are at home needing education, healthcare and other needs? Government now provides most mortgage funds, why not cut out the bank middle man? This can be done at no cost to the state and great social benefit to families.

10. I anticipate that given the weak economic performance in the west that this will facilitate new home-based businesses to develop as the only alternative for many families to survive the coming economic transition and that there will be in fact no choice but to find a way to stabilize the lives of the

people with some economic way to survive. The establishment might very well adopt my reforms offered here, if only to prevent massive impoverishment and resulting social revolt as a means for them to attempt to survive through the coming economic onslaught.

THE NEW JUDICIAL STRUCTURE

The judicial system of lawyers to me is like a swamp filled with human leaches and other social parasites feeding upon working class labour, production and creation, of wealth. Most lawyers work is but overpriced routine administration processes any clerk could easily do in civil law, these matters should be attended to by notaries, as most legal work could and should be performed by them. Most of what lawyers do is to agitate matters already hostile. Lawyers make these matters worse by incitement and circulation of offense upon individuals. When lean and efficient Libertarian Government takes over, removing unnecessary judicial interference in citizen's private affairs will be accommodated by a simplified and streamlined process utilizing standardized forms and administrative reviews. The saber rattling of lawyers is completely superfluous and makes things worse. Threatening and cajoling people as lawyers do is completely unnecessary stress upon litigants and only pads lawyer's billings with nonsense. It prolongs proceedings unnecessarily, and in no way enhances the process of justice.

A LIBERTARIAN FINANCIAL STRUCTURE | RESTRUCTURING SELF-RELIANCE.

Much as industrialization has led to the suburb being created, the new future of insecure contract work will require fundamental economic structural reorganization to maintain social peace. A new future with a self-reliant libertarian home ownership social security system will be implemented as a necessity. Centered upon a Government home and land securitized consumer banking system being created.

1. This Government Bank will provide exclusively, interest free line of credit type consumer mortgages, and small business, mortgage securitized start-up loans for all citizens, based upon equity built up. This would be exclusively Government funded, without the nation's central bank charging any interest.

2. This new system will be outside the current speculators realm as a "Parallel Banking System", to circulate new money into the economy. Consumer home loans would be supplied as life time interest free mortgage lines of credit, which cannot exceed the equity of the home asset.

3. This shall be a new very low-cost type of social security program based upon broad home ownership. This shall be in effect for all citizens as a floating account balance that cannot exceed the home's value. These mortgages shall be interest fee free floating debt instruments for life, with no connection to commercial business banking. Instead of paying central banks interest to circulate money, money circulation would start with mortgages and connected line of credit loans from the Government based upon home equity.

4. This national mortgage finance company shall conduct mortgage loans and small business start-up loans exclusively. Mortgage loans need to be nationalized in order to create this new form of social security program that will replace current welfare programs with a new form of homestead loan system.

TYPES OF BANKS

Two types of banking will be conducted by separate kinds of institutions.

1. Commercial Banks and lenders that would consist of existing banks that would conduct all types of loans as they presently do but be prohibited from consumer mortgages and any financing involving residential consumer properties. Business mortgage banking needs to be separated from consumer mortgage loans.
2. All mortgages on a citizen's principal residence will be interest free and direct from the Government mortgage bank.
3. The rationale for Government mortgages is that, in reality Governments already through middle men, distribute and supply mortgages to circulate money into the economy.
4. Government funding all mortgages through the central bank is not a novel idea given most mortgages indirectly already come from Government.

5. Though this would severely affect the liquidity of banks. Banks would need to raise capital on the capital markets though securities offerings.

There is really no need for the bank middle man in the mortgage process, since it only adds to the cost of home ownership needlessly.

PARALLEL BANKING

A parallel mortgage banking system needs to be implemented to deal with the loss of working-class upward mobility and prevent social discord and unrest, due to mechanization of manufacturing into the future. The future of working will be a growing self-employment movement. Because of inevitable precarious employment. Home based companies in the future will be able to achieve production with minimal labour input, even part time employment would thus enable self-sufficiency. This new Government perspective on home mortgages is designed to create self-reliance, enable citizens to fund any new small business ventures they desire by availing seed capital.

1. To enable self-reliance and entrepreneurship, provide security for all citizens because incomes will become more precarious in future years.
2. To ensure some type of social security that will be necessary.
3. This approach is one that will provide the lowest cost in terms of taxation upon citizens to maintain social

harmony, consumer security and political stability long term.

4. This would also be to disable consumer-based mortgage backed securities, which the Government would assume ownership of the consumer loan portion.

THE FUTURE OF WORK

The working class can expect in future years, increased mass robotic mechanization of all work processes, insecure contract work, and short-term jobs. Thus, opportunity to develop various self-reliant small-scale home-based business can only be possible with secure low-cost home ownership to stabilize the economic situation of the working class. Otherwise there will be a possible social collapse due to fundamental economic and business changes currently in process. Not dealt with this could cause a collapse of western civilization. There must be a pressure relief valve given to the people to ease the economic transformation. Taxation I would expect as a source of Government revenue will decreased in sync with wide scale employment dislocation, preceding such an economic collapse of employment opportunities due to the computerization and robotics revolution in technology underway.

Based upon non-compulsory principal payments, monthly payments that can be extended and postponed as the citizen desires up to lifetime payments for shelter. This new Government system will replace the current welfare state social agenda with a libertarian system designed to encourage citizen independence and self-reliance with very little funded social programs beyond this mortgage program. The guaranteed home ownership loan provision shall be a lifetime completely flexible loan operating like a suspendable line of credit with payments the mortgagee shall determine as necessary. There is always the long-term erosion of this debt that will erode its principal value, thus making such loans easy to repay in twenty years or so. This new type of social support system centered upon a new system of land financing will include, removing tax based social welfare, yet encourage self-reliance, with shelter security and a flexible payment ability. The major expense of shelter needs to have its cost reduced since it currently disproportionately turns average people into indentured slaves for life in western countries consuming thirty to forty percent of net incomes, in lean economic times this payment program will be a tremendous economic boost also. If we do not implement such a program massive homelessness will become a huge problem. This is a way to provide relief and an opportunity for citizens to have a base to use their talents towards self-employment from home.

Too much capital is being wasted in the home allocation process and speculation by house flipping, rather than development of productive enterprises. That process needs to be amended to diminish flipping that does not create wealth to a more stable system that promotes entrepreneurship. Without mortgage worries, it is expected that entrepreneurship and real productive wealth creating business will flourish.In the residential ownership and construction economic sector, too much capital is being wasted, and not enough goes into new business and entrepreneurial economic growth activities. The disproportionate diversion of the wealth of the nation state has been diverted to enslave the working class currently and in the past with mortgage loans; it has always been too exploitive. Both Family financial security and self-employment of all types can be made possible by these homestead loans, where in equity from a home or home business, mortgage down payment is treated like a personal line of credit that citizens can utilize throughout their lives to provide home security or to pay down and draw upon at will as a Government line of credit for other purposes. This is in my opinion is truly a revolutionary social program. Homelessness will cease to exist and both entrepreneurship and innovation will increase. I will explore this again later in this book. Obviously, some will not be entrepreneurial, but I have noticed that entrepreneurism is really not rare, but rather a normal human condition since the dawn of history. It is a part of human nature in fact, repressed by lack of opportunity to grow, from micro businesses. Because current society and its exploited debt-based system limits opportunities.

THE WORKING-CLASS STRUGGLE

The bourgeoisie have been selling out society for their own financial benefit for far too long. They have become disconnected from the working class and failed to see that in fact they are over privileged working-class workers with white collar jobs and Government influence, which are well paid. These privileges and opportunities are now going to come to an end as their layers of self-promotion, corrupt institutions through law in abusing everyone has run its course, an economic revolution is about to sprout, and we must prepare. The working class in reality need jobs and a guarantee of personal shelter, food security, and the Government needs to get out of their personal lives. This will revolutionize and energise western innovation, leading to revolutionary economic change in the west. By promoting working class independence and self-reliance through a home / equity mortgage security program, this will eliminate indenture by interest, and thus eliminate social program dependence, reducing Governmental need for taxation to fund citizen's livelihoods. The working class in reality needs jobs, as the great welfare system is now terminally ill. The working class are the people who literally built every nation in the west. All they ever wanted was as Franklyn D. Roosevelt used to say is: "A square deal" let's start regarding shelter, meaning mortgage finance reform. In point of fact there always has been a greater philosophical connection between the one percent and the rugged individualism of the working class. While they are lifestyle worlds apart, they are connected by a philosophy of:

1. Workers want a "leave me alone Government". A get off my back perspective and shared belief in libertarianism.

2. Both the working class and the wealthy do not like the "middle men". The bankers, lawyers, judges,

politicians, or other elite in the media and Hollywood who are seen as interlopers and social engineers.

3. Home & property security would replace virtually all welfare state programs and reduce all personal debt and income taxes as a result and reduce Government involvement in our personal lives.

4. Funds raised from land use and other royalties and Government revenue after the cost of state administration will be distributed like annual dividends to all citizens regardless of age. Children's share is to be applied for education, healthcare plans and other child development determinations of the parents in trust. According to family needs each family will determine distribution of these funds.

Western society is facing tumultuous times with the technological revolution. Enormous employment dislocation is on the immediate horizon. This situation can be delayed, but it cannot and will not stop. The future will necessitate a new economic model that reforms the old and restores a sense of security and prosperity within society. Most importantly entrepreneurship must be encouraged to fill the enormous void mechanization will create. Self-determination and self-reliance will help grow the economy. Family sovereignty will replace state dictates and interference in the family and economy. It has always been entrepreneurial activity that is a natural human condition that has developed the economy.

Essentially, we must trust our fellow citizens to be innovative again and build a new economy and to ensure they have the tools to do the job.

THE ECONOMIC REVOLUTION

Social change without a vision is very dangerous, since it can lead to Civil War. The use of forced violent Government repression is not and will never be a solution and only lead to a new "dark age" and a war of attrition, where no one wins with wide scale terrorism and all it's tragic consequences, which no-one of any class or social strata will be immune. We will have no option other than this type of social reform, because of impending mass under employment without this type of reform. The west cannot and will not survive as a civilized society; if this erupts. Perhaps Islamization and the tyranny of Sharia-law is being implemented by certain western Governments in an attempt to return to a repressive society of the type the west experienced in the past. I don't believe that this elitist idea could work and will only create civil war. Further complicating a problematic circumstance.

THE MECHANIZATION REVOLUTION

New comers to the west not from our heritage; lack cultural perspective and understanding. This strikes to the core of a nation's identity, ignoring culture is destroying society. Because my society has lost its way from its roots, and its foundation; it is now rudderless. Ruthlessness, with a loss of historical affinity, the soul of a nations being is in essence about cultural connection. The loss of common heritage, and history of our cultural "story", our history is the very foundation of our society. The drifting western nation state and its identity convoluted, has been a very dangerous development, undermining our social confidence, and thus resulting in minimal economic development. Because low skilled, poorly educated migrants add no economic value and only displace domestic workers. Technologically based innovation is needed under the current economic conditions, not unskilled labour. In recent decades in most developed countries, workers are finding that work is far scarcer in the form of good paying reliable jobs, with decent wages sufficient to raise a family with. Stay at home unemployed youth have been displaced by immigration from entry level jobs are not getting any real-world work experience.

Feudalism lost out to industrialization, now the last vestiges of feudal land tenure needs to be replaced by this new "entrepreneurial revolution" in self-employment. We need to encourage innovation and rejuvenation, and that people are independent as Libertarian citizens.

THE BETRAYAL OF HISTORY

Companies manufacturing products invented here, created and perfected here in the west, built by citizens living here have had those jobs taken away. Their technologies exported, and their jobs relocated. Their facilities have been relocated elsewhere; workers are not happy! Meanwhile our Governments have impudently just let industry leave with our creations and achievements. We now import those products that are our inheritance, which we once created, are now imported from foreign lands. What made the west great was our ability to create. To this day inventions from innovative individualistic western cultures fuel the world's development. Our industries leave our nations to take advantage of others for abusive and exploitive working conditions, for that which is not a living wage or civilized working conditions. Westerners for the most part have been the world's innovators and creators. The template of the modern world is the imitation of the successful innovations and industry of the west. There is something that does not sit right in the mind of allowing an industrialist or their ancestors, who choose to live here in this culture, having so little respect or concern for the workers from whose labours they have earned great wealth. They have so much disregard for their fellow citizens, as to take this away from us as a society; - it is like an act of treason. There is a perverted sense of arrogance and self-righteous detachment in our society that self justifies such psychopathic behaviour. It has become infectious, in that even those in Government accept money from foreign nations to legislate against their own people's interest. The sad part is that peoples in the west are amongst the most betrayed upon earth as a result. While some national Governments are self centered, they still have regard for their society's best interests. Industrial production in the west has largely been transferred to other nations. Industrialists speak of globalism, and worldwide free trade, in an effort to have the ability to import the same products tariff free, with obscene profits! They want their cake and the ability to eat it too. This is all being done to enslave the population. Granted, western Governments, society and culture, have increased the associated cost of the production of manufactured goods with regulations; requiring environmental responsibility, unionized working conditions that protect workers from injury, providing wages that are sufficient for workers to provide a good quality of life for a family, with generous pensions. Generally, this has meant clean environments with less pollution, healthier populations, and greater personal security upon the streets, relatively free from crime in the past. Kidnapping the wealthy for ransom does not occur as in some third world nations with higher crime rates, all this made the west a physically safer and much more comfortable place to live if you're wealthy. The wealthy overlook that they have more security in many ways in a more egalitarian society.

GOVERNMENT ATTACKING FAMILIES

If you're a man, given the high level of Government betrayal and duplicity in the west, Government betrayal takes another insidious form of social engineering, villainizing men and thus the integrity of the family unit that has been all too common a form of discrimination and outright bigotry, and enforced by western Governments in that they pander to the majority female vote that has been used to rule over western nations, and represses men. It's an interesting dichotomy when a group claims past repression, while being the majority voters that governments pander to with laws, all the while abusing the opposite gender with legislation to obtain advantage and making posture of being the underdog. It brings forth reminders of the Biblical tale of Eve advising poor naive Adam to eat the fruit of the tree of knowledge; then Adam gets punished into exile because of her bad advice. In war throughout history when your tribe loses, the men and children of the village are always killed in the takeover, and the women become concubines of the victors.

In western nations women virtually almost always get the custody of children and men lose their parental rights in the courts in this system of bigotry over ninety percent of the time. This system sees men as a guaranteed income source. A privatized welfare extortion racket to force others to pay the Governments welfare costs that would result from their policies, thus they need to interfere in families to ensure men are forced to pay for the Government undermining the family. The Government acts as a heavy-handed extortionist collection agency. While the co-owner (father), is responsible to pay for and support their property, in the case of children. In pragmatic reality, women own the children, and men are forced through Government coercion to pay for decades for that which the courts clearly say in their decisions is not the man's right to in any way to parent children equally, except as a financial support liability, an obligation. Concerning child support men are basically expected to pay and have no rights or say in child rearing, their parental rights are discarded for commission of no crimes, and no wrong doing. While the state moves into the man's home in a financial coup d'état, against men's biological parental rights, that are not respected. It's called custody, but within its definition is the extinguishing of the father's natural rights to be a parent with any authority or say regarding raising their own child. It's a clear unmitigated bigoted human rights violation against men, as it is clearly gender biased, that hurts the working class.Meanwhile, western Governments do not enforce civil laws, they make exception when it comes to interfering into private family matters. The Government acts like a surrogate father or "sugar daddy", is more apt a description. It's a privately funded surrogate Government welfare system that makes pretence that all men are pejoratively, lousy fathers, villains and scoundrels, who the state sanctions to be alienated from their children, their parental rights stripped from them. Men are turned into walking ATM machines and little more. A Government enforced extortionist cash for life lottery system replaces paternal love and care due to the resulting parental alienation. Women don't stay with their husbands anymore, when they can get free money guaranteed by Government, interference by extortion. Government enforces this income system. Western marriages have become a money-making enterprise for women who can toss out the man and still keep his income. Better yet, have children with different men and have a variety of payers in this business model. Government supporters think this system is benevolent, this system has no benevolence, it is a great act of anti-male and anti-family tyranny! This is not the function of Government to take sides or interlope into private citizens lives! Clearly with such benefits, is it any wonder with the Government's incentives for divorce, that western birth rates plummeting, and divorce has become an everyday occurrence?

Clearly the only change has been Government sponsoring family destruction and incentivising it with financial rewards. Once again it is clear Government and their Courts are incentivizing family destruction and doing grievous and treacherous damage to society by incentivising this family destruction, by trampling upon men's rights to equal child custody. Governments and certain women see men only as an income source now of no value to their children, despite numerous psychological studies demonstrating that this has severely damaged the children, which the divorce industry ignores. The "controversial" writings of America Author Ann Coulter provide many grim statistical facts regarding female single parenthood. Particularly grievous, is the betrayal and pejorative message to men being perpetrated by Governments in their interference into private civil law matters, and resulting attacks by Government using the full force of the state in acting as a collection agency for this travesty, destroying men's self-esteem; Once again Government is a tyrant! The Government viciously attacks men if they are late to pay due to job loss, or other financial difficulties, this extortion and child ransom, destroys men's credit, removes their drivers licences, suspends passports, seizes wages and bank accounts disabling them to pay their rent, and is responsible as one of the greatest causes of homeless western men; resulting from this Government tyranny. A lot of women see it as an entitlement, often times destroying men's' lives because of Government heavy handed extortion assaults. It is not sufficient that the father has had his parental rights relegated to that of a visitor with less say concerning the raising of his children than the lowliest Government official; they also continue to relentlessly and doggedly, pursue him for decades afterwards. Jeopardizing his employment by harassing employers, they also ensure he cannot move on in his life by continued Government harassment. In this civil law matter, Government is clearly outside interlopers, involving themselves with no invitation. Governments in the west are right now; destroying men's credit and ability to borrow money; cancelling their drivers licence thus their means to acquire a living; and often putting men in prison for a private civil matter such as this; if they do not pay this extortion. Overwhelmed and hiding in their bruised pride and self-esteem, many of these men commit suicide from the harassment, resort to drug and alcohol addiction, due to all the Government repression and years of being harassed and attacks by the Government. Having financial difficulties, these men (working class) cannot afford lawyers, and thus often end up in jail with a criminal record.This politically motivated Government interference in a private civil matter takes advantage of old customs of men being providers and makes them slaves. Meanwhile the resentment and embarrassment cause men to abandon their children's need for a father in their lives.

Many men move on from marriage failure to try again, by remarrying and creating new families; in these actions the Government also often destroys those families through harassment, as a result of their relentless Government attacks, thus often puts pressure upon new families, causes marital problems and stress upon those families with prior children in particular, that are trying to move on with their lives as often these families are struggling financially, particularly in today's economy. Clearly Government is anti-family, anti-children, and will sell its sole to any voting block it can pander to. Men of good character get absolutely no equal recognition in the western legal system as parents, even if they sacrificed their careers to be stay at home parents. There is a book called; Courts from Hell – Family Injustice in Canada, By Frank Simons. He explains the multi-Billion Dollar legal industry child custody cases are for lawyers and their motivation is to maintain this very lucrative business for lawyers that hurts children. This tyranny also harbours the multibillion-dollar judicial industry, an army of psychopathic lawyers, with a vested interest to perpetuate the system, they make a very comfortable living by scavenging other people's children's psychological welfare and pilfering the wealth of families. The multiple means by which Government betrays their own people in their self-interest over the public's best interest is the modern tyranny of national Governments. This circumstance clearly demonstrates why in so many of their actions, that Government must be controlled and restricted in its activities, otherwise it becomes a murderous tyrant in people's lives and for national economies.

What is often overlooked is the negative impact this family discord has upon children, the family, the people involved and the economy, in a society were psychopathic lawyers have traumatized men, so they now join groups like; "Men going their own way (M. G. T. O. W)". Often young men, traumatized by their fathers being villainized and not trusting women, raised exposed to a mother who expressed a negative impression of men by degrading men, like a feminine Nazi or Ku Klux Klan member, generated by their spite filled single mother. These young men, seeing all the bigotry a man must deal with, refuse to have children which has become very common amongst the youth in western nations who refuse to get married. It is not industry that has reduced the fertility rate of people in the west, it is mental illness caused by the trauma of the Government created family situation I have been describing, and so far, that is of issue. The way the word "divorce" is now thrown around in relationships as a rock at men, this smashes the marriages basic foundations. The normalization of family destruction, which is easier to get out of than a car purchase and sale contract, the dysfunctions are many and all reveal a very sick society in the west.

LIVING WITH TREASON

Have no doubt, the same people who export industries could live anywhere in the world, but they still for the most part continue to live in the west and enjoy those benefits and off shoots. The reason being they are mortal beings and also realize poverty is full of hazards. The present-day horrors of Chinese cities and the degradation of the environment might create cheaper products, but it also is equal to killing your own people to take short cuts to wealth. In fact, many Chinese industrialists recognize this, and want to leave their own country after destroying their environment to come to the west.

THE HOME-BASED BUSINESS REVOLUTION

Prior to the industrial revolution, there were primarily work at home economies of custom-made products. Items made in the home, varied from food gadgets to blacksmithing, clothing to medical and other services. Shop keepers lived upstairs from their business, there was little separation of work and home, and business was a family affair. There were shop keepers and trades who usually started from their home workshops. Let us not forget that Apple and Microsoft had their genesis in home garages.

The big transformation came in the post WWII period with the decline of the home business/shop keeper and low-cost cookie cutter manufacturing eliminating a lot of repair shops, making things cheaper to replace than repair. Though a lot of these businesses would still be pragmatically viable, commuting to work is preferable if only due to bribery of craftsmen with company pensions, high wages, holiday pay and a number of other incentives voluntarily introduced by industry. All of which is gone, now with globalization and mechanization by corporations more focused upon the bottom line. Companies have demonstrated resentment toward these payments they themselves often introduced to induce people to work for them in the first place. Historically reliable industrial wage jobs were seen in the west as wage slavery from a cultural perspective. Workers had to be induced with higher wages to take those "wage slave" jobs as an incentive, and the story of Henry Ford and the foundations of the Ford Motor Company, paying higher wages points to this fact. The second relevant aspect of this wage boost was it was the act which signalled the creation of the Great Western, "Middle Class" and 9 to 5 jobs.

Traditionally you sold things, not your time. But, in good faith the working class came to see that perhaps working for wages and big pensions might offer a better life, and it did for many decades of prosperity; – the golden age. Thus, industrial jobs though very trying, became more acceptable, even though much of it in assembly lines was mindless repetitive work. Steady, well paid, benefits and reliable work was a part of the contract with industry. One of the only western nations that has maintained their middle class in recent decades has been Germany. The Germans have done this through a preference to medium size companies that build products and create both value and quality products, protect workers' rights and combine school education and unions to be partners with industry. I believe there was also a strong sense of national identity attached to these traditional industries, and a history of industrial collaboration with other parts of society not seen in other nations, that had maintained "Pride of workmanship"; a term seldom heard these days. Why other nations could not or would not emulate this success with few exceptions such as Japan, points to a dishonesty within many western nations' administration and society. The fact is, despite unionization, most western Corporations felt a corporate responsibility towards their homeland. When the founders died over time, and others took over these Corporations, psychopaths took control. Social responsibility was replaced by extravagant executive pay, poor customer service and a culture of greedy self-righteousness, few of the corporate founders ever had. Thus, the future grew dark and foreboding as industry left North America to fulfill psychopathic financial profit motivated ambitions.

PROTECTING FUTURE INDUSTRIES AND JOBS

The old dirty industries are now gone offshore, but we in the west are still the same people as the descendants of so many industrial creations. We need to brush ourselves off and move forward towards our rebirth. Part of our rebirth must be provisions that prevent this type of industrial raping and espionage from ever occurring again. Libertarian nations need to make it a mandatory legal requirement in all corporate charters and law that in the future that all corporate charters contain a shareholder provision for companies exceeding twenty-five employees. In the national interest we must mandate that employees must initiate controlling voting rights over 50 percent or more of all a corporation voting shares going forward upon the founders' death. This may be the only way to maintain domestic industry. No employee would vote to export their own job and remove domestic industry, because they earn a living wage. The truth is the employees' more than public shareholders, have greater claim to a company's shares for their valuable labour contributions beyond wages, due to the companies' wealth being surplus wealth, from workers productivity. Usury of the nation's human resources must be hindered into the future.

Public and large corporations are run by employees. Corporations are a Government creation that limit personal liability, thus the Government can mandate any changes they desire that benefit society in exchange for this freedom from liability. Corporations despite law stating they are persons are documents in essence, granting special rights to be excluded from liability; this is a big Government subsidy for industry. The nation develops human resources that build companies, and Government incentives often finance companies. Surely this is not a one-way street.

Industry is changing, once again due to the western technology revolution from continued creative innovation. Mass production is due to be replaced by production on demand, and custom 3D printer manufacturing. Thus, many of those old industries will be replaced with these new micro industries, with the advantages of customized, computerized, micro robotic assembly on demand, no industry, no need for retailers either. To ensure these companies do not exploit workers to build something, then export it after taking all the social benefits of western society. New rules need to be initiated upfront for the Government in the creation of corporations to ensure employees have sufficient control over the company's shares to prevent the export of their jobs. This is not repressive or anti libertarian, it is anti-exploitation. Clearly the problems are multilayered, but essentially are created by Government corruption and social treason, for vested self-interest, interloping into the private and personal affairs of others in many inappropriate ways. Government dependency in the economy is now living past it's; "Best before date". We need to grow up and become self-sufficient again and stop lamenting over the past. Internet product distribution services like Amazon.com now enable the sale of homemade products world-wide. No longer is the reliance upon local markets limiting home based business. A craft made at home can now be sold worldwide, thus new opportunities and a new unrecognized economy has opened-up. The world can be optimistic again.

Until you personally navigated the edifice of your nation's actual political and judicial system, and have pragmatically experienced its operation, you know nothing of what you are advocating;

- You're merely assuming to know.

7th Chapter
THE WESTERN CULTURAL REVOLUTION

I wonder if given the pragmatic concepts of the" Overton Window" if that which I present here will be socially accepted, given that there is so much that could be perceived as radical or be too far ahead of its time. I also wonder if we will finally wake up and come to acknowledge reality as it presents itself and accepting that:

1. Equality does not exist –It is a denial of reality.

2. Equality cannot exist in this world – An impossibility due to natural variation.

3. Equality never has in the past or will in the future be possible – A delusional idea.

4. In reality all we live in a world of diversity between individuals, mental faculties, mental perceptions, genders, and races; even within all groups and minorities. Current human rights concepts have become senseless, as they have devolved into repressive reverse discrimination and divisive acrimony.

Author Charles Murray in his book; The Bell Curve" clearly demonstrates that IQ's vary by race and culture, while controversial modern brain science via biological genetic analysis and brain imaging is finding that we are very unique on an individual bases, thus we commonly misunderstand each other in very fundamental ways as individuals.

1. The old genetics and eugenics theories of the past century are being cast aside as false ideas by scientific fact, more and more every day as evidence mounts.

2. Diversity and spectrums in individual human traits are increasingly being proven as a more accurate scientific perspective to view human beings.

3. We are all unique in a myriad of ways!

4. There apparently is no normal. Normal is an average filled with variation, and diversity. Averages as in math, are a series of different sums divided by the total.

5. Human beings can be compared to the numbers that create an average of a sequence of numbers that can represent different personalities and characteristics.

6. Once we accept that we are all different, and that variation is the rule of our existence, perhaps the time for humanity to truly advance socially has arrived as we cast away our ignorance in believing two-hundred-

year-old ideas of equality that is a total falsehood, whose time of scientific ignorance has passed.

We are not equal, we are diverse! Thomas Jefferson's, two-hundred-year-old "Declaration of independence", founded upon the ideas of John Locke are completely wrong. All men are not "created equal" in any way, and science has proven this! All men and women are the products of biological diversity. We must mutually respect our differences and cherish our diversity as individuals not as groups, but as individuals. We are not groups; the current "group think" is totally wrong and inaccurate. I see the foundations of western civilization as long overdue for a radical revision of our outdated notions. Current social policy right now in law and beliefs are the equivalent that the sun circles the earth. We need to learn to see the world as a place of complete diversity and variation and change our constitutional rights to reflect reality. Western society is supposed to be based upon scientific advancement of knowledge and society. Western society is not a religion, it is based upon validating claims proven to be physically true. This reliance upon science is the essence of the western renaissance and reformation, somehow our society has regressed and forgotten its foundations.

All humans are created in complete diversity as individuals needing respect, far more than groups. We must respect all variations within the biological spectrum. All individuals have the right to self-determination, privacy in our determinations of what is best for each person, and to be treated with respect and dignity. To the present day; there was once a great technological and civil society in the west. At a time when honour, respect, and family values were social graces, and respected in what was a place of civility that was admired around the world. A world that came to an end in the early nineteen-eighties and has been on a downward slide ever since. A time that existed when:

1. Parents taught and enforced manners, respect for elders was taught in the home by parents raising their children as we have done since the first human learnt to stand upright clasping onto Mom and or Dads hands.

2. Honouring the family and the meritocracy of employment disappeared as it was undermined by Government sponsored "social communistic equality" of all ages, and thus created a new social barbarism.

3. This new Government sponsored bigotry brought on by political correctness was far worse than the former structure, as the former social structure was worldwide and the product of natural evolutionary custom. This new social communism is a socially engineered construct that villainizes men, and creates outright male discrimination, that is in no way subtle or even gender equality based.

4. Merit and excellence are no longer recognized, and thus as in all cases were qualifications and standards

are lowered, poverty and social disintegration is the end product.

Civility was also destroyed by the Government, in diminishing the authority of the family. The multi-billion-dollar judicial industry and related social interference industries of Government experienced an economic boom in their personal incomes as a result. Living off the carcasses of psychologically damaged children, the bigoted judiciary created, by removing father's parental rights and extorting them for money, the family court system is one of tyranny for all men who enter a court room. Lawyers graduate to become judges in the incestuous legal industry by self-promotion. Family destruction is the judicial interloper's agenda to fund this industry, they make absolute and tremendous personal financial fortunes. These embedded practitioners enrich themselves personally by destroying other people's families. It is a vile industry of vicious psychopaths by:

1. Being provocateurs and interlopers into what are strictly private matters.

2. Inciting people with high handed insult, threats, and posturing towards defendants with insults at a moment of distress and difficulty in a family.

3. Government sponsors this business engaged in by thousands of lawyers their actions demonstrate that

they are psychopathic social parasites, within the political system.

4. This army of psychopaths ensures women have unequal parental laws and exclusive rights before the courts, for equality would remove their incentive and thus destroy their business model.

5. Men meanwhile are lied to by lawyers telling them the system is not discriminatory or bigoted against them.

6. Meanwhile the statistics prove this to be an absolute unmitigated lie. They nonetheless circulate lies of parental equality to their foolish clients, which the statistics do not bear out as having any semblance of reality.

7. No crimes are committed in most cases, only parental desire to maintain their rights. Yet without valid justification or crime being committed, in a total disregard for all the tenants of the Magna Carta and all principals of equality and impartiality before the courts. Contrary to English based constitutions guaranteeing equality of the sexes, men are forced into courts and their parental rights challenged without legal bases, removed for trumped up reasons outside of regular court processes, which can only be seen as demonstrating judicial bigotry, and vested interest.

8. Parental equality in the west is pragmatically a great big lie!

9. The reality is that men over ninety percent of the time loose most custody cases under the bigotry of the Courts in almost all western nations. Put on trial where in no crimes are involved.

10. This is a human rights travesty of justice going on in our own times. How can they justify legally baseless, and crimeless court trials?

11. The legal industry is having a field day accessing all the families' wealth and enriching themselves at society's grave expense. The tremendous damage being done to children, as their fathers parental rights are involuntarily castrated from their personhood and never considered, as are volumes of studies that prove this is very harmful to children.

12. The multibillion-dollar judicial industry interlopes into family finances with impunity and extricates family wealth transferring it in billings and expenses delivered to themselves. Family equity that in the end is expensed out to the psychopathic judicial industry needlessly. This is a very profitable extortion racket that uses children, parental love and human emotions as hostages to enrich themselves.

IT'S ALL ABOUT PROFIT

The psychopathic judiciary do not care to consider the social damage they invoke, instead they only see profit for themselves; - and it is a very profitable industry! They take equity from the family via this scam to enrich themselves, respecting no traditional principals of law, or constitutions of society, of which the family is a fundamental common law foundation. Thus, the result is what we see in the west:

1. An entire society going extinct from low birth rates.

2. Angry disengaged fathers stripped without valid justification of their parental rights, and emotionally distraught about being relegated to the role of visitor to their own biological offspring.

3. Tormented delinquent children raised without benefit of an intact family or involved fathers.

4. Because of judicial abuse, most men simply get the message that they are pejoratively villainized and must pay extortion or be villainized further by Government, it's a complete no-win situation for men.

5. This is Darwinian proof that by destroying the nest of the family, you destroy society's desire and ability to reproduce. This is now undeniably proven in the west.

6. The majority of youth now particularly men have no desire for marriage, little trust in women, and particularly marriage, because they have seen this tyranny in their own families.

Other cultures see this as a warning of the consequences of adopting current western Governmental judicial systems as being highly corrupt; even socially toxic! This is the ultimate punishment for corruption in Government. Western nation's extinction is clearly in progress and the judicial arm of Governments turning law into an industry that seeks to bilk citizens of their money and destroy the family in the process is reprehensible to say the least, if not outright social treason.

RECKLESS DISREGARD FOR HARM TO CHILDREN

For children to be socialized and educated from infancy by the employees of a psychopathic system that has no legitimate biological vested interest in the future success of the children in this world, is the lowering of standards to the lowest of the low. It takes a family to raise a child's foundations, super mom is an unproven myth, with an oppressive agenda. Simple social graces such as respect for others and manners, have become old school, and we have entered a barbaric age of minimal mutual respect for differences:

1. No longer is there social respect for earned status with each other personally, or in business.

2. No longer is there social respect for the law, as it has discredited its workings.

3. Social disintegration is the product of the current "Social Communism" being espoused in society.

4. Business, commerce, and Government have become a shark infested cess pool, where contracts and laws are given no respect by Government, Courts and agencies.

5. Honourable politicians no longer exist; all have been subverted in the public perception. Western countries have become societies run by pirates.

6. Government exercises political speech control for political purposes with politically based laws, exercised under the ideology of political correctness.

7. The boundaries that used to exist between parenting and education have been breached by Government becoming an uninvited interloper into families.

8. Education is no longer about necessary fundamentals. Politics has entered the education system, and Government indoctrination has become part of this system in a complete breach of parental trust. Children hungry for guidance are now indoctrinated at school with "correct speech". Personal matters of

gender and sexuality are now not taught by parents, but rather the interloping state.

9. An undemocratic agenda of globalism for which the people never consented is now the priority of Government.

10. There currently is in the west a Chinese style "cultural revolution" taking place. Western Governments now resort to force, rather than law, as the greatest western Governmental program of human rights violations invokes its venom into society.

11. Freedom of conscience and speech is seldom ever respected any longer or is permitted in the new western dictatorships at the present.

12. The ancient social custom of teaching children mutual respect and manners has come to an end in the west for the most part. Every person regardless of age or familiarity is now referred to by their first name. This is Governmental parenting from the schools, teaching disrespect for your elder's wisdom, starts with disrespect in how elders are addressed.

13. The Government loves undermining all institutions of society except themselves. So they permit children to use first names with all school officials and teachers to undermine the authority of elders.

14. These schools do not respect their obligation to request parental consent because parents have little individual control over the current system, as their school choices are limited by a one size fits all state attitudes towards education. Designed to create socially conformist people.

15. This is not good in a democracy, since this system promotes "group think". The same regimented type education that can lead to people who as adults become programmed to following orders as in Germany, under the third Reich, with horrible consequences and human rights/diversity disrespect of others.

16. A diverse education system of state funded charter schools controlled by the parents would have a much more useful outcome for a society operating as a democracy. Respect for diversity is the single most important advancement society needs to acquire.

17. Human rights legislation is, about having respect for diversity, not acquisition of special rights and privileges for select minorities.

GOVERNMENT SHOULD NOT ACT LIKE THEY ARE A RELIGION

Governments in the west are now trying to get rid of the biological designation of "mother" and "father" in the Canadian Province of Ontario birth certificates from the Government are now replacing the words Mother and father with the word "parent". A seeming innocuous change until you consider its implications. A term in their new laws defines that a "parent" can be anyone the Government chooses to be the parent. Even the Government itself can now be a "parent". According to one Government Minister in that Canadian Province, the Government is a "co-parent". Government now portrays itself as God in its ability to choose who your parents are. Biological reality now has no bearing upon the social communists, they renege in their responsibilities to enforce laws and are servants to vested interest. What else is a Government that acquiesces in its fundamental responsibilities but; - incompetent?

A NATIONAL GOVERNMENT'S RESPONSIBILITY TO ITS CITIZENS ARE:

1. To respect and to abide by the nations Constitution.

2. To ensuring the law is applied and enforced, without discrimination and not simply decreed.

3. Provide equal justice and law enforcement for all their citizens, regardless of rank or position.

4. Protect the environment and purity of foods production.

5. Protect citizens from abuse or mistreatment.

6. To obey the determinations of the nation resulting from referendums, and to hold referendums when

sufficient number request one as per the nations constitution.

7. Respect the diversity of citizens, ensuring equal opportunity based upon personal merit.

8. Promote and enable economic growth and opportunity for citizens.

9. Defend the nation from foreign manipulation or interference in its domestic affairs.

10. Provide diverse education opportunities for the youth to become productive members of society.

11. Promote social harmony, peace and social order.

12. Be non-discriminatory and non-biased, equal application in all laws and actions, regardless of wealth or status.

13. Respect and promote the family and parental authority as fundamental in that the compassion parents have for their children is a valuable resource in children's development.

14. Protect children from damaging abuse.

15. Promote family values as a fundamental building block of society.

16. Respect for home and property rights of citizens as being inviolable.

17. Respect for the citizens privacy in all effects and matters of activity, unless under investigation for criminal activities.

18. To not make any legislation that does not reflect pragmatic reality within society, or attempts to alter society by social engineering, or not in conformity with the principals of respect for diversity and individuality.

THE CITIZEN'S OBLIGATIONS TO THE STATE ARE:

1. Loyalty and performance of their civic responsibilities to oppose the repression or abuse of others free expression and control over their lives.

2. Respect for fellow citizens and your rights to liberty, free choice and privacy in their personal matters, within limits prescribed by law.

3. The obligation to not allow yourself to be coerced into unconscionable Government mandates which do harm to others.
4. Service in defense of the nation from foreign aggression, interference or invasion.

5. Loyalty to fellow citizens and the nation, following due process in matters of dispute.

6. Participation and belief in the democratic process and to ensure the democratic processes are implemented and followed as necessary.

7. To be loyal to your family, fellow citizens and the nation's best interests for the benefit of all citizens.

8. To speak up about repression, injustice, intimidation and abuse of yourself and others.

Current human rights abuses started with social communist engineering. Government has no right to engineer society. Society controls Government, not the other way around. It started as minority rights (supposedly for equality), now these minority rights sanctioned in law are removing the rights of the rest of society. So that a homosexual with no biological connection to a child can be on a birth certificate, as a parent. All biological parents now have their parental biological parental rights thus diminished, taken away, relegated to the whims of the nation state, who can insult nature itself with its own determinations of who are the parents of the child. Parents are biological, not elective or selective status. Parenthood is reflective of genetic heritage and are not options. Government is not and cannot be a parent in reality, to behave otherwise is to violate the boundaries of good governance. Having defeated religion by school indoctrination, the

Government is not a supplemental religion or parent; it is not God or a religion. Government is a social administrator. Government should not have any authority to determine who are the birth parents without biological connection, and even change who parents are, - ignoring all reality of biology. Since the dawn of history, Governments always aspire to be their societies worshipped and absolute God. This trend continues to this day and must be pushed back.

The ancient Chinese philosopher Confucius recognized centuries ago:

"The strength of the nation derives from the integrity of the family"

~ Confucius ~

"To put the world in order, we must first put the nation in order; to put the nation in order,

we must first put the family in order; to put the family in order;

we must first cultivate our personal life; we must first set our hearts right".

~ Confucius ~

8th Chapter
THE INDOCTRINATION SYSTEM

By schools insidiously changing social customs, like for example first name use in schools by children to address adults *(seems innocent enough)*. Fundamentally, symbolizes that inexperience is equal to experience. Schools being institutions of Government have no right to denigrate social customs such as this without parental permission to invoke such social engineering.

1. New ideas from Government institutions such as: social communism; political correctness; affirmative action; not being required to "pay your dues" for admission or promotion has been replaced by unqualified; pedigree politicians and queue jumpers over merit.

2. These queue jumpers now have a vested interest in maintaining the new corrupt establishment, and thus needed change becomes hindered by the corruption of nepotism and unqualified political queue jumpers and political mandarins.

3. Meritocracy, qualifications and fair treatment, have now disappeared. Promotions are no longer based upon merit, but rather biased privilege, and social communist preferences. There is no integrity without meritocracy.

Wherever corruption is rampant, poverty is sure to follow. Government, the new indulgent and obliging western spouse of women, now has free reign to indoctrinate the children's blank hard drive to villainize, ridicule their father resulting in demeaning men, as is the current western circumstance of corrupting the youth. Ultimately the state will utilize these indoctrinated brainwashed children for anything they like; including unjustified military conflict, violating other people's human rights and dignity as per the qualms of the social communist nation state, - this is current practice, down the slippery slope, or should I say; "the road to hell; paved with good intentions".

My historically based Socratic condemnation is directed towards the toxic spread of Social Marxism, in that current Social Marxists Professors do not have the decency and integrity of Socrates to drink hemlock tea for the harm their nihilism has caused western society. By irresponsibly teaching the youth Mobius-strip intellectual fraud, thus they personally refuse to take responsibility for the social harm they have produced, with convoluted zero-sum social teachings. This teaching which instead of expanding young minds closes them with intellectual fraud hidden in enigma, taught to the youth ill-equipped to decipher the treachery of those entrusted with their education and responsible for their guidance. This is symptomatic of the current times, that higher education now is also corrupt in not vetting this type of education foisted upon the youth. The tyranny of politically correct speech and name calling are now used like a weapon.

Weak argument always resorts to personal insult without bases in fact. The Government indoctrinated children, who are now brainwashed and indoctrinated adults, use false insult to silence all critics, and thus turn society in upon itself, in typical neo communist fashion. The stage is set for the Government to create Soviet style gulags, repress free speech as is now happening in most western nations to ensure conformity to the Government brainwashed line. The people have currently lost control over Government; - now Government controls you, instead of the way it's supposed to be. Your servant is now your master.

The Social Marxist intellectuals of the Universities and their subversion of western nation states have now created a dangerous repressive nation state that is self-righteous and completely intolerant of opposing views that stifles debate, with political correctness, and their usual social engineering through indoctrination of the youth in an economically failed ideology. By thinking they can implement the social precepts of communism, without the social constructs also destroying western society.

The current globalist agenda of welcoming migrants to Europe, the harbour of social communism and social engineering, welcoming peoples of a different cultural perspective who seek Europeans conquest, might very well in all likelihood lead to removing Western Europe as a homeland for Western thought. There is a strong likelihood Europe will collapse and within a few decades become a series of fifteenth century Caliphates, in another great communist defeat of the ideology. Clearly all precepts of communism, are about to experience absolute social and political defeat matching their economic failure. This will conclusively change our perception to communism to being and seeing it for what it is as a dangerous and insidious nihilistic historically revisionist ideology with false narratives, that destroys nations and cultures leading to economic collapse, defeat, and conquest by others. In a twist upon bigotry, the new bigot's words are now "Racist" and "Nazi", without bases in fact. These words are indiscriminately fired at anyone who voices dissent, because the youth are now brain washed by the state's terminology of politically correct speech, censorship and repression the state has indoctrinated into the minds of children in the social engineered public schools since kindergarten. Let the example of Europe's demise be the final evidence that parents, not social engineers must control education and prevent social engineering. Without Libertarian education with free choice for parents to control their children's education, and control curriculum, the lesson of the destruction of Europe and it's subjugation to foreign peoples will be repeated worldwide by regressive, repressive, societies that are dominated by use of force, as the standard operating model for communism. Leading to Government extortion of the people, and creation of gulags to eliminate political dissent.

TYRANNICAL TIMES WE LIVE IN

This is all about freedom and liberty! It is about those who control, indoctrinate and through censorship and political repression silence opposition making complicit citizens who live in fear; it is a covert dictatorship! A program of state sponsored indoctrination, they have in fact corrupted the youth, and clearly their hemlock drinking moment has arrived. In order to bring in the new social communist ideology, the subverted state needed to:

1. Through indoctrination discredit the old school and degrade elders and respect for elders.

2. They needed to distort the historical narrative to their ideological bend.

3. Clearly elders who know firsthand the reality of historical narrative needed to be undermined with removing respect for age, and life experience, with historical revisionism and social communism.

4. Self-righteous (politically correct silencing of alternative views) in which prejudice is the new state sponsored indoctrination. Through University based "non-evidentiary humanities education" social engineers know the false narrative is important in programming, (as in Nazi Germany and the former Soviet Union it was practiced) creating a brainwashed and complicit generation.

5. Men had to villainized and removed from the home in this social subversion, along with the aforementioned social modifications. Removing the competing husband "the Government" became the co-parent with the mother.

6. The state financially funded the interest group called feminism.

7. They state indoctrinated women into the workplace so that even mothers are removed out of the way of the new state indoctrination program.

8. They proceeded to socially degrade stay at home parenting of children by women. Child care became farmed out and was no longer a "Do it your-self" project. Now the states values could be installed into the children from youth and the ideas of the left became the programming instilled.

9. The stay at home mother had to be socially villainized, degraded, criticized, and belittled by radical feminists who are by no accident heavily financially sponsored by the Government.

10. Government made pretense that women who raised their children were down trodden victims of the male gender. The target has always been a diversion to get parents out of the way, so the state can indoctrinate

the children with their grand social engineering experiment.

11. The Social Marxists maliciously stigmatizing all mothers parenting activities, belittling her intelligence, and claiming mothers were doing nothing but watching TV all day; - which was done to belittle and make good mothers unfairly and viciously a source of ridicule. Thus, stay at home mothers were villainized out of the home.

12. The state wants parents out of the way, so that they could brainwash and program children's minds from the cradle.

13. Getting rid of fathers was simple in that women could be co-opted with a wedge of Government financial incentives, from claiming child support from the father as a financial reward for divorce. Outright grants of Government money called welfare, and even this new "Government husband" offered low cost to free housing and will take care of your children for you.

14. Brainwashed children were filled with cultural self-hatred for their own culture. The state coopted parents by the old divide and conquer strategy.

HISTORY REPEATS ITSELF

It's the kind of Government surely the Nazi's would invoke had they won the war. You and your children are a "human resource" just like minerals, food stuffs, cattle and sheep; the Government utilizes resources for their own purposes.

1. Basically, if you rely upon the Government to live, you sell your children into the Government's slave labour program.

2. The Government has now become the legal co-parent of the family's children, and the traditional head of the family (men/fathers) have been relegated to a French revolution style headless status.

3. There are no fathers any longer, only sperm donors, who of course the state wants to co-fund the family's demise. The states co-parenting by compulsory payments called child support to have men fund their agenda.

4. We no longer have orphans, which the Government has in reality done to most children; we now have insecure single person "families", and clearly a broken society. A reproduction of the African American style victimhood.

5. Families are exclusively: Biologically based upon mother, father and child (children). How does this

insidious interloper we call Government, get their nose in there? We are not cattle or sheep to be farmed by the state. For if this continues this is exactly what people in this society are.

6. Clearly the desire by Governments to control everything has no ethical or traditional boundaries; clearly the nation state in the west is an over controlling psychopath.

7. Daddy's been overthrown and the Government has moved into the master bedroom as both mother and father. Now the raising and indoctrination of the children is like putty in the nation states hands. They can now do with your children as they like with no parental oversight.

8. Does anyone really believe the Government is benevolent? No need for families next, we can all just work and give everything to the state. We have become cattle, the slaves of the state. Remember the state-run residential schools, the catholic orphanages. This negligence in child care will lead to massive child abuse; our descendants will curse the present generation for this social communistic tyranny we fell for, - if this continues. Like the old expression; "Those that ignore history are condemned to relive it".

9. Once again, the Government wants to create Spartan Robots of indoctrinated children to protect the psychopaths that run the state.

10. The child's greatest obligation will be to protect their new parent; - the Government. The greatest tyranny is yet to come out of this. People need to recognize that Government administration is basically a vested interest power matrix, a parasite, a leach on your child and your life.

CHILD:

"It is a good thing the Government raised you, taught you to serve them, and made your embryo donors pay for you being raised by the Government. Make sure to protect your "Government" from your embryo donors, by informing us of anything said against the Government, little child. Now run along little boy/girl, go over to the battle trenches, run towards the opposing sides machine guns; - protect your "family"; -The psychopathic Government.

Welcome to a life of slavery, your children have now become the Governments' livestock!

FAMILY VALUES

Social engineering is routinely funded by Government who use tax funds to covertly sponsor non-populist minority interest groups, and an education-based youth indoctrination program. These actions financially and emotionally hurt millions of good mothers. The honourable time immortal job of mother and homemaker has been viciously attacked by people from dysfunctional family backgrounds imposing their demented dysfunctional family and communist social perspective upon the rest of society.

Western Society has failed to defend and recognize the high level of social contribution and technical skills the stay at home mother position required, mothers and motherhood has been betrayed and thrown under the bus. Most importantly the family and ethical child rearing teaching children to think for themselves, and be independent people, true to themselves, and the value of independent creative thought, has been sacrificed. The right of parents to socialize and raise their children, teaching their children social skills, and protecting them from psychological manipulation by others, has been intentionally corrupted by the Government in the west. Many skills derived from family, like fair play, unstructured play, honesty and integrity are lost, allowing lies and false Government narratives to go unchallenged by brainwashed children in schools and soon to be Government daycares as this ideology infects society.

Some of these children who are now adults, have no foundation in empathy being taught by absentee parents.

University Humanities social narratives with revised anti-family social history, now contaminate millions of adult and children's minds, particularly in Europe, because their "parents, the state" tells them it is so. They believe it, no need to prove ideas like their supposed to be "victims" of the "patriarchy ideology". All this information is coming from indoctrination in school by a trusted parent; - "Government ". – Ha! Being raised by a loving mother is undeniably better than being raised by a daycare. If institutional care is better than parents; then sex with prostitutes is superior to intimate relationships between men and women. Though given the current state of affairs many young men avoid women in the west as they and child bearing has become a dangerous risk to them with no benefits. Gender distrust has set in in the west. We no longer trust each other, and this product is the outcome of decades of Government sponsored feminist attacks on men, that exceed equality to become unearned privilege where men need not apply, thus given the raw deal younger men have bailed out on having a family. If society desires to see things as utilitarian, then there is no need for children either. This at its core is the result of contamination from state involvement in the family that has demonstrated that equality has become an effort that has turned against men. Like everything Government does outside its intended purpose they messed up the family also. Now thanks to Government interference western nation's birthrates are in serious decline and depopulating towards extinction; - if that is not failure, what is? European children, now adults raised under social Marxism, are so indoctrinated and brainwashed one need only look at the current immigrant and migration in Europe to see the results of this. Europeans are so state indoctrinated they fear politically correct pronouncements. Boys are now so feminized; that they are a shadow of their former proud ancestors. They sit by and watch their very nations be invaded and both women and children raped by foreign cultures, which have made it clear they have come to take over and end western civilization. Mass literal rape of their women, and even children is accepted by the police and even covered up by; The Police, Media and Government themselves. In fact, Europeans are being advised to give everything; even their bodies and children as sacrifices to the foreign migrant invaders by their Government, without a single bullet being shot. These people have been indoctrinated to believe in Government which is benevolent, and not being seen appropriately; as treasonous. All my presentations have demonstrated state brainwashing taking place, and the mindless robots Social Communism has made of Europeans.

Few things add more high-quality value to the future of humanity than family and old-fashioned stay at home mothers or fathers, who are the center of the family and the glue that holds it all together. The situation in Europe clearly demonstrates, Government cannot be trusted to protect your family. Dual family incomes, absentee parents, women in the workforce have added no value in economic terms to the family. In fact, dual incomes has created inflation in the cost of housing and everything else, putting tremendous stress upon the family by necessitating dual incomes as the outcome. Jeopardizing and destroying the institution of marriage, destroying family life, and doing untold harm to children and society at large. Raising children and attending to their life skills and the ethical education of your own children, being their loving paternal and maternal life coach, is the best preparation for life any child can ever be given. Parental time by a dedicated, unbiased biological parent, and preferably two is the best foundation to build responsible children. Being the center of a child's life, teaching cooperation, fair play and good social values, in working with others. Mothers and fathers built the family team brand and good mothers were at its core traditionally since the very first humans upon this earth; this has always been our most fundamental obligation. Human beings, just as all creatures upon earth take care and raise their own offspring as a life priority. There is nothing we can do with our lives that is more important than our progeny. Exceptional cooking and baking skills, which was common in the past for thousands of years, along with so many other skills, too many to list, passed from mother or father, to daughter and son through the generations. Mothers were highly skilled underappreciated family-based trades' people. Now extinct in the west, the maternal family leadership of women and their excellent administration seldom exists. Her set of domestic skills, from cooking, early childhood education, gardening, baking, pickling produce, all added greatly to the family's economy and wellbeing, are now all largely lost due to the Government and particularly the judicial industries interference and indoctrination of women to imitate and behave like men. The calm stress-free life this division of labours by two parents provided to raise children and bond family has all but been lost to create a society of fools preoccupied with other people's business. The family is cast aside and ignored; in an anti-Darwinian societal suicide pact with the devil. Like Freudian penis envy, women's historical family role and jurisdiction as head of the household, was unjustifiably belittled by feminism and Government; replaced by industrial servitude. The state funded and promoted false feminist indoctrination in school over family realities and values. The home has always been the kingdom of the mother, while dad worked outside the home. This has belittled parenting and impoverished families.Upper class women with servants have always had servants and others tend to their kids by relegating childcare to a servant. They often prefer to work outside in family business operations. This is in no way similar to Government programs. This bears no resemblance to working class families given that their income does not support what is essentially a class divide based upon wealth. The working class have always been multi-talented, do it yourself types. The bubble of the elites is demonstrated in their ignorance of working-class reality.

FAMILY ECONOMICS

Let me clarify one critical point here being that, most women in working class families would in fact prefer to be stay at home spouses, as most come from good well-adjusted middle-class families. But they cannot economically, because the good jobs their spouses once enjoyed no longer exist. What is left has been taken over by women. Most remaining traditional industrial jobs have been pirated away to low wage countries. Then there are uneducated third world immigrants from slums domestically willing to take 2-3 jobs at very low wages, willing to work eighteen hours a day and accept a very low standard of living undermining the middle class. In fact, destroying the "American dream" they came for. The Government knows this, their actions demonstrate their affiliations and loyalty to industrial oligarchs.

The family now requires two incomes just to survive and pay the bills. The Government provides little incentive to maintain and enable families, since they are beholden to industry. The reality of Government handouts is that they give with the right hand and take from the left. To diminish women's desire to seek outside employment, would put upward pressure on wages for all. Bear in mind, the Government is beholden to their corporate financial sponsors and other lobby groups who have made tremendous profits gutting and pillaging the North American economy. Average working-class family never asked or wanted this, necessitation of the two-wage family, and the stress filled depressive life thus created.

235

To make any pretense that this was a populist agenda, which it was not; - The mother wanting out of the home is a false narrative based upon a minority of women, it is just another false Government narrative, promoted by radical Government financed feminism. Many narratives about social changes in the past few decades of Government social engineering have created narratives that are all a Government funded fiction. With an agenda on behalf of their corporate masters, and a made-up narrative from social Marxists Government propaganda has all worked against the family. It is truly peculiar how such seemingly contrary perspectives and agendas can subconsciously melt together.

Radical feminism was created by Government financial sponsorship through tax dollars and special ministries to put downward pressure on wages, by doubling the work force (along with intense immigration). The effect upon the family was a catastrophe of decimated families by adding in the cost of daycare and creating inflation. The reality is that working-class families could not afford to live on current low wages and maintain the creation of future generations of children. Western society has become parasitic upon itself in a trend that has continued for decades. Families are now sinking lower and lower towards extinction. Like cockroach's western society now eats its own. Extreme inflation was inflicted upon housing costs which rose prices to meet the increased income of dual income families. This inflation caused a decrease in family standards of living in the long run, as a result. Families also could no longer afford to have children, in that two incomes that initially raised their standard, then became a mill stone around their necks. Dual incomes only added inflation to the cost of everything; the short-term benefits were thus lost very quickly. Virtually everything Government did in this direction was detrimental to the nation and families. Families are no longer seen as teams and collaborators in the best interest of children. The Government does not see families or respect them, they see individuals. Politicians stuck a dagger in the back of the family, like Judas they betrayed their people for the silver pieces of social division; for electoral advantage. Seat of the pants political interest group social policy has had long term negative effects, that the past thirty years have demonstrated when attached to the power of Government are very dangerous with unpredictable outcomes to the detriment of society. Libertarians believe in organic families and that the Government has no business in our private affairs, other than in crime enforcement should something arise.

THE FUTURE FAMILY BASED ECONOMY

Traditional family household feminine skills in the new economy will be beneficial in the new future I see of a return to home-based family specialty micro business, computer-based robots are going to end most jobs, from factories to vehicle drivers and more. Jobs will become part time. The work week will need to be reduced to twenty hours to spread what jobs there are. This will open the door to new part time businesses by the working class. One business and one home-based job will become a common means of livelihood.

1. There will need to be created thousands of home-based, micro manufacturing and service businesses, selling special and exotic delicacies through online marketing of items made at home like; cheeses, fudge, baked goods, candies; custom furniture, the list is endless. Home based internet business will be custom, creative, artistic and high quality, which lasts a lifetime. The manufacture of home-based crafts will surge. Unlike in the past many of these new businesses will not rely upon the neighbourhood for sales; but rather custom orders to ship around the world. Also, these micro manufacturers will be able to live anywhere in the world, including rural locations. Work life will once again as in preindustrial times be family business and reinvigorate family bonds.

2. Outside home employment will become the exception. Home employment will be contract based and full time, due to internet based globalized industry. Clients will be from all over the world, niche products will with worldwide distribution enable the creation of opportunities to make a good living from such products as never before. Robotic big domestic industry made possible by 3D manufacturing technology combined with other design craftsmanship will make possible

intellectually unique products possible. Business survival will be about unique creativity.

3. Being able to freely manufacture in small quantities and sell home made products on sites like Amazon will simplify business to where if you build it, they will sell it for you, this will create a tremendous opportunity for self-employment via crafts that never existed in the past.

4. The future will include a lot of homemade boutique selling. This is the next Amazon or Air BNB model. A web site that connects custom products from micro businesses with buyers wanting custom products. This will result in a new micro industrial revolution. Facebook is the latest to enter the online marketing business with women now swapping and shopping for clothes, gadgets, household and other used items online. Soon virtually everything will be marketed online. The main hindrance right now is cost of delivery. But that is coming as the distribution model needs reworking to deliver fresh items. It will be online catalogue shopping direct from the home maker (manufacturer).

5. Local shipping warehouses delivering goods like mail is delivered. Perhaps with national tube transport infrastructure to quickly and efficiently ship goods across continents within hours faster than flight. No planes, no trucks, just a tube from city to city and

eventually every house. Amazon type companies are the way of the future. Traditionally micro business was how women raised their own money and they often became a larger enterprise as the children aged. The stay at home parent micro manufacturer is the future.

6. In fact subjugation by the Government-industrial corporate elite agenda betraying the nation's vested interest and that of their family, is coming to an economic end. No longer self-employed at home as women once were, they betrayed their own biological and genetic self-interest by becoming corporate mandarins.

7. The next social wave will see the end of a lot of mass-produced factory imports as custom made micro businesses will gradually change the face of industrial production. A robot in a barn will be able to build computer designed and built, made to order custom cars. Furniture and gadgets, and then sell them online.

FEMINISM | FAMILY VALUES AND THE COMING RETURN TO BASICS

Old social rules no longer apply in this fourth quarter industrial revolution. This western deindustrialization will also be the end of Government funded fraudulent feminism. Individuals will realize that they must do for themselves and eliminate the Governmental funded proxy life; the financial shell game that really has come to an end; the "gig is up" and the necessity is to get real. Having specialty Ministries for women is a disgrace; where is the Government "Ministry for Families"? Soon every western nation will need one to readjust society after the current prototype ends either voluntarily, or by extinction via its own nihilistic hands. Should extinction be the result, those that follow us will judge feminism in very harsh terms along with communism, as another grand failed social experiments. Clearly the façade of desiring equality, traded for a social power grab and dislocation of men cannot in the real world succeed long term, since the investment in child rearing requires in practical terms a partnership, which women needed to cultivate throughout history pragmatically. Alliance with a single-minded bruit has great advantages to those he patronizes, and women's Jungian archetypes from history still seek to gain this patronage from the bad boy, who symbolizes the resource rich innovator to whom loyalty must be sworn. Least a competing woman take him from you, for loyalty is a scarce resource the women could barter, to keep the man on side when other women came knocking on her partners door; to get a; "piece of the (your) action".

Now feminism has tossed out this primal strategy of women to obtain resources exclusively and beat her female competition and put on the table an offer to men of realized male promiscuity, which always harkens to men anyways. I wonder, if this play into men's nature and biological advantage to mate with many different women has really been of any advantage to women, as she has lost exclusivity. The female mating strategy to find a good reliable mate/partner and to sell him on the advantages of sticking around and investing in her offspring physically and emotionally, hording his resources for your offspring's advantage, is a good feminine strategy; this has been the biological and pragmatic necessity of our species throughout history. That leads to your kids getting everything when he dies first, now the new wife walks away with the treasures. To the male there are greater advantages to avoiding monogamy and spreading his biological investment (seed) amongst a variety of women; this is to his biological advantage, not hers. The true competition for women is biological, it is competition against other women. This competing with men agenda of feminism has been completely wrong, because the lesbian feminist leadership faction failed to realize; that there is a biological symbiotic reason for the pair bonding with males; in addition to most women being irredeemably attracted to men. The primary battle women have always faced is other women, in their competition for resources for their offspring. Feminisms' logical outcome has come to fruition as it was always lineally headed in this direction. The hostile relationship feminism has created has given men permission to breed leave, rebreed and then leave, breed and leave again. This has led to serial monogamy, the very thing that is counter to female desires to capture and milk the man's resources like her private cow. The male cow has now gone feral. Men now feel justified and socially un-judged by others of their gender in this de-civilization of men that has occurred as a result of feminism. Thousands of years of feminine efforts to reign in male sexuality by seduction and the desire to take ownership of male resources has been undone in a generation. The key to this is the greed of feminism in that it was unbalance and turned into a psychopathic, winner take all ideology. Taking men's jobs has only transferred his work; not his wealth onto to her. So women have become overworked since all her traditional parenting roles still remain.

Feminism was a movement that if it had prudence, it would have kept men engaged by mandating equal parenthood and tying down the man in childrearing by creating an obligation, even if it cost them a bit of money, the benefits would have enabled her greater career success by freeing her up. But they foolishly missed that opportunity in a generation that was a reckless power and money grab, arrogantly done through Government extortion. If the goal was ever equality, shared child rearing with male participation, which has risen significantly compared to post WWII males, is where feminism lost the gender war, and demonstrated an incapacity to be social leaders. Historically prior to the industrial revolution all men were stay at home fully participating parents, who are just as capable to raise children. Male harm to children is factually and statistically extremely rare, statistically non-existent in fact, it is so miniscule, contrary to urban legends.

Compared to child abuse by women of their own genetic offspring. Men are gentle caring and very loving benevolent parental giants; like silver back gorillas when it comes to their own biological children.

Introducing a non-biological step parent into the life of your children in humans as in any species, is a totally different matter. Since biology trumps everything else in child rearing, especially in males and I have seen this in women also. Women won and children lost big time. In ancient times the policy of conquest by war was always, kill the men and male children, and then rebreed the females to create your own children. Sounds crude, but you will find this going on in primitive societies even today in cases of war. Currently, in this subverted legal framework the talk of men is how to get out of these obligations, because it is a raw deal that feminism has offered of winner take all and leaving the man battered and bruised, naked on the floor castrated and in a fetus position. In a winner takes all proposition women are clearly the victors; congratulations to feminism you won, and now your society is going extinct this is feminisms' legacy; you killed your own family! We are going must go back to the eighteenth-century family team to survive. Home based enterprise is the future. Old school Feminism is Passé. All creatures upon this earth, even a virus understands it is a biological imperative to reproduce itself. Feminism is the creator and root of western social and ethnic biological extinction, by attacking the traditional allies of women being male partners and cohesion of the family. Radical feminism and its co-opted alliance with Government alone is responsible for the current malaise of the west as it espouses its own extinction, as compared to all other historical social movements that have desired reproduction rather than extinction. Clearly it is a dysfunctional philosophy based upon nihilistic self-hate of your own society, it has become a cancerous tumour within the body of western society, killing our society from within the body politic and society itself.

Raising children has always been a family team effort, and the loss of the team in custody laws is state sponsored child abuse. The subversion of the family by the judiciary arm of Government to extort money from men does not even come close in terms of value to a present and engaged parent as a positive influence upon the child. . The jails are filled with the failures of single mothers who lose control of and destroy their children's lives. In the spite filled Government created custody industry where lawyers live off of the avails of family destruction. The successful record of poor intact families raising responsible well-balanced children has long been known, as is the failure of single mothers. Single motherhood is nothing to aspire to as statistics and psychological studies prove, it damages children in so many ways. Dual parenting has never been absolute, and neither are all parents perfect, but we must start Government in the history of human rights violations, once again got it wrong, and history will condemn them for causing this mess also. Like residential schools run by pedophiles and child abusers, where in children were murdered by the thousands and molested in considerably larger numbers, in Canada. This has occurred repetitively at other times in other nations where the Government interfered in the family. It always turns out to be an exploitative disaster story.

WHERE WESTERN CIVILIZATION IS HEADED

Feminist philosophy in terms of a historical perspective is increasingly seen as a failed experiment. Darwinian science and philosophy in historical recounts will relegate feminism to become a footnote movement that did not result in successful reproduction or society and thus genetically became extinct and has led to the downfall of the pre-eminence of western civilization.

Where Islamic and other fundamentalist religious peoples become a large portion of the population by demographic reality this will lead to the shrinkage of western society to enclaves and ethnic tensions will lead to a world in constant danger of civil wars breaking out; just like the Middle East. Islam in all likelihood will overtake most western European nations and reintroduce a reverse renaissance, of Western history in these countries, reverting the west back to the 15th century. By implementing Sharia law that will successfully replace western laws by sheer numbers of new citizens, in reproduction of children where Islamic peoples overtake Christian populations. Western nations will regress socially five centuries. North America and certain commonwealth nations other than Great Britain will watch Europe's disintegration and abuse of Europeans that remain and realize that Koran phobia is a prudent fear. You might not like this truth, but this is the predicted future for many Western European countries right now in demographic reality. Within perhaps less than one generation, based upon birth rates.

MINORITIES

The truth is that Government is subverted by radical feminist groups which have the ear of the state. In order to understand this majority that pretends to be a minority movement, you need to consider as previously stated why this group in reality has become state sponsored as a hate group towards men, which their actions clearly demonstrate. Most of the current young feminists have serious emotional and psychological problems from childhood rape by a family members, a father figure, emotional or other abuse, that may be a pattern repeated with spouses and relationships derived from their minority dysfunctional families and background of nihilism and gender hatred that they clearly demonstrate is usually founded is some form of adverse personal family history. Their animosity towards men and the family, comes from their ill families and even abusive mothers and family heritage. There is the largely non-breeding homosexual portion of this group of radicals, which come from families like everyone else. Heterosexuality is where families come from for the most part, this is undeniable reality. Typically, due to mental illness these minorities alienated their families due to post traumatic stress and their uncontrolled mental anxiety issues, based upon their bad experiences with what are in fact criminals. The psychological damage they suffered is coming from dysfunctional families. This is a damaged handicapped group of women, and some men from similar backgrounds. They perceive male-female relationships as power based and abusive, because that's what their dysfunctional families demonstrated to them as normal. Radical feminists are by far a minority, and a quandary to the rest of society. They are anti male hate groups, a form of dangerous bigotry. Their normal state of being is they subconsciously want to strike back at all men for perceived harm. If they focused upon prosecuting their tormenters, they could do far more to protect women than all their rhetoric.

UNBALANCED IMMIGRATION

Coming soon; Sharia Islamic law will be enforced in parts of Europe within a generation, if nothing changes from the current immigration and demographic trajectory. This will result as listed below in changes based upon this new population's political demands and culture, we can expect this population to request Islamic law compliance, the destruction of feminism, gay rights and to repress most other western based human rights. Do to extreme social disruption I can see Visa requirements being imposed upon these nations as a travel requirement by other western nations. Western cohesion will implode do to this change. Unless there is some sort of forced exodus of Muslims, as has happened in Europe in the past. Here is the future, as the Koran will mandate, and all Muslims must obey as mandated by their religion, and all non-adherents will have to abide by should they achieve majority population status. Women will be brutally repressed like never before in western history. Physically beating women and wives even in public places is accepted in every Islamic nation, as is having many wives, western Islamic nations can expect the same permitted by law. Along with Marriage to minor girls as their religion permits. Where Islam establishes a majority of the population, as in most Middle Eastern countries, public flogging, and I would expect executions will occur. The Koran mandates these changes. Many in the west think this is another secular faith; Islam is not secular, or tolerant of secularism; once demographics are on its side! The Koran is a document of religious faith and Islamic law. The Koran is believed to be God's undisputable commandments of how to live, that must be obeyed by all Muslims literally. Islam means submission to Allah and the Koran's commandments and laws literally! Over the years I have worked with many secular Muslims with no issues, most having arrived as authentic refugees from Islamic nations, who appreciated the west for its Liberty. So, it is possible to welcome and integrate secular Muslims into the western world, based upon my experience.

FUNDAMENTALISM

Many Muslims will say there are no secular Muslims, and that those who claim to be secular have abandoned the faith; this is true under Islamic teachings and fundamental beliefs. Integrating Islam peacefully in the west would require a lot of effort. This would require: Government intelligence services monitoring and deporting radicals. Stopping the arrival of any imam and mullah that are foreign born and engage in hate filled racist preaching and deporting those that do. Insuring that religious indoctrination of the youth, does not fall upon hate of others and that tolerance is taught. Muslims need to be reminded that they should be creating a new life in America and they need to let go of the past. Limiting Islamic Immigration to insure it remains a minority population

AFFIRMATIVE ACTION

Like dinosaurs, only the bones of western civilization will remain, and future civilizations will muse about gender based affirmative action as a bigoted attempt at equality, which in fact, being bigoted against men, does not and cannot exist anywhere. In evolutionary terms only successful reproduction counts; otherwise you go extinct. No need to argue the point; no other culture is to blame for the decline of western nations. Don't blame Islam, it is following its' credo. I am not opposed to equal rights, I am opposed to the special rights at present. Political correctness is muzzling dissent. This is causing the collapse of western civilization, and given its trajectory, free speech will be banned within the next decade or less. History will condemn many western European nations' people as fools, who accepted a Trojan horse. The extinction of the west will be laughed at in the future for this naivety. The clock is ticking towards the point of no return. We will see what happens in the next few years to a decade. It is not that Islam is so aggressive or even powerful as they may think. The issue is the Social Marxist, politically correct, mentally ill nihilistic society they are coming to is committing suicide.

We need a revolution every 200 years, because all Governments become stale and corrupt after 200 years.

~ Benjamin Franklin ~

The end of democracy and the defeat of the American Revolution will occur when Government falls into the hands of lending institutions and moneyed incorporations.

~Thomas Jefferson ~

9th Chapter
RANDOM THOUGHTS

THE END OF THE MIDDLE CLASS: The initial Canada – USA Free Trade Agreement was a fine agreement between Canada and the United States. Both nations traditionally being the other's closest friend with traditional allied militaries; sharing continental defence; each other's traditionally biggest trading partner; brother nations with intertwined histories born of the same parents; sharing the same culture and language; and both having industrialized economies. Both nations built the same automobiles, by the same manufacturers, which was founded upon the free trade agreement under the old "Auto Pact Agreement", after WWII. After the war Canada agreed not to develop its own auto industry, if they had this agreement to share production of United States cars, both countries having similar unionized and well treated employees at that time, under similar health, environmental, and safety laws. There were few trade disputes, and little employment dislocation starting from the heyday of Detroit auto manufacturing to recent times. Both nations are siblings, and share more in common than dissimilar with each other, including the territory of northern continental North America than with any other nation, even their parent the United Kingdom. Then they added Mexico under the North American Free Trade Agreement. A third world low wage country was added to our bilateral free trade deal. That one act undermined both Canadian, and jobs in the United States. Once you have a free trade deal with an unequal partner; how does decent working conditions compete with corrupt conditions in the third world; where there is very little to no regulation? From an incremental trial balloon of equal free trade, the way was opened by a trick for Globalization. This is only one small part of what was being foisted upon the working class via a series of big lies. The union fight against the Canada-US deal was without merit, unlike if it questioned Mexico being a part of it. So, the opposition fought the loosing that battle against trade between equals. After the unions lost that battle, the road was paved to open the market to the world. It was a well strategized battle by the globalists to trick the unions and others who would have fought this battle tooth and nail if Mexico were in the first deal. But trade amongst equals is hard to object to, unlike with un-equals.

The Unions lost the battle to stop free trade. This was a carrot dangled and never the objective, as the Mexican and other third world deals were intended by industrialists to get cheap production into North America as the long-term objective. Being skilled negotiators they knew only incremental implementation, as Government often does, was how the public would be tricked into the global trade agenda, with its long-term catastrophic effects upon working class employment and lives.

We the people have since had our faith in Government destroyed. Learnt that our Governments no longer represent us, and instead have been hijacked by big business and even foreign sponsors of politicians, this is a worldwide phenomenon at this time. What in past generations would be cited as treason, now receives a blind eye. I am concerned that, given how we citizens have become aware of this betrayal, as demonstrated by voter actions in the ballot box. That if change does not come soon, an "Arab spring", type revolt, or even civil war type conflicts in the streets of the west are very possible, due to the polarization of politics and the public awareness of the betrayal by politicians and by enemies within the nation co-opted.

THE BELEAGUERED MIDDLE CLASS

The "one percent" is a recently coined expression that identifies the ruling oligarchy in western nations. Their wealth exceeds the wealth of the other ninety-nine percent of people in the world. Working class poverty is increasing as the western middle class is being impoverished by deindustrialization to off shore sources. Mass unskilled immigration is flooding the west after exporting manufacturing industries to low wage countries. Clearly the elite have launched an undeclared war against the western working class, to push down their standard of living and wages:

1. The social contract has been breached by the wealthy elite and the intellectual elite in unison.

2. The working class are under attack from both the left; distracted with minorities and no longer the friend of

the working class or unions. They have been abandoned and stabbed in the back.

3. The human rights distraction of Social Marxists who seem determined towards social nihilism of the founding peoples of western industry, and replacing North American populations with easily exploitable illiterate, low IQ, third world migration.

4. Now new technology and innovation that is going to leave all these groups unemployed.

5. This is installing the conditions with incompatible immigrants for a civil war in few decades to match Syria's current mess.

6. Our political system has been coopted and subverted by national career politicians who increasingly are the employees of large corporations and the oligarchs, not elected representatives of the people.

7. Working class alienation with the system has never been higher.

8. This makes the current political climate very volatile.

In nineteen seventy–seven this exact situation was cited by the Economist, and former member of the administration of John F. Kennedy at the time as, the coming "Age of Uncertainty". The book by the same name is worth a review, as we are now living in Galbraith's, predicted; "Age of Uncertainty". Brought about by consolidated corporate power usurping Government taking over the nation state just as Galbraith predicted. I read this back in 1977 then at the age of 14. The question; what will we do at this point, in this current Age of Uncertainty? As I recall, Galbraith did not have anything to say about the technological revolution, obviously other than Star Trek fans, few conventional economists were contemplating this issue either. We do sit at a social and economic cross road and the future is uncertain for all. Immigration to the west may be no solution at all and given the way western economies are developing technologically this may prove to be a political disaster of social unrest in a few years. We can already see the disaster this new corporate imperialism has created in false flag wars launched over the past decade, using national militaries from coopted Governments representing corporate agendas. We see the "Open Society Foundation", of Billionaire George Soros and family, using the western government strategy of creating by funding; protest movements to suite their agenda. Thus, the grass roots are being undermined by pretense. The silent majority, ever desiring to live in peace, are starting to speak up and talk of civil war against their Governments. This is smoldering in virtually every western nation.

The establishment has become so condescending towards the working class. I would compare their arrogance to the court of Louise XVI and the French aristocracy's isolation in the posh social bubble of the

Palace of Versailles, who were impervious to reality around them. I really think a bloody purge of the elite might very possibly come about in the not too distant future, as a spontaneous outbreak. It reminds of the spontaneous collapse of the former Soviet Union or The Russian Revolution. My concern is not the reign of terror that will mainly affect the wealthy, and certain career politicians. I hope that, enough people will seriously advocate Libertarian reform as I put forward herein as a serious alternative; as I propose here in this book. I hope that peaceful democratic and necessary reform takes place as I formulate herein this book instead. Working class alienation, distrust, and cynical fatigue with western governments has never been higher than the current trajectory. This makes the current political climate as volatile as an overturned jet fuel tanker in the middle of a major highway in terms of danger. The lines have been drawn and it looks like the corruption is so pervasive now that people will come to the conclusion that none of the current players can be trusted. It is just as likely that some unknown radical populist, in replication of Adolf Hitler's Nazi Party coming into power in one western nation after another is possible. Definitely we can expect a purge, but will it be by proper law and order of election or revolution? People forget their history as easily as it must be remembered that Hitler was elected to office. The German's like to say that; "History repeats itself".

The corporate worlds attempted coup d'état of western Governments, I think will be a brutal lesson for them, as I don't believe the population will voluntarily put shackles upon themselves as the elite delude themselves. Law and order are only possible with a complicit population. What happens when society turns on the establishment on mass? Unpatriotic globalism certainly will not be the cohesive glue that can stop it or control it. Being raised as a child by two parents who lived through the Second World War, with parents from both sides of the conflict, I am the last generation who were given firsthand knowledge of that horrific experience. Growing up exposed to two sides of the story and having spent a half century studying the essence of the conflict, I believe this gives me a different perspective to analyze the current situation and warn that evolution of politics is normal. That it is what we do now in preparation, which can make all the difference in the ultimate outcome given this historical perspective. The spread of industrial ability since the end of WWII has seen the emergence of:

1. A renewed German and Japanese industrialization along with post war modernization.
2. The collapse of the former Soviet Union, and sudden emergence of a market economy.
3. The emergence of communist china from an agrarian society to a manufacturing power house.
4. The emergence of the south Asian tiger economies.
5. The industrialization of Brazil, India also many other countries and
6. The creation of the high-tech economy.

It is the sixth item noted above that is the wild card in all of this change. While some things have been engineered, like globalism and open borders. Some aspects like the directions of the high-tech economy are open for debate. These are examples of entire economies rebuilt with and without state support creating new industrial economies that enable those with drive and initiative to become new entrepreneurs. The post war industrialization is concrete evidence that the right economic, legal, and political conditions are all that is required for business to flourish; "the right conditions". The entrepreneur is essentially like an herbal weed in a garden. Entrepreneurship will always pop up in a bare space of soil where conditions are ripe, even in pretentious and corrupt communist nations like China. The post war period further demonstrates that entrepreneurs are not that special, and neither are their corporations; - they are all very easily replaced. Much like Government arresting organized crime or drug dealers jail a dozen, and two dozen pop out of the woodwork, because opportunity for wealth is there. All it takes are the right programs and availability of capital that is within the ability of all Governments, the elimination of corruption and stability of life for entrepreneurs to pop up out of the wood work. The fuel of entrepreneurship is capital. The mission of Government will be how to get capital in the hands of new and expanding small business. There is only ever a scarcity of entrepreneurs where there is a scarcity of four key entrepreneurial resources:

1. Social stability in Government, which does not overly harass the people.

2. An honest legal system with integrity and enforcement of the law.
3. Availability of capital resources to entrepreneurs and business of all types.
4. Personal financial security and Liberty with the availability of all types of knowledge, that becomes an instrument of progress and innovation.

Make available these "four business resources", and the economy will grow, people will prosper, and society will become wealthy. There is no necessity for uncontrolled free trade or globalism as economies will develop internally that benefit the nation. Given these facts and the reality that these four elements are all it takes to have a prosperous economy anywhere humans inhabit because:

1. Entrepreneurship is a natural human characteristic.

2. Entrepreneurship is a part of all human culture and human nature, where free people exist.

3. This does not of course mean that trade deals, or even open borders between certain nations are not an economic advantage, as in certain ways it can be very beneficial for exporters.

Economic decline occurs where any or several of the following occur:

1. There is some form of repression, meaning corruption that forces people to reduce their initiative for fear of being robbed.

2. A corrupt legal or political system prevents investment and long-term planning, thus creates the impoverishment of people and nations.

3. Show me a corrupt nation, and I will show you a very poor nation or a nation in decline.

4. Show me a wealthy nation that has become poor, and I will show you a nation with raising corruption in Government and or society.

5. Economic decline can be delayed in corrupt economies, if capital is available very cheap and easy, to offset the corruption just cited. But it is flighty and uneasy investment, looking for safe havens to hide profits. Thus, it is used where available, then runs for shelter if it can be hidden from the sight of authorities. The current trend for the real-estate investments of; Russian Oligarchs and Chinese Elites in western counties, amongst others come to mind. They rape their own countries and buy real-estate overseas as insurance, as a golden parachute; just in case.

Corruption in all its forms is a death blow to all economic prosperity. Given the fact that all resources, are within the domain of Government. There is a clarity this information provides that: Failed economies are the product of failed Governments. If all the money utilized to subsidize citizens with social benefits were given over for utilization by entrepreneurs and the four key resources were made available: Capital; An honest judicial system; Social stability and Knowledge to entrepreneurs, - economic prosperity in any country is sure to follow. This is a very significant point, since as I continue explaining, there are certain types of people that we as a world and all societies need to focus on to initiate real change and improvement in the world as will be explained.

THE RAVAGED CONDITION OF WESTERN DEMOCRACY

Worldwide even in the third world, there is a perception that Governments in the west are democratic, this perception is complete false. The theory in western nations, at least according to their constitutions and popular history is that the "people" control the nation state. Many naive people in these nations believe this popular myth. The naive do not understand that in order for politicians to get elected they require funding, and most often this is from corporate donations. Clearly covert bribery for Government policy is paid to political parties which is a subversive influence and counter the purpose of the nation state. Clearly this breach of an elected official's fiduciary responsibility and is in fact an act of treason in any nation, but until countries deal severely with this practice by requiring law and order, the practice of Government for sale will not stop.

1. Commonly politicians in the west leave public office much wealthier than when they arrived.

2. Various types of corruption that the media hides from the public goes on with politicians. Indeed - the era of the career politician has in no way served the public interest.

3. The fact regarding the way the system operates is that it provides far more benefit to the politician than the constituent, in that the politicians benefit financially from under the table kickbacks and in providing careers to mediocre and basically talentless individuals who become not only corrupt, but also pretentious towards the public.

4. Politicians and advocates in positions of authority that really could change the world, but rather are subservient to their sponsors, thus the system is one of fraud.

MODERN SOCIAL ENGINEERING

I like many founding people, in western nations, have found my national Governments have repeatedly betrayed and are currently undermining the domestic population. This appears to be the judiciary along with politicians. Irresponsible Government is all too common in this day and age. Mass immigration has been introduced to compensate for extremely low birth rates that do not approach replacement. This circumstance is the product of Government mismanagement, not industrialization as the Government controlled media likes to misrepresent. Government in the west has the deluded ideology that the resolution to every issue is to toss money at it.

LOW BIRTHRATES

The core source of low birth rates is the fact that western Governments over several decades have initiated legal changes in the status of families and marriage, the system now does not support family values and culture.

1. The result is that the family is being undermined by subversive national laws that have had a very negative impact on the family unit. The alteration of Government away from family values to making laws for political expediency rather than the people, has created a divisive culture that has been toxic to families.

2. Individualism in a vote getting divide and conquer strategy by Government has been a betrayal of the fiduciary responsibility of the nation state to the institution of the family. The pursuit of power and affluence in a divisive multicultural, individualistic social agenda in the form of laws, at the expense of heritage, tradition, empathy and identity has created a heinous social gender division promoted by Government and their Government funded feminists

that do not carry any semblance of family values. The result of Government legislation and family interference The creation of a social war based upon claims of gender equality, that's turned into extra gender privilege, at the expense of the other, that has been subverted by gender politics to become a power play of men verses women, and destroyed the foundations of the nation state; -the family.

3. Government has socially engineered a new creation: A masculinised version of some sort of mythological Amazon woman in denial of her true being, denying the reality of two genders; one being feminine and one masculine - thus different.
4. The current feminist agenda is not about equity, it is about political and social power, it villainizes certain women and the masculine gender. Like Nazi villainization of Jews with the same hate and spite filled attitudes. But in this case towards men, in this case as in Nazi Germany, the many sit back and say nothing of the Kristallnacht against men applying for jobs.

5. In complete disrespect of nature, feminists of today overlook the obvious physical and brain differences created by natural evolution for a comic book fantasyland of wishful thinking that does not pragmatically reflect reality. Ignoring differences, which are obvious to all but the blind and unscientific,

they like all fanatics make pretence that the genders are equal.

6. However, equality of genders is more elusive than equality of individuals. Communists have always forced their egalitarianism and imprisoned their detractors, because they refuse to see the scientific facts. They live in a fifteenth century haze without pragmatism in a world of ignorance that validates that once again it is but a minority that always advances humanity. This denigrates all women because it diminishes the perception of women's intelligence to Sharia law levels as being worth half a man's opinion.

7. Seeing every person as reflecting diversity rather than stigmatizing men which paints a much more respectful picture of women than the degradation of equality and all its precepts.

DIVERSITY

The ideas of 17th century philosophers currently dominate the constitutions of western nations, along with pre-feudal political and legal systems. A great deal of new knowledge has scientifically come to light and yet it is not currently being taken into account in our governing systems. Metaphorically, we still govern ourselves convinced that; the weight of an object determines its rate of descent, because we have not applied science to social ideas in the humanities, such as:

1. Psychological research has scientifically revealed that; "all people are not created equal".
2. That every human being has a different mind to match our different bodies.
3. That within every variation of cognition we are a "spectrum".
4. That there is no normal and only variation exists, and "normal" is an average of variety.
5. Due to these scientific fact's equality does not exist, and our obligation as people really resides in learning to and applying the principals of respect for all diversity.
6. Even within apparent diversity there is additional diversity.
7. That our dysfunctional societies are the root cause of most mental illness.
8. That brains function differently and are plastic in their development.

This knowledge foundation if taken to heart changes all aspects of our very concept in the west of human rights, from the requirement for individual rights to an updated perspective of respect for all diversity. The need to live and let live and respect for diversity is an all-encompassing human right need. Human rights require not a code, but only one legal constitutional principal of mutual respect throughout society. This respect entails, the requirement for:

1. The unbiased provision in the application of law in as few pieces of legislation creation as possible, without any bias or abuse, under the assumption of innocence until proven guilty.

2. Respect for privacy, diversity of opinions and their expression, either privately, interpersonally, or in public.

3. Respect for diverse ability, and to provide opportunity based upon the qualities of merit and good character.

4. Respect of each person's decision to protest and defend their integrity against false incursion by Government or other authority.

5. Respect for and application of law in full equality, to apply to all citizens without any exemption.

6. Protection of the family and its integrity, as the foundation and incubator of the nation and its protection from all corruptive influences.

Respect is the only human rights law required, which is a far more valid quality of equality, than any currently espoused, by divisive human rights legislation, as is currently practiced. The current delusional equality, which exists everywhere in the west, is more the stuff of 17th century philosophy than being realistic, as the world is filled with variation in every man, woman and child, both in our bodies and in our mental capacities, we are all not equal! All differences are given in different measures to each individual of all races, creeds and cultures and also gender is a variation. We need to recognize that current human rights laws are devoid of science-based evidence that justifies the legislated biases they contain. They are purely philosophical ideas that have become a divisive religion enforced by Government impositions. That being regressive they keep humanity historically frozen into the past, by emphasising discrimination as a never-ending reality; even once it is in the past. Human rights legislation paradoxically enforces that they are motivated to end, by forever keeping it contemporary. These legislations have become sacred cows of victimhood, locking humanity into opposing sides, creating an historical pendulum. When social and cultural Government policy adheres to ideology, as is the present case, it is clear to see that the intent and the result have been in contradiction, as the result it will create is even greater discrimination. This recipe for new discrimination is thus created once the perversion of the false justice system acts upon such inaccurate manifestations as rights, and moves the historical to become the contemporary, the entire contextualization becomes contaminated with opposing agendas and vested interests. In making these matters "rights" we now enter into, not equality, but the creation of privileges that lack all merit in obtaining the best person of quality based upon merit, rights are similar to cronyism or nepotism, since anything less than merit is always regressive and a violation of those who have paid their dues and are the correctly deserving of opportunity.

Anyone who has inside perspective to the inner workings of the judiciary will tell you that the system is highly incestuous; with politicians coming from the ranks of lawyers, Judges being former lawyers, and all belonging to self-regulating law societies as I have previously stated. Thus, human rights legislation gets distorted by the judiciary for profit. We need to rethink this entire abused notion of "rights". This can be seen as barbarism, because there is no evidence of pragmatic, scientific, or enlightened thinking, to justify the entire notion of specified rights attached to groups, as presently convoluted.

1. We are different and live in a world of diversity!

2. Once we embrace diversity, we will as a species respect each other.

3. This is all the human rights protections we need is summed up in one word: - RESPECT!

Thinking you can replace discrimination with favouritism is an oxymoron. Once the judiciary got their hands onto this whole concept of human rights, this has been transferred to be the equivalent of self-righteous indignation towards others. Special privilege for certain groups; Reverse discrimination foisted upon the innocent for perceived injustice, invoked by contemporary inhabitants upon the ancestors of the downtrodden. We can only move past history and learn from its lessons, and not repeat them, we cannot change it. Germany tried to correct history and were inflamed by historical revisionism by Adolph Hitler regarding WWI. The outcome was WWII and loss of millions of lives wasted over a grudge that the Germans let fester. Revisiting history to correct it to one's liking is a vile and sordid idea, whenever attempted. It creates guilt for perception of ancestral crimes; -now that's unjust!

The concept of social evolution, due to the fact the legislation would not exist in the first place if the perceived discrimination were not ongoing, is the inherent danger in these laws. The remedy is the illness. Human rights legislation, because humans live by past memory, only perpetuates inequality and is a danger of creating social backlash. There are cultural and physical needs similarities we all have, this is as close to equity and common cause for social cohesion as humanity ever gets, or humanity will ever reach for a tenacious social cohesion. This is why nations make sense; in that nations bridge the human diversity gap for common cause. "Rights" are a diminutive legal construct of ideology, and a coercive term. "Respect" is a condition of the mind which "Rights" attempt to; -but fail to covey. I would choose "Respect" as a condition of treatment rather than having "Rights" concerning any matter.

EQUALITY OF OUTCOME

A person wanting equality of outcome implements victimhood to obtain competitive advantage, due to being aware of truly being inferior.

If I am not truly inferior, then I do not warrant equality of outcome, and thus this is not bigotry but lack of merit.

Either way respect is always implied. Rights garner disrespect as they convey a message of victimhood, inability and lacking in merit. - rights over merit signifies inferiority.

RIGHTS REPRESSION

Laws provide privilege to isolate groups and exclusion of others, these are not rights, but bigotry against other groups within society. Human Rights Laws cannot achieve the obligations to have respect towards others as an outcome attached to those rights. Thus "human rights" for one person becomes repression upon another, these privileges are tyranny and devoid of justice.

SOCIAL COMMUNISM

Social Communism is a derivative of unscientific movement started in the University Humanities programs in the western world. It is a uniquely western version of China's Cultural Revolution of history. It has infected intellectual life across North America and Europe with an unfounded pro feminist ideology that is anti-intellectual, meaning not founded upon the principals of vetted science. Starting in the mid nineteen eighties the politically correct movement and its repressive postures started with censoring how people speak with Marxist political views cushioned and hiding as "Politically Correct Speech" censorship.

1. Governments in Western European Nations and Canada have found this political manipulation useful to create Communistic ideologically based Commissions and Tribunals like nineteen sixties style McCarthyism in the United States of America. To push their agenda outside of main stream Courts and the authentic legal system.

2. To enforce their Social Engineering Scheme Western Governments have been funding Government departments, and University Humanities Programs of this Nature to justify their social engineering agenda.

3. In a twist upon Fidel Castro's announcement in the nineteen sixties that he is a Communist. Canada's Prime Minister Justin Trudeau has advocated for Government social engineering by announcing; " I am a Feminist" he put society on notice that all men need to accept the Governments social engineering program to diminish men's roles in all facets of society.

4. In a communistic type purge of men to remove them from societies ruling structures. Never since the signing of the Magna Carte have western nations so blatantly been so bigoted and discriminatory.

5. The social communist movement has had a detrimental effect upon western thought by its repressive desire to control the free exchange of ideas.

6. The entire concept is based upon censorship that started with words, then moved onto ideas.

7. The movement has proceeded far past traditional feminist views desiring equality with men. Now it is flipped upside down, to espousing females are

superior in a form of National Socialist gender-based bigotry. Demonstrating impunity to breach all social conventions, such as the renowned; "Slut Walks". They do this in the belief that women are not bound by any social conventions and have a right to walk out in public with a bare chest and that men are repressive because they should not sexualize female nudity, counter to all scientific psychological research and understanding of the nature of the genders. When an ideology makes pretence that biological reality does not exist, it has become delusional arrogant and has crossed the line into a form of mental illness.

8. The movement runs counter to all psychological research and is in the vain of an anti-male; extreme feminist ideology; that is anti-intellectual and being taught in the universities. That they seek to silence intellectual talks and opinions, which run counter to their particular ideology. This is not in the open tradition of discovery and debate of universities being places of free thought, this is fascism.

9. Clearly individuals who attend universities or administer universities, who seek this censorship should be expelled from places of higher learning and discovery, as intellectually unfit.

10. It is anti-intellectual for the establishment of any place of higher learning to permit such censorship and thus

tyranny against diversity as this behaviour is about domination and control, more in tuned with fifteenth century ecclesiastics, than a place of intellectual development. This disruption should not be permitted to try to censor the search for truth and debate.

11. Like the Chinese Cultural Revolution, the Social Marxists, the politically correct movement is not organic, or to be considered a populist movement. It is a particular philosophy that has been created by the Frankfurt school with a social and political agenda. Taught in university humanities studies, without any scientific bases; it has a corrosive impact upon society, as it is a diminutive socially corrosive ideology.

12. The social communist, current feminist movement has nothing in common with the call for equal human rights movement in the sixties. It was primarily funded by Government and certain private sector organizations dedicated to undermining social cohesion.

13. The movement is one of extreme radicals and has been very effective in providing Government with the false pretence, that this is an organic movement, rather than a group of people being used for the agendas of others, who are much more sophisticated in intellectual capacities.

14. This idea has been pragmatically discredited by the product of their actions. They have done so by denying their own feminine natural self, and the need to collaborate with everyone else in society including men.

15. In an attempt to become as much as possible their perception of men, masculinising femininity; devoid of the wonders of what it truly means to be a woman is disrespectful and degrading of the diversity of women.

16. These new Government sponsored feminists with their historical revisions have sold their souls for the shallow barrenness of ideological social fascism and fanaticism.

17. Denying and losing their connections with the feminine creation of all human life, as the mothers of all men and women, as they have become detached from their organic material responsibility as life givers of all children, both male and female.

18. Tainted by a preoccupation of themselves with mythology of masculine financial ambition and social power. Humanity is being socially robbed of real femininity with a false unnatural transgender definition that defies physical reality and nature itself.

19. This pursuit of Government to conduct unnatural changes that undermine society, damage the foundations of family values and civilization. Men and women are naturally intended to be partners, not rivals as this movement espouses baseless social war based upon unproven rhetorical hypothesis, in ignorance of scientific evidence to the contrary.

RIVALS OR PARTNERS

Perhaps you might think I am being harsh upon the contemporary radical feminists. I am opposed to its elementary, to none intellectual and anti-intellectual bases, and is only a fanatical philosophical ideology that is politically based and created for espionage purposes. I have observed and admired their best qualities and their most reprehensible. The very essence of the decline of the western nations commenced with the decline of women.

1. Women, who compete with men, instead of working with them.

2. Women who do not mould and cultivate the next generation of children to influence the world with their more universal perspective.

3. Women who fail to realize that family and children are a very personal contract with their own genes as an extension of themselves.

4. The failure of both genders to appreciate that both parents in equal measure work to provide children with balance.

5. That any suggestion of war between the sexes is the suicide of society this battle is a nihilistic suicide pact.

VARIATION

The finest human being I ever was a woman of emotion, feeling and empathy. She had very little education, and prioritized giving to the world rather than taking. We call such peoples "saints". People like mother Mother Theresa in the slums of Calcutta who give to the world at their own altruistic expense. It seems education distorts the world, often with unnatural idealistic hypothesis and political concepts that are like science fiction outside the realm of reality. The reality of different social strata and ability, ill-legitimizes all communistic ideas of Karl Marx and his unsubstantiated theories of creating social equality. Equality is a ridiculously impossible fantasy that has hypnotised generations.

1. The reality is that there is no equality. Life, Nature, God and Charles Darwin has only provided an enormous selection of variety. Different personalities, different genders, different races, different cultures.

2. There is no standard like widgets of industry. Everything is a constantly naturally evolving world of

variation. We are not equal widgets from an assembly line mould!

3. The best we can hope for is equality of opportunity for all matters with integrity are based upon merit, and respect for variations. The covert reality of egalitarians is to promote inferiority since they cannot compete with merit by pretence of conspiracy it is a corrupt idea that it thus degenerate's society by inferior administration.

4. There is no need for specific human rights, but rather human rights are about respecting the dignity of differences, and the permitting of a natural social evolution.

5. Race, gender, and religion are matters of personal determination we can alter and do alter at will.

10th Chapter
CULTURAL CONFORMITY

The nation state is always seeking conformity and the globalists seek unity where there is none, it is merely a consolidation of authority for corrupt intentions. Politicians in this day and age travel rudderless upon a sea of vested interests financial sway to and fro. Courts and the legal establishment provide no reality for their tyranny, only rule of law which is subjective. Thus, without any compass of intention the only outcome can be authoritarian social stratification because of misguided and harmful social interference with no determination of the outcome. Western societies manipulations unlike architecture has no proven engineering techniques, only the purpose of social subversion without authentic purpose based upon integrity other than the maintenance of positions by careerist politicians that do not care about the social outcome which they create with no purpose other than providing themselves with a job and narcissistic wealth.

GOVERNMENT VS. FAMILY

The net result of Government interference in family affairs as social engineering by Government has been destructive to families and extraordinarily damaging to children. Many children of "The Daycare Generation", have grown up to see the terror of the state's damaging interference by use of force, have sworn off ever having families in the future. Like child labour, slavery, protecting labour from abuse. All of the abuses of citizen in history are not so much social abuses, but Government abuses. When human rights are violated it is almost always the abuse or neglect of Government authority with abusive laws and or an abusive judiciary. Historically lawyers prosecuted those who wanted to end slavery, reform labour laws, change gender-based laws of Government etc. Lawyers have always been the foot soldiers of tyranny. Today the Government's tyranny continues with human rights becoming perverted to become minority privilege, rather than the intended removal of biased distinction. The clumsy and mentally disturbed nation state fails to see they have no solutions; these reforms must be organically generating. That by accepting distinctiveness, supplemented with the realization of respect for variation, that this should not be used as an excuse for the promotion of minorities and the repression of others. Promotion of minorities without merit can only lead to conflict or civil war for its repression of the majority. It is the manipulation of civilized structure by the weak and unwarranted. The attempt of the betta to dominate the merited alpha by treachery and lies that excuses ineptitude by supplementing this reality with victimhood. The villain is nature, not those of merit who are persecuted.

THE GUILT OF GOVERNMENT

The Government and judiciary are far from having any form of innocence attributed to their vested interest in profiteering from social divisions they create and gain from. The fact is Government, laws, and the legal establishment are almost always the source of human suffering and abuse due to their fanaticism and resulting mistreatment. Undemocratic political solutions are seldom implemented or tempered with balance by their very nature of being extortionist. Government social interference is best compared to the proverbial; "bull in a china shop" when delicacy of approach is more appropriate. Yet Government's sanction historical revisionism, which tars all men with the same perverse corrupt, financially incentivized false narrative, with men being villainized as the purveyors of tyranny of the past. The western nation has convicted all men for perceived crimes of the most lowly and repugnant nature. The enforcement of this Government agenda is not social policy, but rather judicial and legislators profiteering from social trouble making on behalf of "vested interest". This movement is not about equality, it is about a rebellion out of spite and jealously by mediocrity against meritocracy.

THE CURRENT GENERATION

Many men are now entangled in a judicial scam, which has nothing to do with any injustice of the past. The aurhentic protagonist of racist policy, gender inequality, and all other tyranny is always Government, who like to blame others for what in the end is the nation states judicial and legal tyranny, under pretense of innocence by tyrants. Without the tyranny of the nation state's bigoted laws, all discrimination would evolve to filter out of society on its own as citizens would deal with their problems from a community perspective. The reality is that the state cannot be an impartial arbitrator of human affairs, because its concepts are not based upon the true nature of the human being. The Nation state is an extortionist bully by design from the first day of Governance, and a globalist state would be more remote and worse by far. nation state mandates serve its own agenda of political management the states people suffer as the national Government has its own mental dysfunction in being without moral influence or compass. Its only capacity is cohesive use of force upon citizens as it is not democratic currently it substitutes consensus with brutality in many forms. There is a natural human right to have the nation state constitutionally relegated to stay out of citizens private affairs. Few things are viler than the uninvited interloper for s/he is a trouble maker without right to involvement. Government that exceeds its fiduciary responsibilities is always a tyrant. People have rights not Government, Government has fiduciary responsibilities.

A NEW CIVIL RIGHTS OBJECTIVE & PERSPECTIVE

Western Governments need to restore their respect for human rights by being respectful of the natural order of human affairs, respecting variety and diversity of people, stopping the bigoted discrimination of affirmative action, Allowing society to evolve naturally by society maturing on its own terms, at its own pace, and not using socially

corrosive force or social engineering techniques, which creates festering resentments amongst people. To say something is a "RIGHT" is to create laws that will arise to enforce those "RIGHTS" by implication. If you have a "RIGHT" then that must remove some of other peoples 'RIGHTS" and freedoms, since rights are in essence repressive towards other's freedoms. Rights are the wrong word; "FREEDOMS" are more appropriate. "RIGHTS" subordinate others by creating a privileged class based upon perceived disadvantage, which is doubtfully universal. Rights are tyranny by minorities, by these privileges called "RIGHTS". Human rights are an oxymoronic term and a source of repression. The Magna Carte created rules of Government, not rights and was sufficient and superior for centuries.

THE EXTINCTION OF WESTERN NATIONS

This forth coming extinction of western nations like dinosaurs, has all come about as a result of Government incentives for men to be extorted by threat of Government violence. Force founded upon gender human rights exclusion laws and Government financial incentives thus are undermining family unity and western society. Corrupt politicians promoted divisive social policies intent that this will get them electoral votes. There is no evidence of this social fracture benefiting any political party or carrying much more than a small minority of the nation's votes during elections, but thanks to these policies homeless men roan the streets of every North American city. Instead of pro-family policies, western nations have adopted a system of severely persecuting men for having children, savagely dividing the genders thus the family. The sick, cynical, and grave mistrust this has created originated by misguided, from the hip, Government social policy and is all Government generated. Feminist studies in universities are fascist anti-male hate indoctrination programs of historical revision, based upon women's Government sanctioned "rights" to mistreat and degrade men for claimed misdeeds of their ancestors; - this is truly bazaar! The fact is women are the majority of voters but still claim victimhood? A great deal of attention is given to historical revisionism, victimization and the acceptance of unsubstantiated and bigoted feminist social ideas enforced by totalitarian western Governments, without regard for the big picture affects upon children and fathers, without benefit of pragmatic facts. Truly western nations are suffering from a form of sociological mental illness. Psychological studies have proven these policies have severely hurt children. All of these studies are ignored by feminists', courts and their collaborations who are financially benefiting and incentivized, they refuse to hear the facts. There is clear evidence that the Judiciary has shown favour towards false narrative. Elevating a minority cases of individuals from dysfunctional families making pretense that these rare situations are common, which evidence has proven are in reality rare and exaggerating statistics out of proportion. Family policy is being determined by a small minority of dysfunctional people from dysfunctional families and psychological issues, supported by a profiteering judiciary that has a vested interest in misleading society. Reprehensibly those with vested interest are exploiting the family unit for their personal profit. A multibillion-dollar judicial industry is behind all of this corrupt and destructive behaviour. In many regards like the psychiatric industry and their practices in the nineteen sixties and seventies with its; forced involuntary sterilizations, lobotomies, electro shock brain damage to people, Over use of medication, restraint and indescribable abuses of patients without factual evidence, for their suppositions. When theory supplements verified research, tyranny always results, as this is then unfounded politics, all of this is out of control Government and demonstrates the need for Libertarian reform.

THE MULTIBILLION DOLLAR FAMILY LAW INDUSTRY

The multibillion-dollar family law judicial industry today is like the work house of Oliver Twist, abusing society to support their own corrupt wealth creation program; supported by their biased, self-regulating, private club called; "Law Societies". Something I call; "The Judicial Mafia". They are our old social Nemesis that legitimized slavery, child abuse and all human rights violations of history to this day; they are the historical psychopathic enablers of all crimes. The judicial industry routinely twists the facts and use family problems for personal gain. Damaging others in a completely unscientific game of debate without the need of validating the espousing of corrupt and false undefined narratives, like the "best interest of the child", used to steal the parents' natural rights away from the additional protections of a second loving and caring parent. Sacrificing children's protection for biased political agendas, and primarily their own financial vested interest and condescending attitudes. While their personal bank accounts are overflowing with money from this state sponsored extortion racket of leveraging parental love of their children for profit. The system is truly parasitic; a medieval based primitive way to seek the truth. Basically, utilizing the same techniques as 15th century witch trials and inquisitions, they are an outdated manner of reviewing the facts of any circumstance that hurts society, as it completely fails to produce any form of justice. We need to modernize this primitive feudal system by:

1. Reducing the cost of all litigation by mandating all litigants and defendants submit full case briefs to the court and then appear in court to explain their case and written testimony. The elimination of most trials and the need for trials and basing litigation upon documented evidence submissions.

2. A modern evidence-based system of making it mandatory that, all cases that go for trial as matters of abuse issues require proper rules of evidence and reject all hearsay.

3. A document-based system that respects the Magna Carta free of Lawyers saber rattling and incitement.

The outlaw of attempts to intimidate litigants with all forms of threat, posturing and removing false drama manufactured by lawyers.

4. Removing lawyers from litigation and replacing them with Notaries who would guide the judge through his/her submitted documents explaining the contents and evidence therein.

5. Stopping of often unjust determinations by singular judges, who fall for drama over facts and commonly overlook critical details submitted by parties in court submissions.

6. The requirement to have proper psychological review of all custody disputes, considering the child's benefit and desires.

7. Proof of parental criminality or proven abuse against family members would be the benchmark in all child custody disputes, without which they are without merit, thus shall not be permitted.

8. Court rooms really are obsolete in a literate society other than perhaps the Court reading a final verdict to explain their analysis. What the law requires is proper impartial analysis not 15th century inquisition tactics as are now practiced. This can be performed by police and psychologists, investigating any illegal

parental accusations to determine if there is any merit.

9. A peer review process having a dozen judges read the case documents. Having each judge provide their written decision based upon the law and the submissions. Then the judges would meet in committee after reading each other's separate submissions and conclusions. Joint determination on the matters of contention in the case, would be a peer review of the applicable law.

10. Custody cases are serious matters of removing or altering biological parental rights, at present such profound decisions are not being dealt with in the level of seriousness they deserve. Parental rights must be deemed un-volatile without criminally proven issues, as a bases.

THE JUDICIAL MAFIA

Currently the state creates problems and litigation interloping into totally private citizen's affairs for vested interests that have financial incentives to make trouble. The courts are provoking violence and injustice; they aggravate family problems, for their personal profit. This currently is a repulsive, demented circumstance, of a judiciary with a vested interest. This demonstrates how in fact the state has become the enemy of the family and child. They are guilty of financial tyranny more than any other source. They are extraordinarily self-righteous, as they hide their dirty deeds in the shadows of secretive "Family Courts". Courts should never be secretive or closed, and in fact they should be broadcast, to keep them honest, this type of recording is necessary. Too many routine matters get put on trial, when law should not be so vague as to create dispute, as though each case were really so different, when they are not. Clear laws would remove most of the requirements for protracted litigation as is the present case. Trials needlessly become protracted and multiply, when laws are vague. This is but another example of what happens when the fifth column of bourgeoisie subvert the nation state for their own purposes. Un-like business, the nation state exists as a fiduciary that should be acting in all the people's best interest. All politicians are the people's fiduciaries. When the nation states politics intertwines its activities with private business, this can only be viewed as corrupt because of these connections.

SOCIAL COMMUNISM'S REPRESSION OF CIVIL LIBERTIES

The common perspective of western Government's has become a series of "social communist policies", for political advantage. A social engineering agenda through force of legislation is at play. These nations have been in a coordinated effort editing, crafting and sanctioning their false scripted historical narrative since the end of WWII. Anyone who refutes the Government script like Nazi or Communist propaganda, regarding any aspect of the official Government social narrative and sanctioned version of history, gender politics, race politics, cultural politics, or the post war holocaust narrative, by contradicting the censored narrative of the Government's official history, takes upon themselves great risk of Government harassment followed up by judicial persecution and prosecution. The strong-arm possibility of being sentenced to jail by the Government for opinions and perspectives in the west for contradicting the Government narrative is a danger zone most citizens refuse to challenge. Due to the fear created by these Government policies, thus all analysis or contrary opinions are taboo and dangerous perspectives to hold, Governments increasingly repress public debate; regardless of your evidence. Contradicting the Government is like telling the Nazi regime of the nineteen thirties Germany, that you love Jews; a simple statement which at that time could put you in jail or cost you your life. Wherein most Germans were resigned to silence, in fear like today in the west. Silence is the option of choice by the majority under repressive Government regimes. Given Governments extra ordinary powers over citizen's lives and unlimited money to force their will, the most optimal and prudent course of action is to avoid such conflict unless you are a dissident. Dissidents are in many instances' agents of change and national heroes. Human rights as they exist legislatively today, have become repressive instruments to dislocate the majority. Human rights laws grant privilege and power to minorities over the majority and are a grossly undemocratic social formulation. A new left-wing fascism has given rise to majority repression.

MEDIA SUBVERSION AND INFORMATION CENSORSHIP

There is more tolerance of different perspectives in the United States of America, than most nations, due to constitutional rights protections of free speech. Though the Government and establishment as a standard operational procedure attempts to discredit alternative perspectives as first as: "conspiracy nuts" or branded as "racist"; like in other western nations. This repression transforms into harassment, like we can see is occurring at the present time with major web sites on the internet.

1. The corporate establishment, the elite oligarchy owns the media as their employees and servants.

2. The political and legal elite bourgeoisie class work hand in hand to repress the middle working class which performs most of the work, pays the most taxes; offers their children for patriotic military service, essentially, they are the nation.

3. Essentially the bourgeoisie and wealthiest 1% do parasitically feed upon the working class. They expend a lot of effort to indoctrinate and manipulate the middle classes perspectives.

4. There is always a conflict between the ideology of the elite who live in a bubble of fantasy, and the pragmatism of the working classes.

THE BELEAGUERED FAMILY

For decades now the Government has been undermining family values and promoting minority rights groups in general. Governments have been engaged in covert social engineering projects with their populations and been funding their own created and fabricated provocateurs and protest organizations, to undermine social cohesion, and to keep middle class wages down by being socially disruptive. Families in western countries are small because of economic pressures imposed to maximize the workforce and its competitive environment. Mass immigration and family disruption has kept people fighting amongst themselves. Helping to keep wages down and maximize corporate profits. By intentionally reducing social prosperity. This can be seen clearly as workers' wages have decreased, executive pay has increased exponentially. Families disintegrate, more workers are imported putting downward pressure upon wage demands.

Most mothers would prefer to tend to their children rather than work, but they are on a financial tread mill that has destroyed family life and is causing high divorce rates as the repercussion.Immigrants are being brought in to increase populations since the number of children being born is beginning to be exceeded by the number of deaths, from failed social policies. Human resources as you are referred to by the Corporate and Government machine have been over exploited. People are not livestock, yet the establishment has always kept them insecure by ensuring that they must start their lives and continue without end in debt. Like I have explained, this goes back to feudalism and Native Americans who could see through the plot. First, they steal the land and without that security you are always will be ill at ease through your lifetime, you're thus intentionally turned into an indentured debt slave. In 2009 when the Bank industrie's Ponzi scheme collapsed. Only banks got bailed out and not one citizen. These actions speak for themselves. Most people build a life based upon social lies, especially when it comes to banking and finance, which by design creates indentured slaves via mortgages and unnecessary debt.

PROTECTING CHILDREN

It goes without saying that the connection of a child in a relationship creates a common cause for a couple since the beginning of time. The same in modern society in that child abuse in single parent remarriages, orphanages, and schools, even in psychiatric hospitals (institutions of Government) it is all well documented as fact in the annals of history. This also makes a rational case for why keeping males engaged by joint custody is In the best interest of the child to provide the child with double protection that is otherwise unavailable by a population that has no genetic vested interest other than to exploit the child for their own ends. A lot of the abuse of children we see today is due to absent parents and decreased parental protection, not just in war, but also in times of peace. Native Residential schools, and the abuses of all institutions historically when parents are absent, demonstrates that without parental protection the lives of children are in grave danger from abuse. This is where in this society the best interests of children are often neglected by our court's systematic bigotry against male joint custody of their own children. The current circumstance gains money for women and the legal industry that has a vested interest in propagating this as it is so financially lucrative for them but puts children in harm's way as the father often sees it's a no-win situation of judicial anti-male bigotry. Regarding his prior relationship, men simply divest themselves of one relationship (like a failed business venture) and establish a new family as men do all the time. Men have this flexibility due to their reproductive options being more prolonged and thus men mutate and create new families easier than women. The courts thus severely leave children in a very vulnerable position by losing 50% of their parental defenders, educational support and protection. Parental alienation is rampant as a result. In fact, if the father were to remain engaged, in a system of mandatory joint custody of the child, the child would be better served. Men would be less likely to reproduce another family if they were more enabled thus would be more engaged and committed to the child. There are many psychological studies that prove this fact. Financial payments and loss of custody (Parental rights) disengages the man from raising the child; not that this is what most men want, -they don't want this. But the system foists this upon men and women also by dishonest lawyers interloping, who think; No custody; - no money; - they don't get paid. They see the man and family homes division as the ultimate payer of their salary; - this is a fact about most lawyers. Government sponsored feminist organizations, and the legal industry, have created this circumstance that in the long run not only hurts, but also damages children. In the short term there is financial gain and incentive for interlopers with their anti-family vested interest. The long-term interest of the child is thus sacrificed and hurt, putting the children in harm's way. We have grim statistics for children of divorce and single parents as a result, that is in fact a creation of Government negligence to keep fathers engaged in the lives of their children and diminishing fathers to the role of visitor in their children's lives. Men remedy this by moving on to create another family. The state can never stop this, as some men even change nationality to avoid the states attempts at controlling their lives. Coercion and force as is currently exercised to turn men into financial servants/slaves for relationships which the state has divested them of, this has been an abysmal social failure. Male reproductive ability ensures that by removing the incentive of joint care for the child, the Government apparatus has once again created a legacy of child abuse, neglect, emotional abandonment issues etc. Socially engineered laws and courts are responsible for all these problems and issues created out of parental alienation by divesting fathers of their role in what is referred to as custody. Parenting is a biological connection that the state has no right to interfere in and is one of the greatest human rights violations of this era in history. Wester society focuses upon minority rights while the majority are abused by the same hypocritical Governments; it's all phony posturing.

> The process by which banks create money is so simple that the mind is repelled.
>
> ~ *John Kenneth Galbraith* ~
>
> *Economist*

11th Chapter

THE NEW ECONOMY IS FORCING CHANGE

Banking laws under the current system, enables theft of the rewards of hard work and effort. By creating systems of exploitation by the very design of the banking industry, huge profits and incomes maintain the upper echelons of human wealth. Money is in reality a fiat system, backed by; the productivity of workers. "Work" being the "Gold" backing the system. Current Governments create money by creating interest bearing securities, and banks multiplying amounts on deposit and loaned via central Bank funds advanced. Loans and debt constitute the new money circulated (from economic expansion) that must be put into circulation to represent the value of increased wealth from new productivity. New money must always be created, unless the economy is in an economic retraction. Central Banks exchange credits with Government for debt that is created in the form of bonds. Seldom average citizens seem to ask; "why is the central bank obtaining interest for something created out of thin air, which is the creation of Government, and not the banks money in the first place?" The authority to create money is from Government, and its backing is the people's productivity, thus money creation belongs to the Government, as the fiduciaries of the people. Why is all money created immediately converted into debt?

Banks profit from money circulation without justification. Governments exploit workers via tax revenues to pay the interest added to the money created. The central banks have been robbing the wealth of the nation's citizens for decades, by receiving credits and interest on money they get for free. The elite have created an artificial system to exploit labour for their own enrichment by coopting Government acquiescence in this scheme. The Banking system is a shell game, whereby Bankers through money transfers, buy bonds that were created out of thin air by Government that in fact represent taxes on citizen's future labour. The Central Bank prints money or issues a credit to the Government in an amount equal to the bond thus created, that includes interest that must be paid back to the central Bank along with the principal. The authority to create money comes from sovereign Governments. Why is this middle man the central Bank profiting in the form of interest from returning money they first got from the Governments authority to create money. In fact, the central bank has contributed nothing, and earns interest from an investment of zero. This is how the false financial system creates an, exploitive and parasitic wealth transfer system. This is how in fact the system is based upon a debt treadmill, because all money created is derived from Bonds which are unnecessary debt. All wealth created via adding interest the wealth is cancelled out and perpetual debt via interest charges is created. This debt compounds upon interest, then interest upon interest, until the interest exceeds the principal many times over. Creating an economy of non-interest-bearing economic capital growth under a reformed banking system would coincide with stable economic growth, without creating inflation. It is in fact the interest charged, and not the debt, that creates inflation, and thus the devaluation of money via inflation. This is the fundamental problem with the current economic growth model, where in banks create currency and multiply it without tangible economic value creations. Interest has no economic value to the economy, it is only exploitive. New currency without bases in real economic substance as in new infrastructure, new housing, or other assets is theft of the intrinsic value of currency. nterest is in fact the fiat portion or bases of currency, which is undermining economic stability of currency valuation. Interest paid to central bankers is not based upon anything new and tangible being created to justify the expansion in the money supply in circulation that interest entails. Central bank interest is a shell game as it is the non-reciprocity of financial inputs to justify the wealth transfer to the recipients this represents.

MONEY'S TRUE RESERVE VALUE

Additional funds put into circulation must match increased economic value in terms of concrete assets from labour inputs, or else it creates inflation. Money circulation attached to new economic infrastructure is the only valid way to justify increasing the currency supply, without creating inflation which devalues money. There are better ways to do this. Banks currently exist from tremendous subsidy and other Government welfare, they pretend that this theft is earned wealth; -which it most definitely is not, as I have explained regarding money creation and circulation. The fact is the current banking system creates booms and busts in the economy because money is created in debt. Remove the interest debt inflation and growth becomes infinite, though restricted to be grounded in tangible inputs and new constructs. Whenever the supply of money exceeds the capitalization requirements to charge interest. This act causes the economy to increase in size and inflation results. The system does not create more revenue sources because interest is parasitic, and thus only hurts the money supply system. Excess money in circulation like interest floats in the economy like oil on water, it thus creates inflationary bubbles that is not a problem with capitalism, it's a problem with the system of money circulation. If the money were put into circulation to create real economic expansion such as new infrastructure or businesses loans, then the supply of money is being maintained in equilibrium. Circulating new currency, without it being pegged to tangible new investment, leaves money lying around where it becomes used for nothing new. Unproductive money only inflates and increases the cost of goods and prices via creating inflation. Bankers will not give this advice, because it would conflict with their interests. Banking is a very lucrative ponzi scheme, under their current economic model of operation. Booms and busts under free enterprise exist because of the current banking systems method of operation; money circulation & creation. The economy booms and busts because when money is added without connected value created. There is no balanced money supply creation regulation for banks to follow. This is to explain that the current banking system is the creator of every toxic economic boom and bust cycle. When money supply, and economic growth are in harmony, then there is little to no inflation. Consumption can expand circulation, but does not necessarily increase wealth creation, because it inflates prices, if not accompanied by something productive that expands the economy as an asset created. Wealth created without balance of increased productivity or value provided in exchange is always inflationary. Assets create wealth because they facilitate opportunity for economic creation as value. Money circulated without value also created, debases currency. Interest is a negative economic factor that destroys economic equilibrium, thus it causes prices to raise, and various economic bubbles due to the inflation it creates, because unless it is paying for something that increases economic output it debases the value of currency which is labour value based. To receive labour (wages) in the form of interest is inflationary wealth creation. This can easily be eliminated by attaching money supply growth to developments and actual economic expansion activities, not multiplying money creation, but rather directly funding business ventures, infrastructure and real-estate purchases. The gold of a nation's currency is the productivity of its labour force. The money from real-estate does not need to be repaid immediately. Since it is the controlled circulation for value inputs. The contribution and security this create in the population is greater national productivity from land security, and new economic activities beyond conventional employment into a thus more entrepreneurial Libertarian economy.

COMMERCIAL BANKING

A lot of consumer banking business would be absorbed in the non-commercial real-estate finance and purchase sector. This isolates commercial banking from impacting the consumer economy negatively. First there would be a self-sustaining commercial enterprise only banking sector, which would charge interest only upon commercial ventures. This Bank as with all lenders would be prohibited from involvement in the residential housing market and real estate consumer loans in any form. Second the commercial banking system would need to capitalize itself via the stock market. They would Supply all types of commercial and business loans. It would operate much like banks function today but be prohibited from consumer mortgages and mortgages or real-estate consumer loans.

THE ESTABLISHMENT

The multinational corporate establishment is separate from the rest of society in that they are multinational; secretive, manipulative, deceptive, cunning and a narcissistic confabulation often without conscience. They are primarily loyal only to their own profit and wealth extrapolation from the working class. Many of these individuals see the rest of us as something to be harvested. They are the predators amongst us, many are psychopaths, eating our life efforts and our production.

Many are the social parasites, which if given the opportunity to; rob, cheat, or scam other people, they will perform these actions of abuse regardless of the harm done to others without conscience; without any empathetic sensibilities. Yet society can but does not vet these individuals to prevent them from moving into positions of leadership in society, due to their natural flaws of character.

EXPOSING THE CORRUPTION

The 2008 financial crises were caused by un-vetted subprime mortgage backed securities derivatives trading. This was the product of banking CEO's in the; United States and United Kingdom, elsewhere where banks wrong headedly hired psychopaths intentionally, who were incentivized to sell these short-sighted junk bonds they created in these baskets of loans.There is some suggestion that those in the human resource departments of certain banks were inappropriately using the Hare psychopathy test, to intentionally hire psychopaths as derivatives sales people and Executives to manage the banks disposal of these financial instruments. The banks directors had no idea what a ride this would put them on. There is also suggestions that using Professor Hare's metrics police forces are hiring psychopaths now. Psychological research is being improperly utilized by the establishment. Essentially by the same people who often misquote, Charles Darwin's "Survival of the fittest". These individuals are in fact "Arrogant low IQ trust fund babies in over their heads; the idiot children of the establishment. It seems certain business executives responsible for hiring, think ruthlessness is a good business characteristic. This abuse of process has backfired as the brutality exposed has only created social outrage and grave economic and political damage. Being short sighted with a short-term gain being a part of a psychopath's pathology, their Banking institutions remunerated them handsomely for selling derivatives. The banks sales staff sold these toxic derivatives (bundled mortgage loans) with vigour to banks worldwide. The "greater fool", was left holding the bag. Which turned out to be the Governments of most western nations. Banking institutions informed mortgage brokers and lenders that they would be remunerated with commissions and bonuses for providing mortgages to any, and everyone who wanted one. This in itself was not the issue, as it was the inflated real estate prices that resulted, which increased payments, and the unfounded speculation with intent to flip properties, that made it an untenable bubble. I was in the property development business at the time, and one senior lending officer told me that the order was out "If s/he breaths, give them a mortgage if they ask"; - no one was refused. The loans were fraudulently bundled by banking institutions with good and bad credit risks combined into securities issued. Sold to other banks and investment firms worldwide as "investment grade" income generating investments for a profit; even the credit rating agencies gave these junk bond securities stellar ratings. The longer the scheme went on, the lower the standards became for these loans.

Until income statements from borrowers became "stated income", and proof of income was no longer even needed, all these mortgages ultimately were fully insured by the Government. The theory they sold to their banking cronies was that the good protected the bad loans contained in these bundled mortgage loans. Investors in these securities were thus protected from the losses of the bad loans by the Government.

The problem was when home purchasers walked away from these loans, because house prices collapsed from the speculation bubble. Since why not buy 2-3-4 houses if the loans are easy to get, it became a gold rush mentality. Banking at the best of times is nothing but a Government backed Ponzi scheme. Bad loans if renegotiated would not have been an issue so long as the borrower stayed with them, which the borrowers were not given the option to do. Banks have no motivation to deal with any mortgage borrower having problems since the Government welfare to banks is easier to obtain in one chunk and thus preferred. The Banks realized it was more profitable to kick the working-class borrower out of the house, then collect the full mortgage loan amount plus penalties from the Government. The Government through Fanny Mae, Freddy Mac and C. M. H. C subsidized banks making people homeless and tossed onto the streets! This scheme would become so large, that it virtually destroyed the entire financial services sector for the entire world and their Government tax payer backed loan insurance! The bank schemers to this day have walked away with grand bonus pay cheques personally for so much fraudulent mortgage business, all without any due diligence, and being the bank that was performing the fraud for profit. Then when in 2008 the banks were on the verge of collapse from the results of too many unqualified home owners not paying. Banks foreclosing on mortgages and ruthlessly throwing people onto the streets did not help either, rather than amending loan terms and working with their clients or granting temporary reprieves. The banks were ruthless in their treatment of the working-class borrowers had no sympathy at all and were vicious and callous, especially considering the banks created this problem via massive fraud on their part. The Government decided the banks were too large to collapse (fail). The Government used the self-inflicted bank failure as justification for a bank bailout with working class people's tax money of the same banks which in many instances was tossing the same working-class people onto the streets. When the Government bailed out the banks, only bankers were at the table, the working class were given less regard than a trash bin in the corner of the room. Clearly helping the borrowers was never considered as the banks wanted an easy solution of more free public Government corporate welfare money. Next came a national tax payer bail out of the ruthless banks and multimillionaire bankers, with working class people's tax money by creating money to distribute to all the banks interest free. Inflating away the liabilities of the banks. Depreciating the value of everyone's money; they should have all been nationalized instead of bailed out! Never in the history of Government and business, has such an undeserving collection of corrupt individuals been granted such undeserved proceeds. Where laws go unenforced, those laws do not exist. The public got an outrageous inflationary public debt that paid for the banker's reckless behaviour. This new bank Ponzi scheme destroyed thousands, and some suggest millions of average citizens' lives and certainly caused many suicides and countless family tragedies. This situation cost many citizens their hard-earned homes, businesses, savings and security.

The western mind has an amazing innovative ability to make juice from sour fruit by using sugar. Government clearly had a misguided sense of empathy in bailing out the perpetrators, which is a point that was not lost upon the people, who were outraged. Other than the brief, "Occupy Wall-Street Movement protests" the scandal passed by as though silently in the night. The people knowing their impotence took a severe hit from the establishment's corruption in this. Grumbling as they did, it would take the election of Donald Trump as a public protest via electoral voting, before the public would give some kind of tangible response to the establishment and coopted Government's unfathomable corruption. This was in many regards the last straw for public confidence in Government, in big corporations and corporate welfare. The reverberations of this situation a decade later, have only festered and become a social infection.

GOVERNMENT AND BANKS

Bankers traditionally work with Government hand in hand, across party lines with political party funding. Government simply shrugged that the banks could not be allowed to fail. They do not realize that this crony act of bank bailouts would create a public epiphany, removing all doubt of who Government really works for.

1. Consumer banking at the best of times severely impoverishes average people.

2. Central banks create money whose value is the future productivity by labour of the people, with the Government's collaboration, who supposedly are the fiduciaries of the people.

3. All bank solvency is the people's future and present labours. Tax payer's ultimately guarantee bank solvency. Taxpayers assume the liability risk and in fact fund all banking.

4. The bank provides no tangible collateralized security for money they receive from Government.

5. The borrower is in fact the only security from the bank. If the citizen borrowed the mortgage loan directly from the Government, the Government would have greater security and society enriched tremendously without the middle man banker. The

bank in practice, really has "no skin in the game", nothing at stake in the process; only profits to gain.

6. The Government could enrich the entire nation's people with interest free mortgages loaned directly without the "middle man banker" who serves no social benefit, only their personal enrichment.

7. There used to be business banking in the nineteen sixties, and there is still a market for that if properly implemented. But once the banks got into consumer loans and mortgages this is where the business model got off the rails.

INTEREST FREE MORTGAGES

The shell game we need to acknowledge is that this system already supplies free mortgage money to banks, who relend this money to home buyers.

1. Why is the middle man not cut out and the Government not granting mortgages interest free to the people?

2. So why do we need banks for mortgage loans in the first place?

3. All the money comes from their borrowing from the Government (people) in the first place. This is how it actually works! Let's not forget it is the citizen tax payer who rightfully should benefit from an interest free mortgage loan. The same person who also

provides the credit to the Government to set up banks in the first place. The same taxpayer who is on the hook when the banking Ponzi scheme fails, as they do with regularity fail and the Government bails them out.

4. The people (Government) guarantees the bank never loses. The bank gains the interest from free Government money that puts the citizen in decades of indenture to pay the un-justified interest payment that is three or more times the principal the bank got free from the Government. I ask again; where is the banks collateral?

5. Added to Interest is often Government loan insurance to insure not the borrower, - but the bank from loss! The borrower adds the insurance premium into the mortgage loan on which is added interest also, thus more interest income for the bank.

6. Basically, citizens lend and borrow their own money, become indebted for decades, so that the middle men can make pure profit from the interest on the people's own money the bank gets for free without offering any security by the bank.

7. Why the middleman / bank is there, and the Government does not lend mortgages directly to the people, is a scandal as old as banking itself, and their incestuous relationship with the Government. A system which once you understand its workings

causes nausea in the pit of the stomach of any thinking person of reasonable intelligence.

ECONOMIC RESTRUCTURING

Generations of people have long been impoverished due to the current home mortgage scheme. Land that is the birthright to inhabit by the nations people requires decades of unnecessary interest and labour being stolen in exorbitant interest that impoverishes generation after generation by design, for what is a very basic necessity. A squirrel, a rat, a bird or any animal, even an insect is in better financial shape than the average human being, because nature does not charge rent or a mortgage. The current home distribution system only exercised by humans upon this planet is an abomination against natural law; even an insect lives better! Native Americans had free land use as do all tribal societies, this is natural. The feudal monarchies under the western feudal land tenure system destroy all aboriginal societies, because the invading culture is a land thief. Every citizen starts in technical bankruptcy, with mountains of debt or a lifetime of paying rent by the obviously intended design of the system, unless they have someone give them the money free by inheritance or good fortune. The human being suffers the first Governmental tyranny and injustice to insure the citizen will be indentured and exploited by the hierarchy; the theft of our birthright to a home/land.

Curiously though, every basic economics book describes how the system works. Generations of people needlessly work for years funding the elite's lavish lifestyles that money in the form of mortgage interest, supplies the banking Ponzi scheme. Bank deposits are always insufficient for banks to live off interest from loans based upon deposits. This myth or urban legend of banks' lending depositors' money has no bases in reality; -ask any economist, it's all no secret. Most people deposit their pay and spend it, pay check to pay check. Banks have always received their money from the Government to fund their operations, or they would all be insolvent. The real money in banking is made in lending free Government money and charging interest. As a ponzi scheme banks require constant influx of new outside money to remain operational. Since their inception banks have used Government money to fund their operations and maintain their existence.

THE NEW ECONOMY

The current economic model does not work very well other than for the wealthy oligarchs. While particularly banks and financial institutions are parasitically feeding off the working class, and transferring wealth to themselves, as they are funded by Government with their working capital, while Government guarantees their solvency with a myriad of Government corporate welfare benefits. Our economy is in disarray with a serious lack of financial balance and virtually everyone lives in poverty to fund the elite feudal lords we still have.

TECHNOLOGICAL CHANGE

The future decline of the economy in developed nations, whether from foreign competition or robotic development is something inevitable that cannot be stopped. Once the cat is out of the bag, he is unstoppable. It is evolutionary change we have here, and though it is to be economically dreaded by the working class for its long term and current implications. Under the circumstance something must be done to restore and maintain a middle-class consumer society or civil unrest and violence will be the outcome. Everyone who can think knows the problem exists, but until now nothing innovative enough has arisen as a solution. The current trajectory is not looking positive for the working class, if we do not balance the current system and make it fairer. The repercussions for radical political change civil unrest turning into revolution and complete destruction of all order is immanent. This economic dislocation could undermine western civilization leaving anarchy in its wake, if not dealt with appropriately.

Human evolution has been given a push to leave the current feudalism for what must be a new economic system. This is good because technology is destroying the value of brawn and replacing it with brain. Throughout history, whenever there is such fundamental change to the means of production as the current technological change, civil unrest follows. This was true of the industrial revolution with the Luddites and it is true now with the current technological revolution. Many of the economic and social reforms I advocate here, could possibly be welcomed by the establishment. It is not that the establishment is reform minded, they may simply be interested in surviving the disruption themselves, rather than a bloody revolution and they do not desire the fate of the house of the former king of France Louise XVI and his associates. Because as the economy falters to provide for the people their needs they are motivated for change, and change can be a very dangerous thing, as it has no predetermined outcome. Like sailing a ship, change sometimes looks for any wind to maintain momentum. Just as in Weimer Republic Germany, the power brokers choose to support Hitler's Nazi party. Though they were not the preferred option, the Nazis could maintain order and control over the communists and other factions rioting on the streets wanting a change. Devils were behind door 1, 2 and 3 either way no option was pleasant. We are as a society reaching a point where we ourselves must realize the old economic model is not working, so we need another one.

CORPORATE LAW & REGULATIONS

Clearly this system needs some critical reform, like every other socio-economic system in history we must also evolve with changing times. Evolution is a necessity for all life upon this planet. Just as Corporations were created by Crown Charters for purposes of joint stock speculation and limiting liability in trade. Corporate law and banking has evolved, and needs to be amended to serve the best interests of all concerned, and the greater good of civilized society. The free enterprise system in order to maintain stability, need not put society's stability in jeopardy for the few psychopathic owners. With a bit of tweaking the economic and political changes as I will suggest here, we can restore and maintain prosperity in the west, in a socially responsible way, without resorting to communism, which is an absolute failure. At some point in the not too distant future industrial productions ownership will have to become more based upon a co-operative model. Governments will need to write new corporate laws, as I will also outline herein.

CORPORATE INHERITANCE LAW

The deindustrialization of America by the children of former industrialist is a sad and pathetic story. Though the current circumstance at present has been caused more by technology than losing industrial capacity. There is something extra ordinarily unethical about the circumstance of the children of the founders of large corporations, built by the employees in collaboration with the company's founders, that the employees do not acquire inheritance rights just like the family has. I would suggest that the employees having inheritance rights is more justified than to the founder's often inept children. I think that laws need to be changed to make it mandatory that the corporate employees share a trust fund made up of corporate shares having voting rights upon the death of the corporation's founders. That there must be a legal change to provide employee inheritance laws of corporate shares to change in law provide employees a right of inheritance of corporate shares into an employee's corporate trust, to ensure domestic industry never again goes off shore and to reward labour that built the company. Present aristocratic like inheritance conventions prevent employees from ever reaping rewards beyond a salary. This kind of salaried exploitation is a theft of employees' lives given the importance of their contribution to the corporation. I am not saying that the family of a corporation's founders should not have inheritance rights. I am saying the employees should share in the rewards also via a Government legislated inheritance trust that never gets diminished. A share trust would be a mandatory succession plan to be implemented in the Charter of all corporations. This would set aside as a profit sharing voting cooperative ownership benefit, with voting rights of at least 51% and profit sharing along with all of the company's shares in circulation, upon the death of the founder(s). This share trust provision would also help redistribute wealth into the community and society in general in an equitable manner to compensate society's provision of an appropriate and educated work force enabling the existence of the corporation.

CORPORATE SHARE TRUSTS

The nation state creates inheritance and corporate governance laws. Since the corporation is considered to be a person. Then the employees become the company's family. The death of the founders being the time to distribute the shares of ownership to the heirs. The employees as a group thus become entitled to in a block of newly created shares to become a "Corporate Share Trust" the corporation would be mandated to create a share trust of at least 51% of all classes of shares created by the Corporation. This shall be an unsellable share voting block that would vote to designate future Directors by ballot, like other shareholders with the same rights, regarding governance and profits of the corporation. By conducting the governance of the corporation, in this way, existing equity should not be reduced, as no new public shares are put onto the market as it is a Trust being created. This would be a new type of share that would be based upon laws called; "Corporate Person's Inheritance laws", to create a trust fund where in a employee block of company shares would be newly issued to constitute by legal mandate an employee's trust constituting at least fifty-one percent of all public and private corporate shares. This share block would be created as an employee's trust fund estate mandatory in corporate charters, with over ten human employees, to protect domestic industry and jobs, into the future. Preventing transferring ownership to a foreign company and or foreign take overs of the company. This would recognize the contribution of a corporation's employees into the future. Rather than any form of Government review of foreign take overs bids of domestic industry, the company's employees would attend to such matters with their shareholder votes. The remaining shares inheritance would be in accordance with the founder's estate desires. These employee trusts would become mandatory, just as we have estate inheritance laws for other persons.

REWARDS AND CORPORATIONS

The fact is most family heirs do nothing to build a company they inherited. Normally they have contributed little to nothing. This has long been a vicious injustice towards employees who may have contributed decades of their lives for the company. This is simply a matter of Government amending inheritance laws regarding large public and private corporations' shares. No preference in the creation of these trusts or future share dilution would be given to senior management, beyond an equal share with all other employees. I am not advocating an individual dispersal of shares ever, but rather creating a Cooperative Trust of a majority voting block which should belong to the corporation's employees under inheritance as a succession right for the employees under national estate inheritance laws. Inheritance trusts should in no way be taxed by the Government. The block will disburse dividends in accordance with the Trust Block membership's democratic determination of dividends payouts. The trust might be prohibited from the ability to break up, liquidate or otherwise disburse the "Inheritance Trust" block.

CHANGING BANKING & LAND TENURE LAWS

Nothing impoverishes western nation's people more than the current banking system. Virtually every major religion prohibits charging interest as usury and thus a religious crime / sin. It is usually called "usury" there are very solid reasons for this, because it is the acquisition of value (labour) for nominal investment, pirating the labour of others. Interest takes advantage of the need and desire of people to have something immediately. The problem is that it is a feudal indenture and a form of slavery of mankind that still exists in connection with land. A home is fundamental to human living thus in many ways a human right that needs to be respected. Tiltle ethically belongs to the nation's citizens / people, and not a sovereign. The ability to multiply ones input by hundreds of percentiles is a trick foisted upon humanity since the dawn of history, we call it "interest". Interest upon home purchases multiplies the cost by two to three hundred percent above the principal. The difference is between an ability to pay in full within ten years verses thirty or more years. As the additional twenty years is interest. Given this fact, is it any wonder the average family cannot afford children, an eventual small business, savings for college for their children, or decent health care given the high payments in this scheme? This is one area of exploitation where the working class desperately needs some relief. Interest is the source of more hardship foisted upon humanity than all wars combined, as the cost is usually astronomical being that it is in fact a tricky form of slavery that entices the needy. Interest does not reflect the cost of borrowing, it is the cost of human impatience and the deception of the wealthy lazy and unproductive people who parasitically feed upon the productive.

CONSUMER MORTGAGES

Consumer mortgages and insecure land tenure laws impoverish the people, putting them into servitude, to make monthly payments far past the refunding of the principal borrowed. Mankind labours for decades to pay interest for two, three or four decades longer than the repayment of mortgage loan principal.

1. People get taken advantage of a second way also, in mortgaging, and expecting citizens to finance that which was stolen; the land.

2. Kings, Lords and Barons assumed land ownership by thug-based theft, calling themselves aristocrats originally under feudalism.

3. Land based debt creation is always the first drive to put people into servitude. Charging a fee for that which by the laws of nature already belongs to the people. That being the land and constructing long term indenture. This is a scam as old as aristocracy.

THE FIRST EUROPEANS TO CAME TO AMERICA

The first thing Europeans did to settle the western territory was destroy the free food of the Buffalo Herds by killing them off, this way they removed the natives, as they were starved out from the land or otherwise pushed off by force. The second thing Europeans did was take over control of the land itself, by force as they did centuries before in Europe. The Native Americans originally had no concept of "land ownership" only "land occupation and use". In Native American culture Europeans were insane! "How could you own the land they thought?" European land treaties to this day ignore the fact that many tribes sold their neighbouring tribes land, and not their own territory, to ignorant Europeans. Many of the treaty claims of land sold to Europeans were fraudulent native tricks; - so thought the natives. They sold their neighbouring tribes land to the Europeans intentionally! The Lakota Tribe refused to accept large farms the Europeans offered for each tribal member. They could see that this was a trap of indenture and that land tenure would be the end of their truly free way of life. The Native life only depended upon having certain skills of hunting, harvesting and planting crops. If no one occupied a certain area, then it was available. Native American tribes were the last group to live as Libertarians in America.

SLAVES ENSLAVING SLAVES

The Europeans who were fully indoctrinated multigenerational slaves, aided their masters in crushing the free native people, because they wanted a piece of this "free land", thinking they were escaping the bondages of European classed society, they enforced its spread. Within a generation the settlers "free land" would lead to their children becoming indentured to the "land debt system". This is how human enslavement to the system, Government, the Crown or any tyrant begins with this greatest theft ever devised;

1. The theft of the land title.

2. Mortgage serfdom with payments of the mortgage until death.

3. Paying to the establishment, for something that they stole from you.

4. Even a rodent upon this earth is freer than the average dumb human being, who is enslaved with his own inheritance.

5. Every creature upon earth realizes that the land is there as the Native Americans did, free for use.

6. If only the establishment and Governments did the ethical thing of arranging fair distribution of land according to needs.

7. But they don't because slavery is more profitable for the lazy.

THE GOVERNMENT ENSURES ITS SURVIVAL BY:

- Co-opting land wealth.
- Dividing society.
- Giving unearned wealth to the undeserving that serve them in repressing others.

LAND USE; THE GRAND SHELL GAME

This is the dirty laundry of so called "civilization" and "Government"; it is savage, brutal and based upon complete lies. The only asset upon land once developed that should or could ethically be sold is:

1. A premium for the location to convenience.

2. Material and labour cost to construct improvements and buildings.

3. Less depreciation due to age and resulting deterioration of those improvements over time.

4. The cost to acquire property should be based upon the efforts, including materials and related costs to construct land improvements and structure determined by appraisal.

5. New homes would have an incentive percentage added upon the price that would compensate the builder for their efforts we call "profit" that the competitive market would determine. By playing one builder costs off the other, and what the buyer is willing to bear given the properties resale price. This will be how value can be determined. Builders would acquire vacant land from the local Government free for development after proving their ability to finance new construction. Existing land ownership needs to be respected without hindrance.

6. These proposals deal with financing and acquisition of land not tenure.

7. What I advise is two separate parallel financial systems. Despite past tyranny cited herein, land reform should not entail any redistribution as that would be tyrannical at this point in time. What I am advocating is only an alternative consumer bank finance system

FREE MARKET BUSINESS

Libertarianism is for the deregulation of business operations, however there will always be the right of society at large to regulate in restrictive ways the necessary regulations to:

- Protect Human Health
- Protect the environment
- Human Resource protection from exploitation

A free market economy should have less regulation and be freer to self-regulate. Interest free and flexible payment loans from Government. Capital would be available from Government home equity lending. Then unsecured business loans would be available. It would be prudent for a citizen to build their home equity in a home then get an interest free loan with voluntary payments to start a business, preferably started from home. Consumer loans would be unnecessary thus the predation upon consumers would be eliminated by constitutional property occupancy and protection laws. You can fail in anything, but your home will always be yours and protected from seizure. It would be more prudent to use an interest free home equity loan that carries no mandatory payments than borrowed business loans. I do not consider business loans as negative. Business is risk-based lending; It is entitled to interest for risk. What I speak of is the separation of personal finance, verses business finance. Each of us is a consumer and can be an entrepreneur. We are entitled to personal protection of ourselves as humans to have security of our homes, just as incorporation protects shareholders who invest in corporations from liability. This security does not apply to all business loans which are unsecure if from a bank. This economic change means: Capital for productive purposes shall be available interest free if home equity exists to borrow from. The feudal home and land speculation system charging consumers' interest for a home needs to come to an end. Home ownership shall be protected from seizure for any reason, including debt, for life, and can be inherited by successive generations thus this equity grows from paying down of the mortgage or inflation, which can be remortgaged with the Government over your life time as interest free loans, using your home to secured interest free loans from any equity built by inflation or paying down the mortgage, kind of like a life time credit card of home equity for interest free money.This program It is not a guaranteed income, this is a home security program that will end homelessness, create community, provide credit for other purposes over the course of your life interest free, enable flexibility by the family to draw on a money in a crises or for a need interest free and total flexibility to pay or not the debt as life circumstance allots. This system is far more superior to Government welfare and handouts as it is self-reliant in bases and involves real debits and credits. Everyone has a fundamental human right, like every other creature on earth to a secure property and a home, free from taxes, levies, or enforceable liens or seizure. Property loan liens would be registered for resale purposes but be unenforceable Government provisions. No need to tax, or have Government involved in our personal affairs or have social welfare. Welfare programs are only necessary to keep social harmony with the poor because the current system makes almost everyone start life as homeless, landless, debt slaves. It is time we as a society remove our chains put in place by mortgage debt. This is not free land, this is interest free land acquisition and equity finance.

THE PARALLEL ECONOMY

There needs to be a paralleled consumer economy created where in:

We all have a right to security of our own shelter and a piece of land on which to live like all creatures upon this earth, like every, plant, bug and animal. This is our terrestrial right to a place of habitation without rent, fee of exploitation, or extortion by others. The only value upon land that is exchangeable is the improvements upon the land. The system would continue as is, except for financing by Government of all consumer mortgages converted to interest free Government held mortgage loans. All existing land ownership titles would remain untouched. Consumer mortgages that would all be nationalized and repatriated from the banks to become interest free trust mortgages with the Government, essentially a universal exchange of paper at minimal cost to the consumer or Government. Banks would not be paid any compensation for this portfolio under nationalization. This is not communism, but rather calling for an end to feudalism as an economic system that levies fees upon the rightful land inheritance of human beings. Past land values would remain in effect as something determined in the free market.

LAND TENURE

Purchase transactions would be based upon a free market as it is now based upon intended use of the land and the organization of such use and need. Interest free Government home purchase loans and the protection of private home property from foreclosure guaranteeing home ownership would constitute a new social contract with all citizens, as a self-reliant tax-free social security system that is universal and available for all citizens, both rich and poor, far superior to all forms of welfare payment. The need for any significant welfare would thus be eliminated since everyone would own a home. This is in keeping with the founding of America, where land grants where resulted in wide spread distribution of the nation's wealth and costs no other person in taxation. This modernization would not be a redistribution or confiscation of land, but rather the provision of interest free land purchase and or building mortgages by the Government, in exchange for existing bank loans. The resulting equity and security for all citizens would eliminate a lot of poverty and over time create equity that could be utilized for productive purposes by borrowing against home equity free and being able to use the eventual equity to pay for child rearing expenses and or start a new business venture etc.

PROPERTY RIGHTS

Land ownership by consumers would also be free of taxation, other than in the case of commercial ventures which would be excluded from the consumer mortgage program. Non-human entities (corporations) would continue as now to pay compensation as a tax for any private gain and other land utilization. Corporations need to be delisted as persons regarding land use. This land scam emanates from feudalism in Europe and elsewhere, where vigilante groups called aristocracies with their kings and queens claimed ownership of the land. They organized what are in fact armies to enforce their vigilante land claims of ownership by force of violence against any individual or outside group who might oppose their theft of Gods' gift to the people of this planet to inhabit. The nation state was founded as a form of mafia, organized crime, land thieving thugs that in their origins to this day are actively involved in thuggery and theft. Only thuggery justifies their existence since they are currently moving away from a reliance of any form of consent in western nations. All too common is politically based extortion, violence and threats of violence in their divide and conquer ethic, created by the state to repress citizens as an all too common tactic of Government.

THE MODERN TENANT MORTGAGE

Currently money for mortgages is given to the banks from the authority of Government as a manner to create and circulate money. Low cost Government money is being given to the banks in the form of mortgages, rather than circulating money directly to those who need the money, this middle man charges interest. This process currently is a form of debt slavery invoked upon the people keeping the working class in debt their entire lives with no reprieve.

CORPORATE WELFARE

Bank corporate welfare is the greatest welfare expenditure of the nation state since the 2008 economic collapse. By far corporate welfare over shadows all other forms of citizen welfare in totality every single year in every western nation. Yet the welfare the Government gives to people living in poverty gets far more criticism. Because the citizens do not understand how the system works, many people falsely believe banks finance themselves without Government handouts. Corporate welfare is financial and other subsides given to corporations by Government for which they very much have the ability to pay, this is actually the most heinous form of welfare, giving public money for private profit is inappropriate. Most large corporations pay minimal tax contributions. The tax code enables writing down virtually everything by expensing activities on the books. Government legislation protects large corporations from liability in a virtually unlimited way. Recent revelations from Edward Snowden and WikiLeaks point to Government using the Governments spy agencies to gather information for domestic industry. Then there has been:

1. Immunity from Government prosecution for crimes and Government assisted union busting.

2. The creation of the corporate "person" giving immunity to the corporation for crimes, yet this artificial person has the rights of a human being.

3. Consumer loan insurance schemes that consumers must pay for guaranteeing mortgage loans, to guarantee the banks and mortgage loan companies by the Government. In point of fact, the net effect is not to aid consumers, but rather inflate the cost of housing. The net return to the economy I believe is negligible.

4. Housing is a permanent necessity, as it is shelter.

5. Mortgage loan insurance should no longer be necessary.

6. Government bailout money to large manufacturers such as the auto sector is common. Should Government decide there is an economic benefit to corporate loans from them, then Government should ensure they receive some of the benefits in the form

of long-term shares or corporate bonds from the borrower just as any other investor would require.

7. Free or very low interest capital supplied by Government. There in hides the fact, that this in no way is any semblance of free enterprise activity and instead is a subsidy.

8. Over paid directorships on bank boards of directorships commonly granted to politicians in Lou of payments and bribes, this practice should not be legal.

9. Finally, I would add lumber, and mineral mining rights that make fortunes from free or low-cost leasehold land from Government, rather Government should require they be shareholders on behalf of the citizens in the enterprise and that this income should contribute to Government as general revenues.

BANKING INDUSTRY FACTS:

They get their free resource (money) from Government authority and charge Governments' interest on their own property; the money created. Essentially citizens' mortgage their lives for real-estate that has interest charged upon it that the bank gets for a pittance and the citizen pledges a life of servitude for that which rightfully should be provided interest free and could be provided interest free by the state. Government mortgage money is supplied virtually free to banks for mortgage loans. The

Government insures these mortgage loans against default, where is the risk for the bank. With no mortgage interest charged to citizens, and the interest cost removed, the savings for home purchases would be on average three quarters less time and less money to pay off a home, citizens would be liberated from debt servitude and thus much more self-sufficient. Most social programs are necessary, because of things like. "The big mortgage rip-off". Money creation is the sovereign right of all nations to control and operate as they wish. Yet they borrow and pay interest on their own property by issuing Bonds in exchange money put into circulation. Money is created by issuing needless layers of debt upon Government. Banking is a highly Government subsidized Government conspiracy. All the money of banks is issued by Government credit. Banks are middle men, subsidized by Government with free money and guaranteed mortgage insurance schemes that are Government guarantees against the banks ever losing money.

The whole system is a scheme of private profit from public money. Government guarantees private bank solvency while only the consumer pays anything for it. All banks are the property of the people, in principal the citizens of that nation whose labour constitutes the collateral and sovereigns. The peoples labour and productivity, along with other national resources, are the guarantee for the value of every currency worldwide. Fiat currency is a false pretense. All currency is a value construct that is resource based upon; human and material resource production, based upon current and projected productivity of goods and services and the demand for those resources that is via trade backing and determining valuation of a nation's currency. Gold and precious metals are unnecessary to back currency, national productivity is the backer of every currency. Without public money no bank in the world could exist. There has never existed since the founding of banks of a truly private institution. Truly independent banks since the beginning of banking have always ended up insolvent thus; - bankrupt! Take any bank and have all their depositors withdraw their money at the same time and there would not be enough money to pay more than 5% of depositors, if that, they are empty shells. Banks do not earn money from lending depositor's money, but by lending out the Government's money. Let me restate that as it is a very significant point; banks earn money from lending out low-cost money supplied on the people's credit. The banks loan proceeds security is not from the bank, though they profit immensely; security is supplied by the person borrowing the money. The bank profits from the borrower's ability to pay the bank. The bank contributes no collateral.

BANK POLICIES

There is no other business that even comes close to the ways Banks operate. Re-lending money they get from Government loans to the bank and how they multiply money on deposit. All banks operate upon Government money and require bailouts from the public purse since at some point, their business model is a failure, since it is Government subsidized in so many ways. In reality banks are a state sponsored ponzi scheme. All Governments are consciously aware this is a fact; banks can only remain solvent with Government sponsorship and periodic bail outs. The reality is that banks are constantly insolvent and even their bookkeeping systems are counter intuitive. They hide this reality as in making other people's money "deposits" and Government money an asset in their reverse bookkeeping accounting systems. Government in fact lends the people's money to finance banks that exploit the people in a parasitic and exploitative collaboration between the two institutions. One is left to wonder, why the profits go to bankers and their shareholders, while the risk and periodic bailouts go to the nation states taxpayers.

1. Banks are a corporate welfare system; No greater business welfare exists than that supplied to banks and the banksters that operate them.

2. Logically there is only one ownership model for banks which would have integrity and not be such a fraud and that is nationalization of each nation's banks, I would not rule out.

3. There is no need for banks in their present form under pretence that they make profit. In fact, banks only circulate capital as Government desires to increase the money supply through loans that do not require a profiteering middle man known as the "banker". Much of this "banking" emanates from the desire to

parasitically unjustifiably profiteer from private citizens and enslave them to debt on over inflated property; Enslaving private citizens to steal their labour and gain from unjust enrichment. Unlike business expenses, consumer expenses are not tax deductible in many instances.

SURVIVAL OF BANKS

I do not overly concern myself with banks, after consumer mortgages are nationalized, they can be cut loose from the system or they could be nationalized. I would let the people decide the banks fate. I can imagine banks being business lenders and self-financing as they would have to change their business model to do what the original intent of their establishment was, to help capitalize business expansion. There is the possibility this could lead to a renaissance in commercial banking, or it could be their death sentence. Government could easily establish their replacement if they cannot survive in this new environment. But such an environment will also require they sink or swim on their own business acumen, with no more Government subsidies.

THE LIBERTARIAN RATIONAL

Starting with the bank of England, Government collaboration in corruption has been a big part of the reason the system is so lacking in integrity, but we can reform this system to make it function with integrity, and that's essential what this book is about. After the Athenians, the second great attempt at Libertarianism was the founding of the Swiss confederation then the

United States Republic, after the first the Swiss confederation; then the founding of the French Republic.

The founding fathers of the United States were utilizing their contemporary educations and the philosophical ideas of the much-respected British philosopher John Lock and others. Great leaders at the right time came together to create a great nation in The United States of America. Men I have been inspired by and admired since childhood; like Thomas Jefferson, whose home in Monticello, Virginia I visited way back in 2007. The United States constitution was a grand attempt to create a system of checks and balances. Clearly in most nations there are no longer balances in that one fundamental flaw exists with contemporary constitutions that being; fully impartial law enforcement. Without full independence of law enforcement by an independent democratically elected law enforcement body corruption creeps into Government. I advocate:

1. Direct democracy based upon the model utilized in Switzerland one of the wealthiest and most stable country politically on the planet earth as a functional and pragmatic Government constitutional model, that has proven it's merits as the best model for populist government, Superior to that of the United States in being both populist and peace loving, having not been in a war for hundreds of years, including both WWI and WWII. A nation that also has provision for referendums initiated by citizens that allows citizen legislation.

2. An independent Senate to enforce laws replacing any "Supreme Court" and political appointees like Solicitor Generals and Attorney Generals. The further from the legislature, and the more remote from the Legislature house the Senate is the better! We suffer not from a lack of laws currently, there are too many already. We suffer from the lack of enforcing and respecting the enforcement of laws, particularly in the highest levels of Government itself.

3. There is a need for structural and constitutional reform in all western nations. Much of this book has been dedicated to eliminating corruption that exists. There is a cultural morass that has occurred in the west as we have slipped down a slippery slope, by a lack of law enforcement.

4. We need to recognize that Government has far exceeded its boundaries and has become far too interventionist into issues that should stay out of in the private prerogative of private citizens. While important matters of law are selectively enforced for Government convenience. I am reminded of the old expression; "Those that attend to the affairs of others are ignoring their own affairs". Clearly it is not society that has an issue, it is the Government that has created so many problems and it is Government the creepy "peeping tom", which has created so many

problems in society as it has far exceeded its mandates.

5. Libertarians have more faith than most people in the abilities of private citizens to manage their own affairs. We don't want control, we want each person to be as sovereign and independent in managing your affairs as possible, because we believe that each person is intelligent enough to make the right choices and do that which is in your own best interest better than an institution or Government, or anyone else.

6. We want the individual to succeed on your own terms. What I have espoused here is individual sovereign property rights. These rights include economic protections where homes cannot be taken from citizens.

7. Libertarianism needs to be competitive with communism and socialism which create a dependency upon Government handouts to pay rents and mortgages. The problem with this is it requires a big tax base to pay for this dependence that is based upon Government extortion. This is not a communistic elimination of private property touted here. This is the creation of a solid formula for sovereign homestead rights, and flexible payment system to enable conveyance of land and in-volatile protection of ownership.

8. The economic security through this system of land tenure rights is based upon independence of citizens, not Government dependence. Libertarianism with this economic proposal to nationalize all mortgages under this plan via a citizen's mortgage trust system I believe provides a Libertarian gift that demonstrates that even welfare recipients would be prudent to take up the cause of Libertarianism, as it is a hand up and not a hand out that would be beneficial for the poor.

9. Libertarians need to realize that a lot of people are dependent upon Government and to simply spout ideas of liberty is not enough, unless Liberty will improve people's individual rights and real-life style beneficially. No person, even the most dependant welfare recipient I think could resist free housing and land in exchange for Government interference in their lives. A small plot of land with a house afford opportunity to have chickens, raise vegetables, and start an auto repair business or other venture, let people's imaginations fly!

10. The protection of the right to inviolably inhabit this land provides greater security than welfare; like none ever in history. This project is sellable on this basis alone to anyone. I believe nobody wants welfare dependence. Let's free humanity from the chains as I have expressed here and live finally as free people with liberty for all.

COMMENTARY

Libertarianism as presented here is more competitive than most Government handouts offered under either socialism or communism. Wealthy people often advocate Libertarianism as a no brainer for them. However, for the poor this is not true, thus Libertarianism has lacked a populist appeal as a result, because in the past it offered the poor nothing; -perhaps even more misery. I believe fundamental economic change in home ownership is the kind of program that could spring board libertarianism into the main stream of politics, since it makes all the financial self-supporting ideas of libertarianism possible, including eliminating taxation for all, and it is in keeping with traditional Libertarian values. The truth is that life's expenses are an inverted pyramid and giving the youth a break on home ownership is a key element in the formula to reverse the demographic atomic bomb the west is facing. Toxic social communism also needs to be brought under reign, and its deceptive advocates removed from all institutions of learning and Government, along with those who profess these ideas must be removed from their employment amass for this betrayal of fiduciary duty.

Libertarianism can finally be a true grass roots ideology starting with the home and the family as society's foundation needing support, to make citizens truly independent. I stated in the beginning of this book with the words; "BE PROUD". To desire to make people proud of themselves and enabling each to carve their own little paradise in their imaginings, and not anyone else's visions. Free from extortion of Government, and independent in economy, I seek to give every individual apiece and taste of personal liberty in their homes that may spread out into the community where they will have a stake and live under a local state jurisdiction with local direct democracy and have a reason to care once more. A Senate as I have presented in the Federal realm, with the right constitutional provisions, would deal with most of the other issues of corruption. In reality it is all quite simple to comprehend. The problem will be those with a vested interest that will oppose reform, by "tooth and nail", since the status quo is currently providing them a very comfortable lifestyle.

> *"All successful revolutions are the kicking in of a rotten door"*
>
> ~ *John Kenneth Galbraith* ~

12th Chapter
CONTROL THE GOVERNMENT OR THE GOVERNMENT WILL CONTROL YOU

The nation state's obligations to its citizens: Clearly over the centuries a common law (tradition) of fiduciary obligations has been created, between the nation state (Government) in western nations, and the nation's citizens.

1. The most fundamental obligation is one of mutual defense and protection. Followed by protection of family, as a mutual protection agreement between the nation and the people.

2. Government protection of citizens private land ownership, fiduciary administrative protection of public land in its administration, utilization and development for the financial social benefit of the people.

3. The regulation of the territory in accordance with the fiduciary best interests of the nation's citizens in fidelity, exclusive of all foreigners, administered by the Government for the benefit of the people.

4. The essence of the nation state is the expansion of early human tribal care and membership of people inhabiting a section of the earth's territory for the benefit of a select group exclusively that is maintained

by the citizen's guardianship and lives in event of war if necessary, with the lives of the people in military service if necessary.

5. The nation state is a reciprocal fiduciary arrangement. The fundamental obligation of citizen and Government administration is an exclusive arrangement with these parties.

DUTIES OF THE NATION STATE

Every national Government has fundamental fiduciary responsibilities such as promoting the national culture and history, protection and defence of their citizens and national territorial sovereignty free from foreign incursion, from foreign peoples, and Governments, in defence of the nation's people's independence and integrity. Governments owe loyalty and to be both benevolent, and altruistic, towards the nation's citizens. To not engage in covert social engineering, manipulation or violation of citizens' rights to privacy in their personal and private affairs. To be respectful towards human diversity as a spectrum within a promoted melting pot society. That all citizens have the right to live without harassment or the imposition of the personal values of others being imposed upon them or their families; limited by the Government responsibility to prevent abuse and prosecute acts of human exploitation or physical abuse of others. The Nation is also responsible:

1. To ensure the nation has a fair and equitable system of laws that are fully enforced. A nation, which will

equally prosecute all breaches of law, enforced to maintain social peace and harmony.

2. To ensure that laws are limited by necessity and for all citizens applied equally, that all citizens have equal legal protections and judicial protection.

3. To treat all citizens equally in practice and law enforcement without distinguishing one from the other, and only based upon facts and evidence under habitus corpus.

4. To defend freedom of speech and conscience for all citizens and prosecute those who would abuse this right by acts of bigotry and racism or acts of treason.

5. To enable and facilitate citizens ability to earn a living by providing basic education and ensuring the means for a non-indoctrinating education.

6. To development of national lands, industry and business, for the benefit of their citizens and the utilization of fees charged to industry for resource development and extraction for the benefit of the citizenry.

7. Ensure the protection of the health and wellbeing of the nation's citizens, by ensuring that natural environments are respected and protected from pollution and contamination.

8. To ensure every citizen has a secure home upon the nation's territory for life, and that ownership of that home will be inviolable by: lien, tax, any other levies or repossession for life, to provide security to every citizen and financial flexibility. That the nation will do this via providing an interest free home ownership loans on a single property and building of the citizens choice, from those lands available for sale in the free market. Based upon income and ability to pay the principal.

9. To facilitate a free market for entrepreneurs to thrive.

10. To represent exclusively the best interests of the citizens of the nation. To promote citizen independence of the individual, and to not interfere in the natural conditions of family unity, by promoting and supporting the family as a necessity of society, as the incubator of future generations.

THE CITIZEN'S OBLIGATIONS TO THE NATION STATE

Loyalty to the nation, fellow citizens and the nation's best interests of citizens. to defend the nation in the citizens capacities with your life if necessary, in event of foreign conflict, incursion or attack, either internal or external to the nation.

1. Obedience to the nation's laws and to seek reform of any laws that are considered unjust or unfair towards citizens.

2. To be independent to the best of your ability, financially and in conscience.

3. To maintain decorum and comradery with fellow citizens.

4. The obligation to promote and participate in democratic institutions.

5. To respect and promote family values and healthy children.

6. To ensure that the health of citizens is not jeopardized by industry.

7. To be independent and ensure that laws are not tyrannical.

8. To speak out against injustice and tyranny via democratic means.

9. To respect and honour the nation's domestic culture and history.

Libertarianism seeks to limit laws and Government to their bare necessity. Libertarianism has to have rules to be civilized, just as the simplest human constructs under tribalism have rules. Libertarianism is about limiting controlling and restricting Government, to simplifying the apparatus of Government, so that it does not become hijacked by vested, special or outside influences as is the present case this book presents. The type of behaviour cited in the prior pages of this book outline the dangers of Government overreach. Libertarianism is the belief that Government rules and regulations have become far too over-reaching in their activities and harmful to society. That Government has become subverted by vested interest that is against the best interest of society and thus Government does have a tendency to become a tyrant by over extending its reach far beyond its intended purpose. The hope in this book is that an alternative is presented here that is intended to increase individual, social and national liberty. The more local Government is, and the more controlled by the people themselves, the more realistic is the Government. The more peaceful the resulting society. Libertarianism is about local control, limiting Government to its most elemental aspects. For the Libertarian as a non-anarchist, rules/laws are seen as a necessary evil that we must temper and guard against all unnecessary implementation.

Govern when necessary,

but don't necessarily govern.

CONCLUSIONS

So why did I write this book?

For over a half century I have had many life experiences as an entrepreneur starting and operating several businesses, as a citizen with a deep interest in politics and philosophy, topics which I have studied in great depth over the years. I have grown tired of the same old social corruption story, decade after decade, playing out in Government and society at large, year after year. Though this book may come across as being negative, which I admit it is from a certain perspective, this is not my intent. The book is intended to be a positive humanist plan going forward, to resolve the issues outlined herein. I have had several decades of pragmatic experience as an employee at times and a business man for several decades operating different companies. With the courts and tribunals, with lawyers on my side and as a self-litigant representing myself in numerous civil law cases and a Federal Court case. I have lost cases to outright criminals, and seen the system turn me into the victim of crime, and I have won cases in a mixed bag of results. This has given me special layman's insights into the inner workings of the system without vested interest. As keen observer of the political system, as an equal parenting advocate, and political lobbyist, I have met with politicians personally and seen how the political system really operates over public perceptions.

In my experience I have found that corruption in the form of vested interest and even the more typically bribery is rampant, and most people are complicit and too fearful in reality to do anything about it. Too often alternative motives and vested interest is often masked as the public interest which in reality runs the world. There is in reality only a minority of people who are the admirable agents of change within society. The majority I feel would man the gas chambers and say they were, "following orders". We can see right now that even professors in Universities, the elite, some of whom object to politically correct social engineering would and do comply with political correctness, demonstrating they are obedient careerists' believe that most corruption can be eliminated with authentic law enforcement, and it is the negligence in enforcement which is the primary corruption that really runs the world. I have tried in this book by designing a Senate to correct this problem that is by design intended to tighten up the system of justice to have more integrity, by making the Senate independent, setting age requirements and term limits for Senators and other details. People's personal needs are far less as we age, and we have more life experience, thus older people tend to be less corruptible in general than the younger and more ethically clear, because they have experienced life and the end of life is nearer. I designed a Senate of older people purposefully, for their wisdom and time in life when people are most wise and independent. The young have less wisdom from age and have more material needs, thus are easier to corrupt, with less pragmatic experience in life. By making legal enforcement a separate independent body of Government as checks and balances, short of divine intervention, to me this is the only way to ensure the honour and integrity of the system and people. This is counter balancing the system by design, to create a separation from politics. It does not say much positive for the pragmatic reality of human behaviour and conscience. It is often stated we get the Government we deserve and by these observations about human nature that fatalist concept may be right for some people, but not all, thus I do this for the few deserving people who have integrity. In order to resolve any problem, we must first identify it clearly. I have observed the old adage that; "Power corrupts, and absolute power corrupts absolutely". I hate to admit this as the truth where people are involved, but in my real life I have found this expression to be true. So how can we fix this circumstance which is self-evident? If we want to correct these problems, I wondered? More often than not, we lack a plan, nations overthrow corrupt Governments and then the issue arises; - What do we do now? I have diligently attempted to outline from my experience and education what needs to be done, which from my half centuries experience, and much deep thought, that the system must have checks and balances upon the power of authorities. I found individual rights to sovereignty and the tyranny of others attempting to impose their philosophies or religious beliefs upon everyone else needs to be addressed that it is at the core of all human problems. That is simple respect for the integrity of others, which encompasses the old adage of; "mind your own business". Which we all too often, people seem to have a problem with observing. It's really in essence that simple, as I have found that most problems are caused by people I would categorize as; "trouble makers"/ "the controllers". They can be complicit collaborators or instigators, either way you categorize your "trouble makers", both categories carry equal guilt. I have over the years met many zombie humans; People who go along with corruption or abuse other people. When I question this, they usually say; "because I need a job". This "job excuse" does not wash any more than Nazi concentration camp guards saying; "I was just following orders" which many did at the Nurnberg trials. Then were sent to the gallows for their crimes. I first read and saw videos of Nurnberg as a child, and even then, it left me in a state of dismay in that this excuse makes humanity truly a pathetic creation. Every child must be educated regarding the ethical crime that complicity in tyranny is shared guilt and does not supply exemption. Something that even many contemporary University Professors need to be advised of regarding political correctness and social Marxism. If you are following orders in a corrupt system, then you have an obligation to assist the persecuted by leaking information to those that can do something or bringing an end to it. You have an obligation to leave and or initiate change by undermining corruption in any way you can conceive. This is your human obligation and responsibility, otherwise turning your defensive attitude towards you, application of this perspective entails that you personally deserve all your misfortunes in retribution for your blind eye to the suffering of others; the law of return. The world will never be a better place so long as humanity accepts corruption and we all know what it is when we observe it and put simply; it is abuse of power. The old golden rule applies of treat others as you would have them treat you.

This book has a very positive message regarding people and places a lot of faith in people's ability to manage their own affairs independently, from family to Government the intention is to encourage adulthood, leadership and integrity in both family and social responsibility. My observation is that tyranny begins when society attempts to control each other's perceptions to line up with our own. Tyranny begins with arrogance, that I am superior to others, and thus must tell them what to do, this is the cause and epitome of much human suffering in the past century. When force is used rather than persuasion, tyranny in all its forms has arrived. Human beings are still in need of rules, but these rules must be tempered with tolerance by limiting the rules and enforcing these basic rules/law equally upon everyone. Democratic application of law prevents law from becoming a tyrant, thus by enforcing all laws equally, we force laws to be implemented with caution. By separating Law enforcement from legislators, we create a balance that prevents elites from escaping the law as they often do in hypocrisy. By moving most day to day Government administration to Cantons (Local Government) we ensure local control and remove arbitrary Government by putting a local democratic face upon local affairs. Balance is necessary in Government and nothing makes people fairer and more reasonable than the knowledge that what you do to others will also apply to you and your family. The natural environment is at least indifferent, but people are interventionist, which starts with individual arrogance and corruption. I believe that left to our own devices that each of us can manage our own affairs, and that intervention into our personal affairs by others and corruption for personal gain within society is the root cause of tyranny. If you want to create a better world, then make the rules apply equally to all. This does not ensure equal economic outcomes, but I have included some critical economic reforms to provide opportunity that with diligence and added effort can create prosperity and protection from becoming destitute and vulnerable to economic exploitation from others. This book has a positive message of having you join me on this voyage to envision a better world, a more peaceful world where we can live in harmony, if we can just learn to respect each other's rights to libertarian independence.

BIBLIOGRAPHY

A Memoir of Jacques Cartier, Sieur De Limoilou: His Voyages to the St. Lawrence, a Bibliography and a Facsimile of the Manuscript of 1534 with Annotations, Etc (Classic Reprint) By James Phinney Baxter

A National Crime: The Canadian Government and the Residential School System, 1879 to 1986 (Manitoba Studies in Native History). By John S. Milloy.

A People's History of the United States: By Howard Zinn

American History: A Survey, 12th Edition. By Alan Brinkley.

Bank Heist: How Our Financial Giants Are Costing You Money: By Walter Stewart.

Canada: A People's History, Vol. 1. By CBC and Don Gillmor

Canada's Residential Schools: Missing Children and Unmarked Burials: The Final Report of the Truth and Reconciliation Commission of Canada, Volume 4 (McGill-Queen's Native and Northern Series) Paperback – December 9, 2015. By Truth and Reconciliation Commission of Canada (Author).

Champlain's Dream. By David Hackett Fischer

Das Kapital: A Critique of Political Economy: by Karl Marx.

Flames across the Border: 1813-1814. By Pierre Berton.

From Dictatorship to Democracy: A Conceptual Framework for Liberation: By Gene Sharp.

Hitler's Banker: Hjalmar Horace Greeley Schacht. By John Weitz..

IMMANUEL KANT Premium Collection: Complete Critiques, Philosophical Works and Essays (Including Kant's Inaugural Dissertation): Biography, The Critique ... of Ethics, Perpetual Peace and more: By Immanuel Kant and J. M. D. Meiklejohn

Justice denied: The law versus Donald Marshall: By Michael Harris

Lament for an Ocean: The Collapse of the Atlantic Cod Fishery: By Michael Harris

Lies My Teacher Told Me: Everything Your American History Textbook Got Wrong: By James W. Loewen

Neurotribes: The Legacy of Autism and the Future of Neurodiversity: By Steve Silberman.

One Flew over the Cuckoo's Nest" was written: By Ken Kesey,

On the Origin of Species: By Means of Natural Selection (Dover Thrift Editions): By Charles Darwin.

Paris 1919: Six Months That Changed the World: By Margaret MacMillan

Real Democracy in Operation; the Example of Switzerland:. By Felix Bonjour.

Rules for Radicals: A Practical Primer for Realistic Radicals: By Saul D. Alinsky.

Samuel De Champlain: From New France to Cape Cod (In the Footsteps of Explorers). By Adrianna Morganelli.

Self-reliance and Other Essays. By Ralph Waldo Emerson.

Snakes in Suits: When Psychopaths Go to Work: By Paul Babiak and Robert D. Hare.

Stasi: The Untold Story Of The East German Secret Police: By John O Koehler.

The Age of Uncertainty: By John Kenneth Galbraith.

The American Invasion of Canada: The War of 1812's First Year. By Pierre Berton

The Americans: By MCDOUGAL LITTLE.

The Canadian Securities Course 1993. By The Canadian Securities Institute.

The Collected Works of Rene Descartes: The Complete Works Pergamum Media (Highlights of World Literature). By Rene Descartes.

The Communist Manifesto: By Karl Marx and Friedrich Engels.

Courts from Hell - Family Injustice in Canada Paperback – Dec 27 2007. By Frank Simons (Author)

The Gulag Archipelago 1918-1956 I-II 1973. By Solzhenitsyn Aleksandr I.

The John Locke Collection, Nov 6, 2014. By John Locke.

The Naked Ape: By Desmond Morris.

The Origin of Species: By Charles Darwin.

The Peoples of Canada: A Pre-Confederation History. By J. Bumsted

The Prince: By Niccolo Machiavelli

The Power of Myth Paperback: By Joseph Campbell (Author),. Bill Moyers (Author)

The Rise and fall of the Third Reich: A History of Nazi Germany. By William L. Shirer.

The Robber Barons: By Matthew Josephson.

The Second Treatise of Government and a Letter Concerning Toleration, By John Locke.

The Social Contract (Penguin Books for Philosophy). By Jean-Jacques Rousseau.

The Swiss Model – The Power of Democracy: By Venelin Tsachevsky.

The Trial of Louis Riel: Justice and Mercy Denied a Critical Legal and Political Analysis. By George R. D. Goulet

The Wealth of Nations: By Adam Smith.

Thomas Jefferson: Writings: Autobiography / Notes on the State of Virginia / Public and Private Papers / Addresses / Letters (Library of America): By Thomas Jefferson and Merrill D. Peterson.

Thomas Paine: Collected Writings: Common Sense / the Crisis / Rights of Man / the Age of Reason: By Thomas Paine.

Two Treatises of Government (Everyman). By John Locke.

Unholy Orders: Tragedy at Mount Cashel: By Michael Harris

Walden and Civil Disobedience. By Henry David Thoreau.

Without Conscience: The Disturbing World of the Psychopaths among Us: By Robert D. Hare PhD.

. Parental alienation is rampant, 297
"Men going their own way (M. G. T. O. W)", 194
"Middle Class" and 9 to 5 jobs, 196
"mother" and "father, 212
"Racist" and "Nazi", without bases in fact, 222
15th century inquisition, 290
15th century witch trials, 289
17th century philosophers, 267
2008 financial crises, 88
3D printer manufacturing, 199
a chance to be elected, 62
a common historic identity, 70
a constant in-flux of competition, 75
a covert dictatorship, 223
a culture of greedy self-righteousness, 197
a culture of victimhood, 148
a desire for less Government intervention, 143
a division of social strata, 142
a façade of independence, 108
a fiduciary conflict of interest, 154
a fifth column, 71, 130
a form of long-term national sedition, 103
a form of wage repression, 76
a functional social model, 24
a grudge that the Germans let fester, 272
a lifetime completely flexible loan, 181
a man's right to freely accept or enter into a relationship, 58
a media of Government shrills, 108
a murderous tyrant in people's lives and for national economies, 194
A nation state is a common connection, 74
a nation's ancestors, 128
a new economic model, 184
a new Libertarian resurgence, 155
a new unrecognized economy, 199
a normal human condition since the dawn of history, 182
a person's private business, 60
A PLAN FOR CHANGE, 4
a power game, 50
a power grab, 61
a preference for globalism, 76
a preference for non-traditional candidates, 155
a pressure relief valve for dictators, 117
a pretence of popular support f, 57
A public highway system, 170
a roaring laugh, 160
a serious internal enemy, 71
a severe repudiation, 139
a shark infested cess pool, 210
a silent majority, 61
A square deal, 183
a state sponsored movement, 43
a system of repression, 70
a thick Russian accent, 159
a time proven anti-discrimination recipe, 110
a travesty of justice, 93
a tube from city to city, 239
a tyrannical dictatorship, 63
a very dangerous development, 61
a very grave imposition, 57
a very irresponsible ideology, 162
a very perilous future, 27
a very profitable industry, 208
a worthy future goal, 63
abandon their children, 43
abandonment, 30
abdication, 57
ability to reproduce, 208
absentee parents, 231, 232
abuse, 34
abuse or mistreatment, 213
abuses started with social communist engineering, 216
academic administration, 153
Achilles tendon, 48
acquired larger brains from Neanderthals, 117
acquisition of special rights and privileges, 212
actions speak louder than words, 51
activist judiciary, 92
actor, 29
Acts of treason, 3
acts of treason against their own people, 107
Adam, 189
Adam Smith, 151
administrative reviews, 176
Adolf Hitler's Nazi Party coming into power, 258
Adolph Hitler, 62
adulterous boyfriend, 54
advance themselves, 94
advantage that is unearned, 25
affection, 45
affirmative action, 45, 56, 219
affirmative action into positions of power, 56
afford to have children, 236

African American, 40
African Americans, 113
African nations, 46
Africans in Portugal, Italy and Spain, over the centuries, 117
Age of Uncertainty, 257
age restriction, 98
agenda, 285
agenda of feminism, 242
agents of evil incarnate, 54
agrarian society, 259
alienation, 256
all civilizations eventually collapse, 131
all has been a delusion, 133
All men are not "created equal", 203
all men are pejoratively, lousy fathers, 190
aloof Governments, 67
already come from Government, 178
alternative perspectives, 47, 79
Altruism, 26
always been implemented without consent, 103
Amazon, 239
America, 27
American dream, 235
American Natives, 118
Amish, 120
an absolute travesty of Justice, 144
an act of treason, 187
an anti-national act of treason, 70
an army of psychopathic lawyers, 193
an echo chamber, 108
an extraordinary level of historical illiteracy, 127
an intervention, 66
an uncaring society, 103
an underhanded vote buying scheme, 131
anarchist, 166
anarchists, 19
Anarchists, 23
anarchy, 19
Anarchy, 24
ancestor's legacy after four hundred years, 126
ancestors, 27, 46
ancestors past settlement, 120
angering, 45
angry mood, 49
animal husbandry, 55
animals, 37
Ann Coulter, 191
annual dividends to all citizens, 184
anti male, 37, 38
anti male form of fascist attack, 58
anti male hate groups, 248
anti-democratic, 45
anti-democratic administration, 45
anti-democratic forces, 65
anti-exploitation, 199
anti-family, 147, 231
anti-government, 19
anti-immigrant racist attitudes, 117
anti-male bigotry, 52
anti-male discrimination invoked by Government policy, 144
anti-male feminism, 150
anti-male hate indoctrination programs, 287
anti-male sentiment, 52
anything less than merit is always regressive, 271
apartheid created by multiculturalism, 105
apex of libertarianism, 25
Apple and Microsoft had their genesis in home garages., 195
apprehensions, 86
appropriate, 29
arbitrator, 285
arbitrators of social peace and justice, 65
archaic judiciary, 54
argument, 47
aristocracy, 133
aristocrats with hemophilia, 118
army of lawyers, 32
army of psychopaths, 206
arrogance, 187
artificial social divides, 148
as anti-racist as it gets, 111
Asian tiger economies, 259
assembly lines was mindless repetitive work., 196
at home Dad, 38
at the expense of the middle class, 62
attacked, 230
attitude problem, 84
Attorney General, 98
audacious insult and degradation upon us, 127
authentic, 28, 30
authentic free thought, 47
authentic love, 45
authentic social justice, 102

authentic working-class leaders, 135
authenticity, 30
authoritarian, 20
authoritarianism, 34
auto manufacturing, 253
Auto Pact Agreement, 253
autocratic rule, 153
average man, 52
average of a sequence, 202
avowed communist, 154
backlash, 152
bad decisions, 54
bail out banks, 88
bait and switch, 42
Balkan style racial cleansing dangers, 128
bank interest, 167
bank middle man, 175
BANK POLICIES, 336
Banking industry facts, 334
banking reformation, 52
bankrupted, 10
banks create money, 299
barbarism, 271
based upon merit, 68
based upon wealth, 234
basic economic structure, 87
beacon of light, 28
become corrupted by too much authority, 102
being pragmatic, 18
being repressive, 155
being spoon fed, 47
being the underdog, 189
being treated with respect, 60
belittled by feminism, 234
below the poverty line level for 20 years with no wage increase, 76
benefit of foreigners, 73
benevolence, 41
benevolent, 45
Benjamin Franklin, 252
Berlin wall, 153
Best before date, 199
betrayal and duplicity, 188
betrayal by politicians, 255
betrayed, 53
betraying, 45
bias, inequality and injustice, 100
biased privilege, 219
Biblical tale of Eve, 189
big pensions, 196
big tent, 13
bigoted discrimination, 285
bigoted human rights violation, 190
bigoted judiciary, 205
bigoted laws, 115, 285
bigoted movements of history, 112
bigotry, 189, 207, 222
bigotry a man must deal with, 194
blk citizens, 209
Biological, 213
biological advantage, 241
biological and genetic self-interest, 240
biological designation, 212
biological diversity, 203
biological extinction, 244
biological imperative, 244
biological investment, 242
biological offspring., 208
biological parent, 233
biological spectrum, 203
Biologically based, 226
biology trumps everything else, 244
birth parents without biological connection, 217
birth rates plummeting, 191
birth right, 72
birth right to own and use property, 167
birthrates, 38
blatant reverse discrimination, 61
blatantly bigoted, 56
bodies of Government would be independent, 99
born in corruption, 49
boundaries of parenthood, 57
boundaries regarding your privacy, 57
bows and arrows, 120
brain damage, 35
brain washing, 19
brainwash and program children's minds, 225
brainwashed, 34, 49, 130, 221, 230, 232
brainwashed and complicit, 223
brainwashed children, 220
brainwashed in the schools, 130
brainwashing, 34, 41, 48, 162, 232
Brazil, 259

breach of Constitutions, 102
bread and circuses, 10
breed, 242
Brexit, 2, 137
British Colonies, 121
British or American territorial take over, 119
broad stroke amendments, 96
broadly accepted, 160
brutal, 33
brutal repression, 51
brute force, 24
brutish use of authority, 115
build a new economy, 185
bureaucracy, 41
business case analysis, 82
business case studies, 79
Business Case Studies, 80
business community controlling a global political mechanism, 62
business management, 28
Business mortgage banking, 178
business operations, 234
business tycoons, 26
business was a family affair, 195
businesses, 237
by virtue of having shared his home with a woman, 59
by way of not being elected, 93
C. I. A, 35
Calcutta, 280
camera phones, 48
can of information worms, 48
can the class alliance between the wealthy and the working class be maintained for a prolonged time?, 143
Canada – USA Free Trade Agreement, 253
Canada, 33, 106
Canada's Prime Minister Justin Trudeau, 275
Canadian guy, 160
cancellation, 48
candid about this provocative, 64
candid talk is feared, 63
canoe, 25
Cantons, 96
Cantons could force a national referendum, 96
capital, 25
capital is being wasted in the home allocation process and speculation, 181
capital loaned by the banks, 173
capitulate to impositions., 102
Captain James Cook, 119
captive bird, 23
career politician, 264
career politicians, 256
careerists, 28
Careerists, 29
Carl Jung, 17
cases of endemic social division, 113
cash for life lottery system, 190
cash for life to women, 60
castrated, 244
castrations, 35
catalogue shopping direct, 239
catastrophe of decimated families, 236
catholic orphanages, 227
cause men to abandon their children's need for a father, 193
causes of homeless western men, 192
censored, 47
censorship, 223, 275
central bank, 177, 178
central banks, 153
centralized social communist state, 139
chain reaction, 48
change, 47
changing banking & land tenure laws, 321
character assassination, 47
characterized the working class as idiots, 155
Charles Darwin, 280
Charles Darwin's book, 115
Charles Murray, 202
charter schools, 212
cheaper to replace than repair, 195
checks and balances, 67
cherry picked for enforcement., 87
chicken pox, 118
child abuse, 33, 244
child abusers, 35
child bearing, 231
child care, 14, 33, 34, 35
Child care became farmed out, 224
child custody laws, 141
child ownership, 37
child rearing, 189, 241, 244
child support, 226
child tax credits, 9

child's life, 233
child's upbringing, 36
childcare, 234
childhood education, 233
childhood indoctrination, 43
children, 23, 32, 34, 226, 233, 234
Children hungry for guidance, 210
children learn compassion, 44
children lost big time, 244
children's developmental, 44
Children's rights, 53
China, 26
China's Cultural Revolution, 274
Chinese economic miracle, 83, 84
Chinese Elites, 262
Chinese Government grants, 83
Chinese politburo ruling class, 62
Chinese style "cultural revolution", 211
Christian populations, 246
chronically ill, 27
circulate money into the economy, 178
circumvent the influence of the people., 68
citation that men are poor parents as a complete lie, 144
citizen cooperation, 63
citizen's free will, 22
citizen's principal residence, 178
citizen's private affairs, 86
citizens, 37, 169, 170
Citizens can subscribe, 171
citizens privacy, 215
city of Vancouver, 119
civic responsibilities, 215
civic sense of responsibility, 26
civil matters, 39, 97
civil rights movement, 39
civil service, 155
civil war, 6, 154, 185, 256
Civil War, 185
civil warfare, 129
civilized society, 185
claiming mothers were doing nothing, 225
class warfare, 49, 62
clean environments, 188
clean up our own, 66
Clearly Government is anti-family, anti-children, 193
coerced into unconscionable, 215
coercion, 24
coercion and threat of violence, 91
coercion to pay for decades, 189
co-fund the family's demise, 226
cognitive development, 42
cold war, 156, 160
cold war period, 153
collaborative, 25
collaborators, 237
collapse of Detroit, 49
collapse of the former Soviet Union, 258
collapse of western civilization, 180
collapsed, 163
collateralization, 21
Collectivism, 25
collusion, 48
coming civil wars, 132
COMMENTARY, 343
Commercial Banking, 305
Commercial Banks, 178
commissions of enquiry, 99
common law, 55, **345**
common law marriage, 58, 59
common law principals, 74
common sense, 71
communism, 39, 46
communism's ideological crimes, 136
communist agenda, 50
communist Frankford School, 151
communistic ideas, 24, 46
Communistic ideas, 123
communistic pattern, 50
communistic social engineering, 55
communistic social nihilism, 136
communists, 153
community collaboration, 23
companies do not want to pay a living wage, 76
compatriots, 126
competition against other women, 242
competition for resources, 242
competitive, 13
competitive environment, 18
complacency and collaboration, 68
complete alienation, 129
complicit, 46
complicit citizens, 223

complicit media, 35
complicity, 43, 53
compounding interest, 172
computer designed, 240
computerization and robotics, 180
computerized, 199
concentration camps, 35
concentration camps and gulags, 147
concentration of power, 101
concentration of wealth, 62
CONCLUSIONS, 351
condescending, 155
condescending attitudes, 289
condescencing reality, 155
confidences, 55
confiscated, 33
conformity, 23
Conformity, 23
Confucius, 218
conscience, 52
consequences, 43, 209
consolidation of power, 30
conspiracie, 93
conspiracy, 156, 161
conspiracy nuts, 294
constant lies, 155
constitutional, 52
Constitutional limitation and control of the mega or Federal state apparatus, 139
constitutional rights, 203
constitutionalist, 24
Constitutionally controlling all Government, 146
constructive ideas, 21
consumer mortgages, 177, 178
Consumer mortgages, 322
consumer-based mortgage backed securities, 180
contamination, 231
contemptuous in their actions, 73
contention, 28
contested, 47
contextualization, 270
continued for decades, 236
contract does not any longer exist, 58
contradicting the Government narrative is a danger zone, 293
contributed to the nation for generations, 69
control, 47, 227
control all law enforcement agencies, 100
control exercised, 47
control of the agenda, 143
control over the company's shares, 199
CONTROL THE GOVERNMENT, 345
control the narrative, 47
control their children's education, 222
controlled state, 20
controllers, 24
controllers., 25
controversial, 202
convenient group of minorities, 57
conventional media, 48
Conventional media, 48
convergence, 49
conversation, 158
convoluted zero-sum social teachings, 220
convolution, 47
cooking and baking skills, 233
co-opted, 41
coopted parents, 225
co-parent, 213
co-parents, 32
corporate benefactors, 42
Corporate inheritance law, 318
Corporate law & regulations, 317
corporate mandarins, 240
corporate masters, 236
corporate oligarch masters, 156
Corporate share trusts, 319
corporate shares, 52
Corporate Welfare, 332
corporate welfare scheme, 78
correct legislation, 87
correct speech, 153, 210
correspondence, mail, and literature, 65
corrupt, 28, 220
corrupt establishment, 141
corrupt Government, 82
corrupt legislature and judiciary process, 53
corrupt malfeasance, 77
corrupt motives, 76
corrupt politicians, 39, 154
corrupt politicians buying votes, 58
corrupted, 230
Corrupted institutions, 45

corrupted the judiciary., 141
corrupted the youth, 223
corrupting the youth, 220
corruption, 30, 41, 53, 262
Corruption in all its forms is a death blow to all economic prosperity., 263
cost of daycare, 236
cost of delivery, 239
cost of housing, 233
costs money, 83
costs of raising children, 7
countries, 157
coup d'état of western Governments, 258
court defence, 40
court industry, 39
court perjury, 100
Court precedents, 100
Courts, 36, 91
courts clearly say in their decisions is not the man's right to in any way, 189
Courts from Hell – Family Injustice in Canada, By Frank Simons, 193
Courts to take effect of law, 100
covert, 94
covert plan, 72
covert social engineering, 295
covert terrorism, 130
covertly supported, 157
craftsmanship, 238
create a backlash from the majority, 61
create a vision of the future, 66
create both value and quality products, 196
create laws, 99, **286**
create optional non-profit corporations, 171
create social discord, 69
create social division, 69
created inflation, 233
created out of thin air, 173
creates ghettos as exists, 105
creates more employment, 79
creates this national identity, 74
creating new families, 193
creating opposition and descent, 114
creating resentment, 52
creation of legislation, 87
creation of opportunities, 238
creations and achievements, 186
creative and pragmatic solutions., 79
creative thought, 230
credentialed merit, 149
credit, 191
credit slaves, 42
crime enforcement, 237
crime., 32
crimeless court trials, 207
crimes, 33
criminal actions, 33, 88
criminal courts, 32
criminally, 35
critical thinking, 64
criticize new media, 47
crony, 28
crony clubs, 30
crony judges, 41
cronyism, 45
cruel, 43
crushing personality, 45
crushing the individual, 45
crying, 39
cultural "story", 186
cultural history perspective, 128
Cultural Integration, 124
Cultural integration takes time, 123
cultural warfare, 133
culture, 27, 127, 202
culture does not embrace or comprehend western cultural history, 128
culture hijacked, 139
culture,, 187
cultures of disrespect, 84
current circumstance, 6
current crop of politicians, 64
current system, 97
current world affairs, 64
curriculum, 222
custodial arrangements, 34
custody, 37
CUSTODY, 38
custody cases, 207
custody disputes, 290
custom cars, 240
custom orders, 238
custom products, 239
customized, 199
custom-made products. Items made in the home, 195

damage to society, 191
damage to the family, 32
dangerous, 36, 185, 231
dangerous development, 186
dangerous disconnect, 49
dangerous perspectives, 293
dangerous posture, 61
dark age, 185
dark times ahead, 61
Darwinian, 234
Darwinian proof, 208
Darwinian science, 246
daughter, 233
daycare, 44, 45, 231
daycare generation, 112
dead, 45
deadly lack of children, 2
debauchery, 35
decades of betrayal, 155
decent wages, 186
Deception and greed are their ethics, 155
de-civilization of men, 243
Declaration of Independence, 203
decline, 231
decline of the middle class, 2
deconstruction project, 158
deep in thought, 160
defence of minorities, 60
defend the nation, 71
degradation, 86
degradation of our overall humanity, 103
degradation of the environment, 195
degrade elders, 223
degrading, 73
degrading men, 194
deindustrialization, 240, 255
delinquent children, 208
deluded ideology, 265
deluge of too many foreign nationals, 116
democracies, 29
democracy, 18
democratic ideas, 29
democratic process, 216
democratically elected Senate, 95
demographic, 5
demographic reality, 247
denigrate social customs, 219
deny parental rights, 144
deology, 294
departed their base, 50
depopulating towards extinction, 232
deprogram, 164
descendants, 46, 197
deserted island, 28
designed to extricate money from men, 58
destroy their children's lives, 245
destroyer of prosperity, 46
destroying men's credit, 192
destroying men's self-esteem, 191
destroying men's', 192
destroying their environment, 195
destroying western society., 221
Destruction of the family, 154
destruction of the family in western nations, 143
determinations, 213
detrimental, 237
detrimental effect, 275
detrimental long-term effects, 80
detrimental to society, 83
developments, 61
devil, 234
devised to create social discord, 158
devoted to our families, 68
dichotomy, 188
Dickinson, 34
dictionary words, 50
did not care, 154
did nothing to counter act this sedition, 158
differences, 203
different cost structures, 81
different interpretations and perspectives, 85
different personalities and characteristics, 202
different perspectives, 81
difficult time integrating into our society; most likely never., 132
difficult times for the working class, 110
difficult to integrate, 124
digging themselves deeper, 47
diminished, their human rights, 72
dinosaur, 47
dinosaurs, 286
direct democrac, 18
direct democracies, 17

363

direct democracies following the Swiss model, 146
direct from the Government, 178
dirty deeds, 43
dirty industries, 197
disadvantaged the majority, 61
discarded and betrayed by their own Government, 69
disciplined and organized, 24
disciplined and organized freedom, 24
disconnected from the population, 52
disconnected from the working class, 182
disconnected politicians, 156
discredited, 47
discredited its workings, 210
discredited most of that ideology, 62
discrimination, 51, 124, 188, 201
discrimination against domestic citizens, 72
discriminatory or bigoted, 206
disengaged fathers, 208
disengages, 83
disgrace, 46
dishonourable industry, 90
dishonourable vested financial, 102
disinformation, 106
dis-information, 78
disinformation and spreading dead end philosophies, 159
disinformation policies, 153
disintegration of the social order., 95
displace domestic workers, 186
displace their own peoples, 72
displacing the founding peoples, 72
disposable fodder, 57
disproportionate diversion of the wealth, 182
disregard, 187
dissatisfied in their lives, 44
dissimilarities, 124
distorting and perverting society, 148
distraction, 157
distraught, 208
diverge in values, 120
divergent beliefs, 121
divergent perspectives, 134
diversions, 28
diversity, 53, 201, 202, 203
Diversity, 202
diversity as individuals, 203
diversity of citizens, 214
divide and conquer, 28, 54
Divide and conquer, 154
divide and destroy western civilization, 149
divide in concepts, 166
divide society, 55
divided people, 27
dividend earnings, 171
dividends, 169, 170
dividing society against itself, 139
division is everywhere, 65
division of labours, 234
divisive acrimony, 201
divorce, 191
DNA tests, 117
Do it your-self" project, 224
doctors for instance that drive taxis, 117
documented, 153
Domestic birth, 74
domestic citizens, 71
domestic corporations, 78
domestic heritage, 74
domestic industry, 198, 238
domestic political parties, 78
domestic population, 70, 106
domestic population is homogenous, 124
domestic skills, 233
domino effect, 43
Donald Trump, 137, 152
Donald Trump in 2016, 62
done right with mutual respect, 121
down trodden victims of the male gender, 224
downward pressure on wages, 236
drama manufactured by lawyers, 290
drink hemlock tea, 220
drowning man, 10
dual income families, 236
Dual parenting, 245
dumbing down, 107
dust bin of history, 123
dustbin of history, 169
DUTIES OF The Nation State, 346
dysfunction, 66
dysfunctional, 150
dysfunctional families, 247, 248
dysfunctional philosophy, 245
dysfunctional societies, 268

dysfunctions, 46
easily subverted, 56
east bloc nations, 123
East Germany, 65
echo chamber, 140
economic breaks to those who have children and families, 175
economic certainty, 6
economic collapse, 6
economic communism has been discredited, 136
economic conspiracy, 49
Economic decline, 262
economic depression, 6
economic guarantor, 53
economic ideology, 11
economic migrants, 128
economic pressures, 295
economic productivity, 168
economic reality, 24
economic restructuring, 314
economic revolution, 183
economic situation, 12
economic surfs., 29
economic system, 87
economic transformation, 180
economic tyranny, 24
economically, 37, 235
edited story, 47
Education Charter School Trusts, 8
education of biased social agendas, 134
education opportunities, 214
education system, 34, 46, 164
education to be an individual, 44
educational hierarchy, 153
educational system, 156
educators, 163
Egyptian Pharaohs, 120
Egyptian pharaohs of the past, 64
Egyptian Pharos, 118
elderly gentleman, 158
elders, 223
elected dictatorships, 88
elected officials, 102
election campaign contributions, 98
election of Adolf Hitler, 105
elections, 13
electoral advantage, 237
electoral demands, 54
electro shock brain damage, 288
electro shocking patients, 35
elementary school children, 57
elephant in the room, 31
eliminate indenture by interest., 183
elite agenda, 240
elite crony, 41
elite establishment, 49
elite live in complete arrogance, 142
elites, 40, 50, 152
elites and minorities, 50
elites arrogance, 48
elitist, 28
emergence of a market economy., 259
emotionally, 242
empathetic, 27
empathy, 26, 27, 43, 45, 231
employ western workers, 75
employee's attitudes, 84
employees, 209
empty nest, 7
enable citizens, 179
enable economic growth, 214
enable Government to indoctrinate the children, 143
enabler of criminality, 94
encourage citizen independence, 181
encourage self-reliance, 181
endemic human condition, 113
endowments, 26
enforced manners, 204
enforcement, 40
enforcement of law, 91
enforcing these laws, 146
enforcing these social engineering, 56
engaged parent, 245
engineer our children's sexuality, 57
engineered this social discord, 134
engineering political protest, 142
English based constitutions, 206
enlightened, 51
Enormous employment dislocation, 184
enslave the population, 188
enslave the working class, 182
enslavement, 23
ensure his country was not infected, 158

ensure some type of social security, 179
entered a barbaric age, 209
entertaining, 158
entire social body like leprosy, 65
entitlemen, 192
entitlement and greed, 155
entrepreneurial activities, 6
entrepreneurial activity, 184
entrepreneurial revolution, 186
entrepreneurial struggle needlessly, 131
entrepreneurism is really not rare, 182
entrepreneurship, 25, 179, 184
entrusted positions, 72
entry level jobs, 186
environmental responsibility, 188
epitome of ignorance, 128
equal justice and law enforcement, 213
equal parental rights, 36
equality, 231, 241, 284
Equality cannot exist, 201
Equality does not exist, 201
equality implements victimhood, 273
Equality never has in the past or will in the future be possible, 201
equality of individuals, 267
equality of opportunity, 281
equality of the sexes, 206
equality of treatment, 61
equally all the laws, 96
espionage, 197, 279
espionage planning, 153
espoused communist ideas, 157
espousing these ideas, 73
establishment, 23, 31, 48, 49
establishment's narratives, 47
establishments, 48
ethical child rearing, 230
ethnic tensions, 246
eugenics, 202
Europe, 27, 106
Europe as a homeland, 221
Europe will collapse, 221
Europe's disintegration, 246
European diseases like the common cold, scarlet fever, small pox, 118
European Union, 18
Europeans, 221
Europeans and Asians, 117
even the KGB underestimated, 160
ever-present claim of victimhood, 148
every geneticist knows, 120
everyday occurrence, 191
evidence, 202
evidence of a sick society, 58
evil people, 147
evolutionary, 48
exaggerated narratives, 150
exasperated by legislators, 87
excellent, 233
exclusive determination of the woman, 60
exempt from the law, 98
exempt from the laws, 98
expectations starting in the schools, 125
experience is simple, 66
experimenting, 35
experiments, 35
exploit this western weakness, 156
exploit workers, 199
exploitation of foreign workers, 75
exploitative disaster story, 246
exploited debt-based system limits opportunities, 182
exploitive, 141
exploitive working conditions, 187
exposING the corruption, 306
extinction, 32, 50, 145, 236
extinction is clearly in progress, 209
extinction of family values, 145
extinction of western children, 146
extort money from men, 245
extorting men for money, 145
extorting money, 144
extortion, 36, 166, 172, 190
extortion and child ransom, 191
extortion racket, 207
extortionist, 166, 284
extortionist collection agency, 189
extortionist., 284
extradite themselves, 54
extravagant executive pay, 197
extreme poverty, 46
facade, 83
façade, 241
facilitate usury, 172
facilities, 186

factories, 34, 237
factual via a proper peer review process., 81
failed, 48
failed economic system, 163
failed ideology, 221
failure, 163, 168
failure of political correctness, 105
fair and equitable system, 87
fair play, 230
fake foreign refugees, 132
fake judicial industry, 59
fake liberalism, 52
fake prosperity, 10
falling apart from a foreign invasion, 65
false justice system, 270
false narrative, 23, 223, 236, 284, 287
false narratives, 20, 47, 148
falsehood, 203
falsely depicting all men as bad negligent parents,, 144
familial connection, 128
familial feeling, 74
familial melting pot nation state, 74
families, 32, 33, 37, 235
Families, 237
Families disintegrate, 295
families on trial, 32
family, 7, 27, 230, 231, 232, 236
family and parental authority, 214
family business, 33
family court system, 205
family Courts, 36
Family Courts, 31, 36, 55
family dynamics, 143
Family equity, 207
family finances, 207
family heritage, 128
family incomes, 232
family is a fundamental common law foundation,, 208
Family Law Courts, 31
family life, 20
family matters, 145
Family policy, 287
family relations, 41
family relationships, 53
family rights, 52
family sovereignty, 12, 63
Family sovereignty, 184
family standards, 236
family team, 233
family values, 214, 279, 295
family wealth, 59
family,, 231
family-based trades, 233
fanaticism, 284
farm settlements, 121
fascinating revelation, 160
Fascism, 5
father, 233
father and child, 226
fathers, 225, 233
fathers parental rights, 207
favouring globalism might not be in their interest, 62
favouritism, 271
Fear of Government, 32
fearless risk taking, 43
fed food poison, 77
feed upon the working class, 294
fellow citizens and the nation, 216
fellow citizens and the nation's best interests, 216
female competition, 241
female mating strategy, 242
feminine strategy, 242
feminine victim culture, 149
feminism, 3, 39, 224, 236, 242
feminist agenda, 55
feminist attacks, 231
feminist ideology, 276
feminized, 232
fertility, 32
festers over time, 129
feudal, 29
feudal economic policies, 6
feudal economics, 172
feudal Government, 38
feudal land tenure, 186
feudal surf economy, 175
Feudalism lost out to industrialization, 186
feudally based economic models, 172
few inbred animals, 120
few industrialists, 26
fewer and fewer owners, 107
fictional conspiracy, 160

fictionalized historical narratives, 148
Fidel Castro, 275
fiduciary, 9, 14, 171
Fiduciary Corporations, 7
fiduciary responsibilities, 285
fiduciary trust, 101
filled with good intentions, 116
finance companies, 198
financed feminism, 236
financial advantage, 61
financial benefits, 54
financial break, 175
financial coup d'état, 190
financial enslavement, 44
financial expediency, 92
financial handouts, 6
financial incentives, 225, 291
financial liability, 37
financial reward for divorce, 225
financial shell game, 241
financial sponsor, 56
financial sponsors, 235
financial sponsorship, 236
financial structures, 49
financial support liability, 189
financial tyranny, 291
finding that work is far scarcer, 186
fire would result in an explosion, 58
first day of birth, 44
Flexible Government home mortgages, 167
flexible mortgage loan, 167
floating account balance, 177
food, 74
For a society to be based upon "Justice", 68
for commission of no crimes, and no wrong doing, 190
Force never works as it corrodes good will, 115
forced contract of marriage, 59
Ford Motor Company, 196
foreign aggression,, 215
foreign cultures, 232
foreign influence, 146
foreign lands, 187
foreign manipulation, 214
foreign peoples, 222
foreign sponsors, 255
foreign terrorist claims, 110
foreign wars, 67, 158
foreign workers, 75
foreigners, 69, 74
foreigners and foreign wars, 65
foreigners are given preference for employment, 69
foreigners must earn their place, 111
forethought in a normal mind, 43
forsaking the local founding peoples, 70
foundation, 30
foundation of our society, 186
foundation of the family, 53
foundations for bloody future civil war, 129
foundations of familial culture, 103
foundations of western representative Government, 142
founding peoples, 45, 70, 84
founding principles, 51
four business resources, 261
France, 49
Frankfort School, 141
Frankfurt school, 147, 277
Frankfurt School, 135, 137, 153, 157
Frankfurt school conspiracy, 153
Frankfurt School precepts, 140
Frankfurt school Trojan horse., 161
Frankfurt school's sedition, 156
Franklyn D. Roosevelt, 183
fraudulent common law principal, 59
fraudulent feminism, 240
fraudulent populism, 50
free choice, 166
free choice and privacy in their personal matters, 215
free enterprise, 26
free enterprise system, 162
free lands, 21
free life time meal ticket, 59
FREE MARKET Business, 327
free market society., 13
free markets, 5
free media, 48
free men, 29
free money guaranteed by Government, 190
free people, 5
free speech, 48
Free speech, 5
free speech rights, 89
free thought, 23

free votes, 99
free will, 27, 166
free willed options, 19
freedom, 87
freedom and liberty, 223
freedom from liability, 198
freedom of association, 89
Freedom of choice, 7
freedom of individuals, 48
freedom of optional, 169
freedom of speech, 65
freely choose, 169
French Canadians, 120
French explorer, 119
French Huguenots, 117
French Indian wars, 121
French revolution, 41, 226
French Revolution Reign of Terror, 133
French, Native American, 126
Freudian, 234
From Dictatorship to Democracy, 109
full disclosure, 81
functional unitary state, 63
fundamental obligation, 233
fundamental responsibilities, 213
fundamentalist religious peoples, 246
funded surrogate Government welfare system, 190
funding radical feminist and minority rights groups, 144
fur trade, 121, 122
Furniture and gadgets, 240
future civil wars, 104
future generations, 236
future of western civilization, 86
future social engineering, 134
future years, 180
Galbraith, 256
gangster club, 41
Gas taxes on fuel, 171
gender, 37
gender based divisive, 143
gender biased, 190
Gender distrust, 231
gender equality, 266
gender privilege, 266
gender war, 243
gender-based nepotism to, 149
general good of society, 82
general population, 48
general public, 31
generation, 14
generational foundations, 126
generations, 49
generous pensions, 188
genetic defect from inbreeding, 120
genetic defects, 120
genetic immunities that pass down blood lines, 120
genetic offspring, 244
genetically became extinct, 246
genetics, 202
Genghis Khan, 117
genocidal tendencies, 116
genocide of people everywhere, 123
George Soros, 257
German and Japanese industrialization, 259
German socialists, 5
Germans were resigned to silence, 293
Germany, 196
Germany, under the third Reich, 212
getting mothers out of the way, 44
ghettoized minorities, 110
give everything to the state, 227
give false information, 88
gives away free stuff and money, 128
global federalism, 63
global trade, 254
Globalism, 153
globalism and other communist ideologies, 158
globalist agenda, 221
globalist destroyer, 51
globalization, 17, 150, 196
Globalization, 154, 254
glue of society, 71
golden parachute, 262
good debater, 41
good for social harmony, 112
good in a democracy, 212
good mothers, 230
good of society, 54
governance of the population, 50
Governing apparatus, 94
Government and banks, 311
Government betrays their own people, 193

Government constitutions, 21
Government corruption, 199
Government creates a problem for future generations to deal with, 132
Government creation, 173
Government dependency, 199
Government disappears, 67
Government education, 42
Government facilities and airports, 65
Government funded, 57
Government handouts, 235
Government has moved into the master bedroom, 227
Government has no right to engineer society, 216
Government heavy handed extortion assaults, 192
Government husband, 225
Government ignore the volumes of studies, 143
Government income, 169
Government initiatives, 166
Government interest free, tax free, and with flexible repayments, 175
Government interfered, 246
Government interference, 192
Government is a social administrator, 217
Government is a tyrant, 191
Government is benevolent, 227
Government is not and cannot be a parent in reality,, 216
Government issued money, 173
Government legislation and family interference, 266
Government manufactured justification, 142
Government Ministries indoctrinate multiculturalism, 142
Government money, 225
Government must be controlled and restricted in its activities, 194
Government narrative, 236
Government pensions, 171
Government policy like a toxic soup, 57
Government programs, 170
Government propaganda, 236
Government revenue, 184
Government threats and intimidation., 107
Government tyranny, 108, 192
Government which is benevolen, 232
Government, the new indulgent and obliging western spouse of women,, 220
Governments do not enforce civil laws,, 190
Governments have become totalitarian, 65
Governments have prostituted themselves, 65
Governments regulate individuals, 42
grand failed social experiments., 241
grand social engineering experiment., 225
granting unearned privilege, 73
grass roots local Government, 112
grave expense, 207
great athletes, 43
gridlock, 13
grim statistical facts, 191
grinding their teeth, 45
Group affiliations, 60
group think, 203
group thinkers, 25
growing self-employment, 179
guarantee of personal shelter, food security, 183
guaranteed home ownership, 181
gulags, 36, 222
has cost western societies free speech, 70
has made things worse, 66
have a good work ethic, 139
have any law or constitutional provision changed, 96
have never been wealth creators, 139
Having financial difficulties, 192
hazardous for men, 145
he confessed all this to me, 160
He seemed to laugh it all off, 160
head of state, 102
headed for a fall, 27
headed towards extinction due to these judicial exploiters, 103
heading; clearly, towards extinction, 86
health, 66, 253
health care, 9, 14, 81
health care system, 170
Health Care Trust Corporations, 81
health insurance foundations, 170
healthcare, 81
Healthcare Trusts, 8
healthier populations, 188
Hegelian communist theory, 62
hemlock drinking, 223
Henry Ford, 26, 196
heritage, 74, 185
heterosexual male, 57
hidden agenda, 46
hidden virus, 159
hierarchy, 23, 29
high handed insult, threats, 205
high wage economies, 77

higher crime rates, 188
highly intelligent, 159
high-tech economy, 259
hijacked, 41
hijacked the agenda, 50
hippy ideology, 4
his victim is superior, 157
historical, 234
historical affinity, 185
historical community, 125
Historical connection, 74
historical narrative, 223
historical narratives, 150
historical perspective, 246
historical populations, 73
historical revisionism, 149, 223, **287**
historical social movements, 245
historical vintage, 126
historical wrongs perceived, 46
history, 27, 48
History is evolutionary, 127
history repeats itself, 42
History repeats itself, 258
home and property rights, 215
Home based companies, 179
Home based enterprise, 244
Home based internet business, 238
home employment, 238
home equity, 178
home interest free, 167
home made products, 239
home mortgages, 170, 179
home mortgages,, 167
home ownership, 168, 177
home ownership rights, 6
home parenting, 224
home-based businesses, 175
home-based family, 237
homelessness, 39
homelessness will become a huge problem, 181
Homelessness will cease to exist, 182
homemade boutique selling, 239
homestead, 21
homestead loan system, 178
homosexual, 247
honest judicial system, 263
Hong Kong airport, 158
Hong Kong China airport, 159
horrific, 34
horrific experiments, 35
horror story, 32
horrors, 33, 35
horrors of Chinese cities, 195
hospitals, 35
housing costs, 236
Human beings, 233
human brain, 43
human emotion, 46
human endeavour, 23
human nature, 261
human relationships, 37
human resource, 226
human rights, 39, 201, 207
Human Rights Laws, 274
human rights legislation, 269
Human rights legislation, 272
human rights violation, 31, 55
human rights violations, 35, 39, 245
human rights,, 268
human traits, 202
human vegetables, 34
humans, 233
hundreds of thousands of natives, 120
hurts the working class, 190
husbands, 190
Hutterites, 120
hyperinflation, 5
hypocrisy, 27
ideological, 5
ideology, 23, 276
ignorance of the issues, 133
ignoring culture is destroying society, 185
ill prepared, 66
illegal activities, 88
illegal immigration, 87
illegal immigration, 112
imbedded reports, 108
imbedding reporters, 47
imitate, 28
immigrant, 232
immigrates, 128
immigration, 39

immigration and demographic trajectory, 248
immunity, 30
impact of legislation, 79
impact the working class, 142
Impatience, 42
impending mass under employment, 185
importing European Communists, 161
impositions, 22
impoverished, 154
impoverished by interest payments, 173
impoverished families, 234
impoverishment of people, 262
impregnation of a woman, 58
imprisoned, 36
impudently, 186
impunity, 32
in a responsible, 169
in favor of Immigrant foreigners, 106
in favour of minorities, 83
in no way enhances the process of justice, 176
In pragmatic reality, women own the children,, 189
inability to raise their children, 144
inaccurately, 29
inadvertently infected the natives with diseases, 118
inappropriately make a judge a de-facto sovereign or monarchy, 93
incentive, 9
incentives, 15, 286
incentivising, 9
incentivising it with financial rewards, 191
incentivising marital breakup, 54
incentivizing family destruction, 191
incestuous, 90
incitement, 54
incitement to violent and bloody civil, 129
income tax, 171
income taxes, 22
incomes will become more precarious in future years, 179
incompetent big Government, 155
incorruptibility, 98
independence, 25, 36, 81
independent analysis, 82
independent law enforcement, 53
independent research, 161
independent Senate oversight, 99
independent thinkers, 44
indescribable abuses of patients, 288
India, 259
individual, 22
individual liberty and speech, 51
individual responsibilities, 20
individual responsibility, 20
individual rights, 53
individual's rights, 19
individualism, 3, 24
individualistic rights, 24
individualistic western cultures, 187
individuals, 169, 201, 237
individuals rights, 25
indoctrinate, 39, 223
indoctrinate the rebellious youth, 141
indoctrinated, 2, 28, 41, 43, 148, 163, 164
indoctrinated adults, 221
indoctrinated are becoming un-indoctrinated, 48
indoctrinated by the state education system, 104
indoctrinated children, 228
indoctrinated people, 44
indoctrinated with social sedition, 163
indoctrinated women into the workplace, 224
indoctrinating education system, 130
indoctrination, 20, 23, 34, 39, 41, 140, 152, 216, 221, 223, 227, 231, 234
indoctrination by the school system, 112
indoctrination in academia, 140
induced with higher wages, 196
indulgence, 26
industrial collaboration, 197
industrial jobs, 235
industrial pillaging, 49
industrial production, 187
industrial revolution, 240, 243
industrial servitude, 234
industrialist, 187
industrialization, 260
industry, 197, 235
inexperience is equal to experience, 219
infected, 27
infected western nations, 137
infectious, 187
infects society, 230
inferiority complex, 162
infidelity by a spouse, 71
infiltrate institutions, 156
infiltrated, 156

infiltration, 153
inflation, 237
information wars., 48
infrastructure, 239
inheritance, 40, 72, 187
inhumane actions, 35
initiate controlling voting rights, 198
injustice, 36, 37, 46
innocence, 46
innocent children, 35
innocuous, 213
innovation and rejuvenation, 186
innovators, 187
insecure contract work, 180
inside of a court, 89
insidious, 188
insidious interloper, 227
insidious nihilistic, 222
instead of creating social cohesion, 69
institution of the family., 265
institutional undermining the family, 149
instruments of social repression, 42
insult and discrimination, 45
insult without bases in fact, 221
intact families are be best incubator for child development, 143
intact family, 208
integrate cultures, 122
Integration, 115
integration and intermixing, 112
integration is normally accepted and peaceful, 114
integration of immigrants, 124
integrity, 188
intellectual, 46
intellectual elite, 255
intellectual fraud, 220
intellectually bankrupt, 48
intelligence service, 47
intelligentsia, 48
intended malice, 58
intentional legal breaches, 92
intentionally weeding out journalists, 107
interactions, 148
interest free line, 177
interest free mortgage lines of credit, 177
interest free mortgages, 167
INTEREST FREE MORTGAGES, 312
interest group, 224, 237
interfere in individual liberty, 115
interference in the family and economy, 184
interference into private civil law matters, 191
interlopers, 55
interlopers and social engineers, 184
interloping, 199
internal sedition inside the borders, 158
internal treason, 71
internet based globalized, 238
internet meteorite, 47
interpret legislation, 100
interracial relationships, 114
intolerant fanat, 123
inventions, 187
inviolable property rights, 167
invitation for future fascism, 134
involuntarily castrated, 207
involuntary sterilizations, 288
irredeemably attracted, 242
irrelevance, 11
is truly a revolutionary social program, 182
Islamic demographic conquest of Western Europe, 137
Islamic fundamentalism, 39
Islamic law, 249
issue warrants, 100
it can only be a meritocracy, 68
it has all been a lie, 41
It is a part of human nature, 182
It takes a family to raise a child's foundations,, 209
It will hurt your ego, 64
It will hurt your pride, 64
its very existence is illegitimate, 73
Jacques Cartier, 119
jail sentences, 40
Japan, 197
Japanese Emperors, 19
jeopardy, 34
job creation being close to equal to immigration levels, 109
job loss, 191
jobs taken away, 186
John F. Kennedy, 186
John Kenneth Galbraith, 299
John Locke, 203
Joseph Campbell, 165
Judas, 237

Judges and Lawyers, those that profiteer, 89
judicial abuse, 208
Judicial administration, 53
judicial arm of Governments, 209
judicial bigotry, 206
Judicial business, 91
Judicial establishment, 55
Judicial industries, 234
Judicial industries, 145
judicial industry, 205, 207
Judicial industry, 145
judicial integrity, 98
judicial interference, 53, 59, 102
judicial interloper, 205
Judicial repression, 106
judicial system, 38, 53
judicial systems, 209
judicial systems profiteering, 59
judicial tyranny, 52, 145
judicially created contract, 59
judiciary, 54
Jungian archetypes, 241
jurisdiction beyond civil society, 55
jurisdiction to enforce laws, 96
Justice, 27
justifiable, 33
justification, 36
Karl Marx, 280
keep the state out of the private affairs, 60
KGB engineered espionage program, 153
KGB infiltration program, 156
KGB man, 157
KGB plot to divide western nations, 164
KGB program, 159
KGB sedition project., 153
Kidnapping, 188
kill the men and male children, and then rebreed the females, 244
killing our society, 245
killing your own people, 195
kindergartens, 34
king maker, 152
kingdom of the mother, 234
knowledge of the human rights, 75
labour contributions, 198
lack cultural perspective and understanding, 185
lack individuality, 44
lacking in providing guidance, 93
lamenting over the past, 199
land disputes, 121
land ownership, 121
land tenure, 172
Land TENURE, 330
land theft, 174
land they stole from the people, 174
land thief, 172
land use laws, 6
LAND USE; THE GRAND SHELL GAME, 325
land was virtually vacant, 119
landlord, 29
Large government becomes paranoid, 63
late developing prefrontal cortex, 42
launched an all-out war against 50%, 58
law, 37, 40
law and enforcement of laws, 101
law enforcement, 30, 53, 91, **102**
Law enforcement, 99, 101
law enforcement oversight powers, 147
law enforcement powers, 102
law is applied, 213
law of the land, 92
Law Societies, 90, 288
laws, 30
laws to prosecute domestic citizens who oppose in any way, 106
lawyer, 41
lawyers, 38, 40
layers of self-promotion, corrupt institutions, 183
leaders, 28
Leaders, 30
leadership, 66, 242
leadership role in this world, 66
leading to economic collapse, 222
leading to revolutionary economic change in the west, 183
learning opportunity, 25
leave me alone Government, 183
left wing, 14
Left wing, 36
left wing fascist, 52
left wing gulag society, 51
leftist, 2
left-wing agenda, 51
left-wing politicians, 134
legacy of cultural heritage, 128

legal administration, 41
legal co-parent, 226
legal enforcement, 95
legal framework, 244
legal industry, 205, 207
legal inequality, 40
legal system, 274
legally baseless, 207
legislation by courts, 72
legislation is a scam upon society, 60
legislators, 80
legislators without any constituency, 92
legislature, 40
Legislature, 8
legislature corruption, 53
less likely the business class will control, 62
lessons of the heart, 44
levels of reproduction, 57
libertarian, 50
Libertarian Direct Democratic Cantons, 139
Libertarian historical narrative, 52
libertarian model, 51
libertarian populist movement, 52
Libertarianism demands, 86
libertarianism is experiencing a resurgence, 86
Libertarians see Government as, 166
lie, 160
lien, 167
lies and deception, 46
Life is like an inverted pyramid, 175
life paths, 42
lifestyle, 49
lifestyle worlds apart, 183
lifetime payments for shelter, 180
like a ball rolling down a hill, 134
Like Nazi villainization of Jews, 266
like-minded individuals, 156
limited job security, 108
line of credit loans, 178
lineally headed, 242
literature, 156
little separation of work and home, 195
lives and continue without end in debt, 296
livestock, 33, 42
loans and incentives to big corporations, 78
lobby groups of Lawyers and Judges, 90
lobotomies, 288
lobotomizing people, 35
local and national interest, 77
local business, 79
local elections, 152
local politicians, 146
logic, foresight, 43
logical outcome, 242
lone wolf, 23, 24
lone wolf citizen, 31
look hard to cure our own problems, 66
loose cannons, 107
Lord and Surf, 6
lose control, 48
loss of your home and provide the security, 168
Louise the XVI, 49
Louise XVI, 257
loving benevolent, 244
loving mother, 231
loving paternal, 233
low birth rates, 208
low skilled, poorly educated migrants add no economic value, 186
low to no collateral, low interest loans, 83
low wages, 236
low-cost home ownership, 180
lowering of standards, 209
loyalty, 241
LSD, 35
Luddite revolt was so intense, 63
M K ULTRA, 35
made to order, 240
Magna Carta, 206, 289
Magna Carte, 30, 89, 275
maintain social harmony, 180
majorities, 6
majority female vote, 188
majority of their citizens, 45
majority population, 148
majority voters, 189
make pretence of popular movements, 144
Making laws, 93
male discrimination, 204
male entrapment by pregnancy, 60
managerial class, 26
mandating equal parenthood, 243
manifested in the future, 157

manifesting local sedition, 157
manipulate the minds of the youth, 156
manipulation of the population, 47
manipulations, 47, 48
manipulative, 46
manipulative minorities, 152
manual labour jobs are in short supply, 132
manufacture, 238
manufactured goods, 188
manufacturing, 186
manufacturing a narrative, 48
marriage, 145
marriage against his better interest, 59
marriage contract, 59
Marxist agenda, 50
Marxist class war, 140
Marxists, 236
masculine gender, 52
masculinising femininity, 278
Mass immigration, 295
Mass immigration has been introduced, 265
mass indoctrination, 49
mass media, 48
mass robotic mechanization, 180
mass underemployment, 6
massive child abuse, 227
massive plague, 119
mass-produced, 240
material responsibility, 278
maternal family leadership, 233
mates, 37
mechanization, 184, 196
mechanization of manufacturing into the future, 179
media concentration, 107
media engineer, 46
mediocre and basically talentless individuals, 264
mediocrity, 139, 284
mediocrity fights meritocracy, 136
melt together, 236
melting pot, 74, 122
men, 32, 36
Men are turned into walking ATM machines and little more, 190
Men as a group have suffered the most injuries, 132
men as a guaranteed income source, 189
men lose their parental rights, 189
men lose their rights, 145
men marrying Asian women, 158
men under state sanction, 57
men's nature, 241
mental dysfunction, 285
mental illness, 247
mental illness caused by the trauma of the Government, 194
mentally deprogrammed, 152
mentally disturbed nation state, 283
menu of choices, 170
meritocracy of employment, 204
meritocracy., 284
Mexico, 253
micro business, 237, 240
micro businesses, 240
micro industrial revolution, 239
micro manufacturer, 240
micro manufacturers, 238
micro manufacturing, 238
micro robotic assembly, 199
middle age, 41
middle class, 6, 235
middle man, 173
middle men, 183
middle working class, 294
middle-class lifestyle, 76
migrant invaders, 232
migrants, 221
military commanders, 34
military conflict, 161
military conscripts, 43
milk the man's resources, 242
mill stone around their necks, 237
millennial minds, 162
minimal economic development, 186
minimal employment, 78
minimal Government, 169
minimal mutual respect for differences, 209
minimalist, 20
Ministry for Families, 241
minorities, 6, 56, 201, 286
minorities become the alpha, 60
minorities in their drunken abuse, 61
minorities take over Government, 57
minority, 286
minority biases, 56
minority equal rights, 60

minority interest groups, 230
minority privilege, 51
minority rights, 3, 45, 52, 56, 61, 216
Minority rights, 61
misbehaving capitalists, 62
Mischling, 115
miserable failure, 123
misfortune, 160
misfortune of families, 90
misinformation, 47
mislead the people about society, 144
misleading, 46
misleading narratives, 46
mistreatment, 36
mixed culturally, 117
mixed nationalities, 112
mixed race (Métis), 121
mob justice, 133
Mobius-strip intellectual fraud, 220
money circulation, 177
money free to all parties, 172
money from foreign nations to legislate against their own people's interest, 187
Money's true reserve value, 302
monkeys flinging stones, 161
monogamy, 242
monolithic Government and business, 62
mono-operational world, 62
monthly payments, 180
more political and social grandstanding, 60
mortal enemy, 17
mortgage, 7
mortgage finance reform, 183
mortgage from the state, 21
mortgage indenture, 168
mortgage loan, 173
mortgage loans, 172
Mortgage loans, 178
mortgage payments, 7
Mortgages, 167
mortgages shall be interest fee, 177
most difficult of circumstances, 169
most individuals in jail are the products of single parent households or broken families, 143
Most people build a life based upon social lies, 296
mother, 37, 233, 236
Mother Theresa, 280
motherhood, 230
Mothers, 233
multi-Billion Dollar legal industry child custody cases, 193
multibillion-dollar judicial industry, 288
multicultural, individualistic social agenda, 265
multiculturalism, 55, 70, 133
multi-culturalism, 103
Multiculturalism, 71, 103, 154
Multiculturalism flies in the face of reality, 104
multigenerational, 40
multilayered, 199
murdered millions of people, 168
murderous philosophy, 123
murderous regimes, 168
must have a two-way empathetic relationship, 67
must pay their dues, 122
mutations, 123
mutual respect, 211
naïve fools, 31
naïve ruling class, 164
naivety of human nature, 71
Napoleon Bonaparte, 63
Napoleonic, 54
Napoleonic wars in Europe, 63
narcissistic and detrimental social manipulations., 138
narcissistic financial gain, 89
narcissistic personal financial benefit, 154
narrative, 48, 236
narrative of circumstances, 47
narrative on all issues, 48
narratives, 47, 236
narratives., 48
nation has become so repressive, 63
nation state, 20, 41, 53, 55, 227
Nation states constitute local, answerable Government, 67
national accounts, 10
national corporation, 17
National defense and national money bills, 95
national health care, 21
national identity, 197
National leaders thus live with constituents, 67
National Socialist German Workers Party, 26
Nationalism is not racism, 104
Nationalism is now a backlash against globalism, 63
nations, 28, 232

Nations are a necessity, 67
nations Constitution, 213
Nations that espouse multi culturalism, 71
native, 32
Native American tribes, 119
Native Americans, 296
native born, 17
Native North Americans, 3
native residential schools, 35
natives allied themselves, 121
Natives in America, 121
natives sided with the Canadians, 121
natural birth right, 174
natural evolutionary custom, 204
natural human characteristic, 261
natural human condition, 184
natural human rights, 38
natural order of humanity, 63
natural rights to be a parent, 190
natural selection, 115
Nazi brown shirt policies, 112
Nazi Germany, 223
Nazis, 35
Nazism, 26
ncentivised, 13
Neanderthal bones, 117
need not apply, 56
negative effects, 237
negative social impact, 116
neo communist, 221
nest of the family, 208
never heard, 47
never paid even one cent, 131
Neville Chamberlain, 3
new administration, 56
new bourgeoisie, 50
new economy, 237
new entrepreneurs, 260
new type of social support system, 181
niche products, 238
Nigel Wright, 137
nihilism, 220
nineteen fifties, 6
nineteen nineties, 33
No armies, 161
no child or descendant is guilty of the crimes of their ancestors, 127
no common law bases in fact, 59
no consent, 82
no credibility, 140
no cultural connection, 128
no desire for marriage, 209
no difference between multi culturalism and segregation, 105
no economic benefit, 163
No employee would vote to export their own job, 198
No family values, 146
no firsthand knowledge, 149
no impartiality, 41
No inherited memory, 42
no legitimate biological vested interest, 209
no longer desire to reproduce offspring, 58
no longer exist, 235
no marriage, no right to claim support, 59
no oath of marriage, 58
no parental oversight, 227
no place in public discourse, 60
no political options, 155
no social programs, 166
no sympathies, 155
no title only extortion power over, 173
no way altruistic, 147
non-deliverance after the election, 84
non-discriminatory and non-biased, 214
None of this is racially based, 74
non-parents, 43
Non-profit entrepreneur funding trust, 8
non-profit insurance corporations, 171
Non-reproduction is clear evidence, 58
North American Natives, 120
not a living wage, 187
not an issue of minority rights, 73
not created equal, 268
not popular movements, 57
Not subscribing, 170
Notaries, 290
now Government controls you, 221
now throw this money at foreigners, 131
numerous abandoned villages, 119
obedient regimented robots, 44
obfuscation, 49
objective, 24
obligation, 37, 228
obligation to request parental consent, 212
obligation., 189
obscene profits, 188
obsolete technology, 13
odd man out, 140
odious problem, 87
offensive bigoted insult, 127
official narrative, 23
offspring, 233, 242
old media, 48
old school, 223
oligarchies of the wealthy, 60
oligarchs., 235
oligarchy, 45
Oliver Twist, 34, 288
one ethnic nationality, 111
one people, of one culture, 114
online marketing, 238
only seen the tip of the iceberg, 62
Ontario birth certificates, 212
open borders and globalization, 78
Open Society Foundation, 257
open the mind, 135
opponents in academia, 153
opportunists, 41
opportunities, 87
opportunity, 239
opportunity to develop, 180
optimistic again, 199
opting out of marriage unions, 59
organic, 156
organic families, 237
organic movement, 277
organized imposition, 22
orphanage, 33
orphanages, 34, 35
orphans, 226
our culture and our land, 127
Our freedom of speech which is being repressed, 65
our history is our culture, 127
our own cells (politicians) killing our culture, 65
outright anti-male bigotry, 145
outright bigotry, 188
outsourcing manufacturing, 6
Overton Window, 201
ownership, 37
ownership of male resources, 243
oxymoronic, 286
paid monthly or as an annual lump sum, 169
pair bonding, 116, 122, 242
Palace of Versailles, 258
paradigm shift, 138
Parallel Banking System, 177
parallel mortgage banking system, 179
parasite, 228
parasitic, 236, 289
parasitic brutality of the state, 174
parasitic exploitation, 153
parasitic land ownership, 173
parasitic pilfering, 155
parasitic social strata, 140
parasitically feeding, 49
parent, 213
parent child empathy, 44
parent's natural rights, 37
parental abandonment, 44
parental alienation, 145, 190
parental desire to maintain their rights, 206
parental equality, 206
parental guidance, 43
parental rights, 36, 38, 205, 206, 208, 216, 291
parental rights are discarded, 189
Parenthood is reflective of genetic heritage, 216
parenting, 32, 144
parents, 19
partisan party politics,, 88
partnership, 241
patriarchy, 146, 160
patronage, 41, 241
patronage appointments, 41
pay by subscription, 171
pay now or pay later, 167
pay their entrance dues, 111
paying protesters to covertly make pretence of popular movements for the corporate media, 144
payment of dividends, 168
payroll deductions, 22
pedophile daycare center, 33
pedophiles, 33
peer reviewed, 79
pejorative and condescending, 69
pejorative message to men, 191
pejoratively villainized, 208

PRAGMATIC LIBERTARIANISM
Engineering populist constitutions for the 21st century

penalize current people, 148
Pensions, 14
people are incited to fight and squabble, 142
people do integrate and melt into one people in one nation, 114
People do otherwise interbreed for generations, 113
people like tribal (national) identities, 63
people took a chance, 155
people's best interest, 76
people's personal affairs, 55
perceived past wrongs, 148
perceived slights, 45
perception of men, 278
perceptions, 43, 201
perceptive intelligence, 148
permit children to use first names, 211
perplexing, 27
Personal choice, 171
personal dignity, 55
personal economic growth, 169
personal experience, 27
personal family history, 247
personal financial fortunes, 205
personal incomes, 205
personal independence, 168
personal lives, 54, 55
personal matters, 39
personal responsibility, 37, 168
personal right to privacy, 60
personal security, 87, 188
personal security has disappeared, 65
personally responsible, 7
perspectives, 22, 47, 236
perspectives of victimhood, 149
perspectives on society, 73
perverse corrupt, 284
perverse initiation, 56
perversion, 93
philosophical schools, 17
phony matrix society, 31
phony name of privacy, 31
pilfering the wealth of families, 193
Pinkerton guard's, 26
placated population, 83
places of freedom and human rights, 60
plan, 4
plan for the times, 6
planted like a seed in the United States to circulate sedition, 159
plebiscite, 97
plebiscite and referendum rules, 96
points to ponder., 166
poisoned the majority, 58
Poland, 26
police force, 101
police shootings, 40
policies and laws of Governments, 113
policy to interfere in society, 144
political administration, 25
political advantage, 103
political agenda, 30
political assassinations, 31
political climate, 256
political conversation, 50
political correctness, 39, 45, 137, 147, 148, 153, 156, 158, 204, 221
Political correctness, 58, 122
Political correctness is muzzling dissent, 250
political correctness is tyranny, 69
political disaster, 257
political dissent, 222
political evolution, 29
political expediency, 265
political fraud, 77
political hijacking of the state judicial apparatus, 92
political interference, 88
political management, 28
political matrix, 147
political movement, 152
political office, 30, 40
political parties, 49, 146
political parties of minorities, 155
political reforms, 146
political repression, 223
political stability, 18
political system, 29
political wedges, 103
politically based laws,, 210
politically correct, 50, 232
Politically correct Movement, 140
politically correct speech, 220, 222
politically motivated, 192
politician's benefactors, 42
politicians, 29, 41, 155
Politicians, 30, 282

Politicians stuck a dagger in the back of the family, 237
politicizing private and personal affairs, 142
Politics, 29
Politics has entered the education system, 210
pollute the mind, 162
polluted by vested interest, 65
polygamist, 53
popular elections, 12
popular movements, 57
popular revolution, 51
population, 40, 42, 47
population decline, 110
population divided, 142
populist agenda, 236
pornography and titillation, 55
positions in Government, 153
positive outlook, 58
post modernism, 162
post-modernist ideas, 160
post-secondary education, 141
post-traumatic stress, 33, 42
potential hazards, 81
poverty, 205
power always creeps over time, 94
power and money grab, 243
power grab, 241
practitioner of dominance, 61
pragmatic, 15, 39
pragmatic failure, 169
Pragmatic life, 98
pragmatic reality, 40, 103, 122
pragmatic reality within society, 215
pragmatically a great big lie, 207
pragmatically ignorant, 162
pragmatism, 13
precedence over the majority culture, 70
precedents in pragmatic fact, 94
preferential treatment for employment opportunities, 148
prefrontal lobes, 43
pre-industrial nations, 62
preindustrial times, 238
preoccupied, 234
pressure on wages, 235
pressure relief valve, 180
pretence of benevolence, 46
pretence of independence, 57
pretends to be a minority movement, 247
pretense, 41, 236
pretentious, 147
Pride of workmanship, 197
primal strategy of women, 241
principals of law, 208
prioritization of minority rights, 52
prison escape, 48
private affairs, 54, 152
private citizen's affairs, 291
private daycares, 43
private enrichment, 141
private family issues, 142
private family matters, 190
private insurance, 170
private insurance subscription, 170
private lives, 59
private sector competition, 170
private sexual lives, 57
privilege positions, 73
privileges and opportunities, 183
products invented here, 186
professional politicians, 154
Professor Gene Sharp, 109
profit for themselves, 208
profit motivated ambitions, 197
profiteering lawyers, 37
progeny, 233
project planning, 79
promiscuity, 241
promotion, 28
promoting working class independence and self-reliance, 183
promotion and positioning, 164
promotion of social long-term division, 104
Promotions, 219
propaganda, 43, 106
propaganda style news reporting, 107
propaganda traumatizes, 42
Property financing, 7
property of the Government, 42
property rights, 52
Property rights, 331
property taxes, 167
proportional, 27
prosecutions of criminals, 101
prosperity, 10

prosperous nation, 18
prostitute's pregnancy, 58
prostitutes, 231
prostitution, 30
Protect children, 214
protect workers, 188
PROTECTING CHILDREN, 296
protest movements, 257
proven abuse, 290
provide the lowest cost, 179
provocateurs, 205
proxy life, 241
prudence, 24
Prussia, 34
Prussian, 20
pseudo marriage, 59
psychiatric institutions, 35
psychological adultery, 54
psychological damage, 42, 248
psychological manipulation, 230
psychological problems, 247
psychological research, 276
psychological studies, 245
psychologically damaged children, 205
psychopath, 27, 45, 227
psychopathic, 28, 35, 36, 148
psychopathic and narcissistic personality, 44
psychopathic behaviour, 187
psychopathic corruption, 41
psychopathic individuals, 147
psychopathic judicial industry, 207
psychopathic judiciary, 208
psychopathic nation state, 46
psychopathic or elitist, 67
psychopathic politicians, 43
psychopathic profit motive, 82
psychopathic social parasites, 206
psychopathic system, 209
psychopathic vested interests, 147
psychopaths, 34, 44, 228
Psychopaths, 27
psychopaths took control, 197
public corruption, 100
public discourse, 60
public hearings, 95
public officials, 146
public perception., 210
public retribution, 133
publicly available documents, 154
punishment for corruption, 209
pure genius, 156, 160, 163
purity of foods, 213
put a citizen in jail, 50
put on trial, 55
que jumpers, 125
rabid anti-Semitism, 106
race, 202
race mixing was not illegal, 114
racial and cultural combinations, 126
racial and cultural integration, 115
racial hegemony, 124
racial integration, 115
racial segregation, 122
racist, 26
racist laws and policies, 115
radical, 7, 201
radical and comprehensive change, 63
Radical feminism, 154
radical feminists, 224
radical shift in politics, 156
radio and television, 47
raise capital on the capital markets though securities offerings, 179
Raising children, 233, 245
raising their own child, 190
Ralph Waldo Emerson, 17
rape, 147
rape of female slaves, 113
raped, 33
raw deal, 244
real life, 40
real productive wealth, 181
real-estate investments, 262
reality, 27
real-world work experience, 186
rebelliousness, 150
receive in Government handouts, 78
recipe for future civil war, 71
reclusive, 48
reduce Government involvement, 184
reducing the size of government, 63
referendum, 97
referendum questions, 97

referendums, 213
reflect differences and reality, 125
reform, 28
reformation, 155, 203
reformers, 26
reforms, 169
regimented type education, 212
regular court processes, 206
regular media, 47
regulation, 20
regulation and action, 58
regulatory determination, 141
reign in male sexuality by seduction, 243
relationship, 29
relationships being entered into freely, 58
relegate feminism, 246
relentless Government attacks, 193
reliable, 242
reliable jobs, 186
reliable work, 196
religion, 40
religious based education systems, 128
religious groups in America, 118
relocated., 186
remote elites, 129
removing tax based social welfare, 181
removing the consequences, 54
removing unnecessary judicial interference, 176
reorganization of the state's operation, 41
repercussions, 3
replacement levels, 57
replacing the words Mother and father, 213
repossession, 167
reprehensible, 209
represent their political base, 50
repress domestic population's freedom of expression, 107
repressed by mediocrity, 47
represses men, 188
repression of free speech, 109
repression of the majority, 73
repression of women, 53
repression organizations, 57
repression, injustice, intimidation and abuse, 216
repressive, 51, 201, 286
repressive nation state, 221
repressive society, 185
repressive state, 50
repressor, 51, 52
reproduction rather than extinction, 245
reproductive decline, 103
reprogrammed and brainwashed, 32
require fundamental economic structural reorganization to maintain social peace, 177
requiring law and order, 264
resentments, 51
residential schools, 11, 33, 227, 245
resignations, 41
resource allocation, 41
Respect for diversity, 212
respect for elders, 223
respect for others and manners, 209
respect for the liberties, 24
respect these values, 128
respectable careers, 35
respecting its founding peoples, 69
responsibility, 101
responsibility to ensure the enforcement of law., 91
responsible children, 233
responsible for their guidance, 220
restitution, 92
restructure our economy, 15
restructuring, 12
Results are the truth, therefore necessary to determine the truth, 85
retired, 35
retirements, 35
reverse discrimination, 46, 148
reverting the west back to the 15th century., 246
review all court precedents, 95
revisionist narratives, 130
revolt, 31
revolution, 41, 49, 155
revolutionized, 47
Rewards and corporations, 321
right of occupation, 174
right of succession, 68
right to privacy, 57
rights and dignity, 220
rights violations, 107
robot factory of Government repression, 44
Robotic, 238
robots, 232
role modeling compassion, 45

rose-colored glasses, 31
rudimentary, 147
rudimentary knowledge, 20
rule of law, 45
rule of the Chinese Communist party, 62
rule of the jungle, 9
ruling structures, 275
run by pedophiles and child abusers, 245
Russian gentleman, 158
Russian Oligarchs, 262
Russian Revolution, 258
rust belt, 49
ruthlessness, 26, 27, 103
sacred trust, 91
sadistic abuse, 36
sadistic tale, 33
Saint Lawrence river, 119
sale of homemade products, 199
Samuel du Champlain, 119
sanctity of marriage, 55
Santa Clause, 131
Saxons, Anglos, 117
scale employment dislocation, 180
scam of mortgages, 173
scam perpetrated, 42
school policies, 162
schools, 41, 148, 219
scientific fact, 202
scientific foundations, 150
scientific ignorance, 203
scientific perspective, 202
scientifically based, 79
seat of the pants initiatives, 80
Second World War, 35
secretive human rights violation, 55
secrets, 48
secrets sometimes, leak out, 161
secure home, 21
securitized consumer banking, 177
securitized start-up loans, 177
security and prosperity within society, 184
sedition by infiltration, 153
sedition of the minds of the youth, 135
seditious enemy within the state, 157
seditious espionage, 163
seditious lobby group, 102
see men only as an income source, 191
seed capital, 179
seed for social discord, 105
seek dominance over the majority, 61
segregated as multi-culturalism creates, 111
segregated costs, 81
segregating people based upon gender and race, 104
segregation in all their forms, 111
segregation in the USA, 114
segregationist ideology., 150
seizure or judgement, 21
selective enforcement of laws, 97, 102
self justifies, 187
self-analysis, 66
self-appointment, 54
self-determination, 203
Self-determination, 184
self-employed, 240
self-employment, 239
self-financing, 15
self-funding, 21
self-hate, 245
self-hatred, 84, 225
self-interested policies, 157
Self-interested politicians, 77
self-interested social deception, 155
self-regulating, 41
self-reliance, 179, 181
Self-Reliance, 17
self-reliant small-scale home-based business, 180
self-reliant, 25
self-responsibility, 169
self-righteous detachment, 187
self-righteous indignation, 271
selling out society for their own financial benefit, 182
Senate, 8
Senate Assembly, 99
Senate determination, 101
Senate endorsements, 100
separate from the legislature, 99
separating legislation from enforcement, 97
Separation of legislature, 53
separation of powers, 97
separation of the legislature and the Judiciary, 88
serial monogamy, 242
serious backlash, 61

serious social revolution, 61
servants, 34
seven-year terms, 98
shackles created by the controllers., 138
shadow of darkness, 31
shared child rearing, 243
shift in attitude, 84
Shop keepers lived upstairs from their business, 195
shopping, 239
short comings, 46
short-term jobs, 180
silence all critics, 221
silence opposition, 223
silencing of alternative views, 223
silent majority, 133
silver back gorillas, 244
since the beginning of time, 63
single mothers, 245
single parenthood, 191
skin color, 113
slaughter of innocents, 34
slave labour, 226
slavery, 229
SLAVES ENSLAVING SLAVES, 324
slums, 235
small business start-up loans, 178
small isolated groups, 55
snake oil tonic, 77
So that a homosexual with no biological connection to a child can be on a birth certificate, 216
social activists, 38
social assault and win, 61
social benefit to families, 175
social burden, 169
social change, 76
Social change without a vision, 185
social changes, 236
social cohesion, 104, 134, 156, 163
social collapse, 180
social communism, 38, 136, 204, 221
Social Communism, 153
social communist, 157, 277
Social Communist, 46
social communist ideology, 223
social communist policies, 135
social communists, 46, 135
social compliance, 41
social condition, 56
social conflict, 61
social conscience, 47
social consciousness, 147
social contribution, 230
social control operations, 152
social dealings, 46
Social decorum, 60
social discourse, 50
social disintegration, 205
Social disintegration, 210
social distraction, 142
social divisions, 71
social dominance over the majority, 61
social earthquake, 49
social engineered public schools, 222
social engineering, 20, 38, 39, 46, 48, 51, 82, 83, 169, 221, 236, 282, 292
social engineering program, 153
social engineering program., 57
social engineering,, 215
social engineers, 20, 223
social evolution, 281
social experiments, 11
social fascism, 278
social foundations, 20
social graces, 209
social harmony, 98, 214
Social Harmony, 106
social housing, 9
social indoctrination, 34
social institutions, 45
social integration is slow, 124
social interference, 282
social justice, 148
social manipulations planned, 153
social Marxism, 6, 232
Social Marxism, 2, 11, 45
Social Marxist intellectuals, 221
Social Marxists, 277
social modifications, 224
social movement, 38
social narrative, 141
social opportunity, 56
social organization, 24

social parasites feeding upon working class labour, production and creation, of wealth, 176
social philosophy from the 15th century, 123
social policies, 286
social policies for the majority, 60
social policy, 203, 237
social policy favouring minorities, 58
social position under threat, 61
social problems, 46
social reality, 56
social reform, 185
social research, 82
social respect, 209
social responsibility, 9
social retardation, 44
social rumblings, 3
social security program based upon broad home ownership., 177
social skills, 230
Social stability in Government, 260
social strata, 185
social subversion, 224
social treason, 199, 209
social unrest, 6
social upheaval, 134
social values, 233
social war, 3
social welfare, 53
social-communist fantasy, 103
socialism always fails, 50
socialist, 12
socialized and educated, 209
socialized medicine, 14
socializing children, 44
socially accepted, 201
socially demoted, 57
socially divisive policies, 157
socially engineered, 204
socially isolated, 49
socially villainized, 224
societies worshipped and absolute God, 217
society, 28
society and culture, 188
Society controls Government, 216
society has lost its way from its roots, 185
society is run by psychopaths, 43
society must evolve naturally, 69
society self-heals all wounds, 113
society's best interest, 147
society's best interests, 187
society's social skills, 44
socio-economically separate, 129
sociological matrix, 148
Socratic condemnation, 220
sold a false bill of goods, 77
sold off their positions of authority to others, 154
soldiers, 35
soldiers to put down domestic unrest, 63
sold-out their own people, 154
Solitudes of people, 105
somber and depressed populace, 49
son, 233
South Africa, 46
sovereign elected legislators, 93
sovereign rights, 53
sovereignty, 19
Soviet bloc, 36
Soviet dissident, 156
Soviet era gulags, 26
Soviet indoctrination, 130
Soviet intelligence program, 162
Soviet political system collapsed, 163
Soviet style gulags, 221
Soviet style media propaganda, 108
Soviet Union, 10, 26, 48, 123, 163, 223
Soviet Union and eastern bloc, 62
Spanish inquisition, 55
spanning generations, 49
Spartan Robots, 228
Spartans, 44
special ministries, 236
specific duties, 101
specific trials, 100
spectrums, 202
speech control, 141
speech repression, 50
spite filled single mother, 194
sponsored bigotry, 204
sponsoring family destruction, 191
spontaneous explosion, 133
spouses, 235
spy on our speech, 65
squandered, 40

St. Laurence River, 119
stable system that promotes entrepreneurship, 181
Stalin and Hitler, 26
state apparatus, 19
state coercion, 19
state financed, 57
state indoctrination, 44
state indoctrination program, 224
state interference, 53
state propaganda, 48
state sponsored, 247
state sponsored child abuse, 245
state sponsored indoctrination, 223
states interference, 20
statistically extremely rare, 243
status quo, 5
stay at home mothers were villainized, 225
stay at home spouses, 235
steal land, 172
step parent, 244
sterilizations, 35
Steven King, 32
stifles debate, 221
stigmatizing all mothers, 225
stigmatizing men, 267
strategic bigotry, 150
Street wise, 31
stress upon litigants and only pads lawyer's billings with nonsense, 176
strictly gender based, 54
stripped, 32
stripping fathers' rights away, 144
subjugation, 240
subordination of the majority's human rights, 56
subpoena witnesses, 100
subscription and payment, 13
subscriptions, 7
subversion, 221
subversion against the family, 60
subversive, 38
subversive national laws, 265
subversive philosophies, 135
subvert, 22
subvert the political process, 45
subverted, 223, 244, 247
subverted by interest groups, 82
subverted by multicultural and minority group politics, 135
Subverted by political correctness, 72
subverted Government, 141
subverted individuals, 82
subverted media, 47
succeeded, 153
successful innovations, 187
successful reproduction, 246
successful subversion plan, 163
such things do cause resentments, 125
sugar daddy, 190
suicide pact, 234
super mom is an unproven myth, 209
superfluous and makes things worse, 176
superior offspring, 120
superior working class, 152
support family values, 265
support men, 189
supported by the former Soviet Union,, 158
surrogate father, 190
surrogate husband, 53
Survival of Banks, 338
suspend home payments, 7
suspend payments, 168
suspendable line of credit with payments, 181
sweet election time words, 84
Swiss Cantons, 17, 21
Swiss constitutional governance, 18
Swiss neutrality, 17
Switzerland, 18
symptomatic of social/cultural illness, 58
symptomatic of the current times, 220
symptoms of this malaise, 66
synchronicity, 161
system of repression, 53
systematically and dogmatically deny fathers, 144
systems discrimination, 58
taboos against inbreeding, 122
take care of your children for you, 225
take precedence, 54
take responsibility, 220
taking jobs from the struggling domestic population, 110
Taking men's jobs, 243
tax contract, 14
tax funds, 230
tax payer's, 9
tax system, 14

PRAGMATIC LIBERTARIANISM
Engineering populist constitutions for the 21st century

taxation, 21
taxes you pay, 170
teaching children, 211
Teaching children, 56
teaching cooperation, 233
teaching good manners, 112
teamwork and collaboration, 25
technical revolution, 50
technological and civil society, 204
technological change, 6
Technological change, 315
technological revolution, 63
Technologically based innovation, 186
technologies, 186
technology revolution, 198
template, 187
tendency towards dictatorship and tyranny, 63
terrorism, 185
terrorism everywhere, 65
that has reduced the fertility rate of people in the west, 194
the antidote to racism, 114
the apex of personal development, 25
The Bell Curve, 202
the bosom of opportunity, 64
The Brexit vote, 109
The citizen's obligations to the nation state, 348
the cold war, 157
the coming economic transition, 175
THE COMPETITION OF IDEAS, 5
the contract with industry., 196
the co-parent with the mother, 224
the core of a nation's identity, 185
The current auspices, 45
the current immigration trend, 129
the current social order, 68
The Daycare Generation, 282
the divorce industry ignores, 191
the domestic population, 116, 129
the dominant culture, 125
the dysfunctions are many and all reveal a very sick society in the west, 194
the echo chamber of the elite., 108
the economy, 11
The education system, 44
The Elite will be viewed as traitors, 133
the end of Slavery, 126
the establishment, 75
The establishment, 305
the family unit, 188
the fanaticism of fascism, 123
The feudal economy, 174
THE FIRST EUROPEANS TO came to America, 323
the Frankfurt school, 143
the general population, 49
the globalist agenda, 71
The Government ensures its survival by, 325
the Government's incentives for divorce, 191
the greed of feminism, 243
the immunities passed down to the next generation, 115
the impoverishment of social welfare, 132
the industrial revolution, 63
the intellectual inferior, 157
the judicial gravy train, 145
the judicial industry, 59
The Judicial Mafia, 288
the judicial system, 89
The judicial system, 176
the KGB, 157
the Kristallnacht against men applying for jobs, 266
the land was ripe for settlement, 119
the law and the submissions, 291
the lawyer who depends upon the father to pay his billings, 145
the left's bribery, 10
The Libertarian rational, 338
The loss of common heritage, 186
the majority cannot speak, 70
the man is always depicted by lawyers as a deadbeat parent, 144
The melting pot, 116
The melting pot formula has been largely a success, 110
the middle class has been destroyed, 61
the minority 1% holding most of the wealth, 61
The modern tenant mortgage, 332
the modern tyranny of national Governments, 193
the most vicious and murderous ideology, 123
the nation is a home; not a hotel, 111
the nation state exists as a fiduciary, 292
The nation state hates individualism, 44
the Nazi movement, 115
the negative impact this family discord has upon children, 194
The new economy, 315
the new future of insecure contract work, 177
the nineteen thirties, 124

The normalization of family destruction, 194
the oligarchy, 47
the outcome will be severely dangerous, 61
The parallel economy, 329
the past 30 years, 58
the people themselves, 139
The political classes, 154
the political ruling classes, 155
THE POPULARITY OF LIBERTARIANISM, 5
the pressure relief valve of free speech, 109
The program consists of:, 153
the results of a sequence of events, 85
The risk of multiculturalism is also of civil war, 128
The road to hell is paved with good intentions, 51
the road to hell; paved with good intentions, 220
the roles of Government, 171
the Senate, 96
The Senate, 91, 98
the social division diseases, 158
the social integration process, 125
the soft embrace of a loving parent, 45
the state always has armies and weapons, 62
the state in acting as a collection agency, 191
the state is a disloyal charlatan, 69
The state wants parents out of the way, 225
the states agenda, 44
The strength of the nation, 218
the successful melting pot policy, 71
the sun circles the earth, 203
the system is one of fraud, 264
the system is rigged, 31
the tail wanting to wag the dog, 143
the technological revolution, 184
the treachery of those entrusted, 220
the Trump revolution, 152
the truth is going to hurt your perceptions, 64
The truth lies in the manifestation, 85
the ultimate historical act of treason, 77
The Wealth of Nations, 151
The western nation state, 55
the working class, 76, 137
The working class in reality needs jobs, 183
the world enlightened ones have screwed up, 64
the world of pain, 64
The world's political diseases, 65
theatre, 33
their ancestors paid for, 75
their living in the 15th century, 64
their own demise, 72
their own purposes, 226
their parental rights stripped from them, 190
their Social Engineering Scheme, 275
theme park of university fantasy lands, 140
theocratic government, 40
there is a disconnect, between reality, pragmatism, 131
there is no equality, 280
There is no integrity without meritocracy., 219
they betray their own founding peoples, 69
they had ancestral immunity, 118
they poisoned the well of marriage, 59
they tow the party line, 88
third world migration, 256
This is not healthy for our society, 131
This matrix, 148
this smashes the marriages basic foundations, 194
this system has no benevolence, 190
Thomas Jefferson, 203, 252
Those that ignore history are condemned to relive it, 227
threat of terrorism is the result, 71
tipping point, 47, 49
to buy votes, 73
to buy votes from foreigners, 70
to create a dysfunctional society, 59
to create one identity, 112
to create social instability, 154
to indoctrinate the youth, 154
to not threaten the majority, 61
to obtain resources, 141
to pit one ethnic group against the other, 103
to prevent massive impoverishment, 176
to promote sedition through the Universities, 159
to provide relief, 181
to raise a family, 186
to repress wage and benefit increases, 75
to silence opposition, 154
too focused upon foreign wars, 156
too little, too late, 110
tools to do the job, 185
torture, 147
toss out the man and still keep his income, 190
total waste of education dollars and time, 163
totalitarian, 11

totalitarian surveillance states, 65
totalitarian western Governments, 287
toxic communist, 164
toxic ideas, 161
track record, 113
trade deal, 254
trade deals, 261
Trade Union Movement, 126
traditional base, 137
Traditional family, 237
traditional family values, 56
traditional foundation, 50
tragic consequences, 185
trampling upon men's rights, 191
transgender sex changes, 57
traumatized men,, 194
travesty, 38
travesty of justice, 207
treason, 40
treason against the people, 74
treasonous, 232
treasonous acts, 70
treasonous policies, 133
treasonous vested interests, 126
treasures, 242
treated as a business, 91
treated as a concubine, 59
treats minorities as the majority, 56
tremendous economic boost, 181
tremendous profits, 235
trial where in no crimes are involved, 207
Trojan horse, 250
Trouble maker, 160
true nature of human beings, 169
Trump, 2
Trump has been a pressure relief valve, 109
Trust Corporations, 8
trust fund elitist fools, 109
trusted parent, 231
trusts, 9
Truth and Reconciliation Commission, 33
tumultuous times, 4, 184
turned into common law marriages, 59
turns average people into indentured slaves for life, 181
two incomes, 235
two-faced, 155
two-hundred-year-old ideas, 203
two-wage family, 235
tyrannical by nature, 157
tyrannical elimination and subordination, 56
tyrannical police state, 56
tyrannical state interference, 59
tyrannically, 54
tyrannizing the world, 46
tyranny, 32, 40, 94, 168, 227
tyranny and repression, 123
tyranny in their own families, 209
tyranny of the judiciary, 59
tyranny upon free speech, 50
tyranny upon humanity, 46
tyrants, 28
Tyrants always resort to violence, 157
umbrella, 17
undemocratic agenda of globalism, 211
undemocratic dictatorships, 106
undemocratic law creation, 93
under reported domestic unrest, 63
under social communism, 142
underemployment, 6
undermine social cohesion, 162
undermining the social structure, 154
undermining western civilization, 164
understanding, 276
understanding of a culture, 122
unearned privilege, 231
uneducated, 235
unelected judicial industry, 59
unemployed youth, 186
Unemployment Insurance Trust, 8
unintended consequence, 139, 164
uninvited interloper into families, 210
union support, 52
unionized working conditions, 188
unions, 254
United Kingdom, 253
United States, 2
University, 162
university education systems, 134
university humanities, 37, 277
University Humanities, 231
unjustified military conflict, 220
unmarked graves, 33

unmitigated lie, 206
unmolested, 167
unpredictable, 49
unpredictable outcomes, 237
unqualified, 28
unqualified; pedigree politicians and queue jumpers over merit, 219
unregulated, 90
unscientific, 37
unskilled and uneducated, 129
unskilled jobs, 132
unskilled labour, 186
unstructured play, 230
unsuspecting politicians, 157
US intelligence services, 158
use their talents towards self-employment, 181
using education for political ends, 135
Using media as propaganda, 107
usurious interest, 172
usurious mortgages, 29
utilitarian, 231
utilize the naivety of youth, 156
utilized to advance group agendas, 60
utopian ideas, 94
values of the working class, 142
variables, 81
variation, 202
variety of choice, 15
verge of collapse, 27
Versailles fool's paradise,, 109
very harmful to children, 207
very lucrative business for lawyers that hurts children, 193
very wealthy, 38
vested interest, 47, 65, 82, 91, 219, 240
vested interest power matrix, 228
vested interests many of foreign origin, 86
vestiges of communism, 50
vicious psychopaths, 205
victim, 160
victimhood, 6, 148, 162
victims, 231
vigilant to watch for controllers, 25
Vikings and Britons, 117
villainized, 224
villainizing all men as brutes and abusers, 150
villainizing men, 188
villains and scoundrels, 190
violation, 37
violence, 31, 36
violence that the state can muster, 57
violent Government repression, 185
Violent Government repression, 109
VISION FOR THE FUTURE, 4
visitor, 36
Vladimir Putin, 157, 158
voluntary subscription, 166, 170
vomiting, 33
vote getting scheme, 58
voucher-based education, 171
wage slavery, 196
wages, 235
wages of his factory workers, 26
wake up, 47
waking up, 49
wanting to confess his sins, 158
war, 23
war of 1812, 121
warehouses, 239
We are not cattle or sheep to be farmed by the state, 227
We are not groups, 203
We are not nations of immigrants, 127
We have become cattle, 227
we have entered a dark age, 106
we must trust our fellow citizens, 185
Weak argument, 221
wealth, 30, 41
wealthier than when they arrived., 264
wealthy nations, 46
web site, 239
Weimar Germany, 105
Weimar Republic, 115
welfare, 54, 169
welfare extortion racket, 189
welfare programs, 178
welfare state, 168
welfare state programs, 184
welfare state's, 5
well-adjusted, 235
well-balanced children, 245
were not exposed or deported, 156
were used as a tool to create social hatred, 134
western children's minds, 163
western civilization, 10, 32, 203

western civilization., 246
Western cohesion will implode, 248
western cultural realities, 128
western culture, 128
western dictatorships, 211
Western Europe, 46
Western European Nations, 274
western freedoms, 47
western Government, 42
western Governments, 188
Western intelligence, 156
western judiciaries, 41
Western marriages, 53
Western marriages have become a money-making enterprise for women, 190
western nation, 30
western nations, 27, 39, 40, 62, 264
western nations has no boundaries, 60
western people, 103
western renaissance, 203
Western Social Communists, 123
western social constructs, 3
western societies, 46, 87
Western societies, 45
western society, 27
western society now eats its own, 236
what lawyers do is to agitate matters already hostile, 176
what the future may bring, 62
When racial issues become protest movements, 114
when the wind goes in our direction, 138
when your tribe loses, the men and children of the village are always killed in the takeover, 189
Where and how has domestic peace gone, 65
where is the banks collateral, 173
where we have been and where we are, 66
Wherever corruption is rampant, poverty is sure to follow., 220
white-collar, 152
white-collar crimes, 40
wild animals rent, 174
will need one to readjust society, 241
will revolutionize and energise western innovation, 183
will sever all loyalty to the elite, 133

window dressing, 42
winner takes all, 244
with minimal labour input, 179
wolf packs, 24
women, 37, 235
Women, 190
women become concubines, 189
women virtually almost always get the custody of children, 189
women's unequal treatment, 58
work at home economies, 195
work processes, 180
work week, 237
workers are not happy, 186
workers productivity, 198
working class, 9, 49, 77, 131, 142, 152, 180, 234, 235, 238, 254
working class and unions, 50
working class families, 234
working class in reality need jobs, 183
working class switched loyalties, 155
working classes economic woes, 58
working conditions, 75
working-class, 235
working-class base, 50
working-class families, 236
working-class people, 129
working-class silent majority, 133
working-class upward mobility, 179
world is an imitation, 66
world of diversity, 271
worldwide communication, 152
worship the state, 64
WWII, 19
young academics, 154
younger men, 231
your rights to liberty, 215
Your servant is now your master, 221
your utopia is my hell on earth, 157
youth in western nations who refuse to get married, 194
YouTube, 156
Yuri Bezmenov, 156, 158
zero income tax, 171
Zimbabwe, 46

www.ingramcontent.com/pod-product-compliance
Lightning Source LLC
Chambersburg PA
CBHW060106170426
43198CB00010B/790